ROYAL HISTORICAL SOCIETY

STUDIES IN HISTORY 68

CHURCH PAPISTS

¶ The signification.

*H*E which preacheth in the pulpit, signifieth godly zeale, &
a furtherer of the gospel: and the two which are plucking
him out of his place, are the enemies of Gods word, threatning by fire to cõsume the professors of the same : and that
company which sitteth still, are *Nullifidians*, such as are of no
religion, not regarding any doctrine, so they may bee quiet
to liue after their owne willes and mindes.

Stephen Bateman, *A christall glasse of Christian reformation*,
London 1569, sig. G4r
(Bodleian Library, Oxford, Douce B. Subt. 266)

CHURCH PAPISTS

CATHOLICISM, CONFORMITY AND
CONFESSIONAL POLEMIC
IN EARLY MODERN ENGLAND

Alexandra Walsham

THE ROYAL HISTORICAL SOCIETY
THE BOYDELL PRESS

First published 1993

A Royal Historical Society publication
Published by The Boydell Press
an imprint of Boydell & Brewer Ltd
PO Box 9   Woodbridge   Suffolk IP12 3DF   UK
and of Boydell & Brewer Inc.
PO Box 41026   Rochester   NY 14604   USA

ISBN 0 86193 225 0

ISSN 0269-2244

British Library Cataloguing-in-Publication Data
Walsham, Alexandra
    Church Papists : Catholicism, Conformity and Confessional
    Polemic in Early Modern England. – (Royal Historical
    Society Studies in History, ISSN 0269-2244; No. 68)
    I. Title   II. Series
    282.42
    ISBN 0-86193-225-0

Library of Congress Cataloging-in-Publication Data
Walsham, Alexandra, 1966–
    Church papists : Catholicism, conformity, and confessional polemic in early
modern England / Alexandra Walsham.
        p.   cm. – (Royal Historical Society studies in history, ISSN 0269-2244 ; 68)
    "Royal Historical Society publication" – T.p. verso.
    Includes bibliographical references and index.
    ISBN 0-86193-225-0 (alk. paper)
    1. Catholics – England – History – 16th century. 2. Catholics – England –
History – 17th century. 3. Reformation – England. 4. Church of England –
Membership. 5. Catholic Church – England – Membership. 6. Persecution –
England – History – 16th century. 7. Persecution – England – History – 17th
century. 8. England – Church history – 16th century. 9. England – Church history –
17th century.
    I. Title.   II. Series: Royal Historical Society studies in history ; no. 68.
    BX1492.W28   1993
    282'.42'09031 – dc20   93-3896

The paper used in this publication meets the minimum requirements
of American National Standard for Information Sciences –
Permanence of Paper for Printed Library Materials, ANSI Z39.48-1984

Printed in Great Britain by
St Edmundsbury Press Ltd, Bury St Edmunds, Suffolk

I know thy workes, that thou art neither colde, nor hote. I would thou were colde, or hote. But because thou art lukewarme, and neither cold nor hote, I wil begin to vomite thee out of my mouth.

Zeale and fervour is commendable, specially in Gods cause: and the Neuters that be neither hote nor cold, are to Christ and his Church burdenous and lothsome, as lukewarme water is to a mans stomake, provoking him to vomite, and therfore he threateneth to void up such Neuters out of his mouth. – Apocalypse iii. 15–16, *The New Testament of Jesus Christ Translated Faithfully into English*, Rheims 1582.

I know thy workes, that thou art neither cold nor hot, I would thou wert cold or hot. So then because thou art lukewarme, and neither cold nor hot, I wil spew thee out of my mouth. – Revelation iii. 15–16, *The Holy Bible, Conteyning the Old Testament and the New: newly translated out of the originall tongues: & with the former translations diligently compared and revised, by his Majesties speciall commandement*, London 1611.

Contents

The Society records its gratitude to the following whose generosity made possible the initiation of this series: The British Academy; The Pilgrim Trust; The Twenty-Seven Foundation; The United States Embassy's Bicentennial funds; The Wolfson Trust; several private donors.

Acknowledgements

This book is a revised and expanded version of the thesis I submitted for the degree of Master of Arts at the University of Melbourne, in July 1990. At that time, as I prepared for further postgraduate study on a different subject in Cambridge, its eventual publication in this form could not have been envisaged. There are, consequently, a number of people who must be thanked for their contribution to making the appearance of *Church Papists* possible.

I am grateful to the supervisor of my research in Melbourne, Dr D. E. Kennedy, for his incisive criticism and his sensitive guidance through difficult stages; to Charles Zika, for his continuing interest and encouragement; and to the late Laurie Gardiner, from whom I first learnt of the existence of church papists as a raw undergraduate in a stuffy lecture theatre one summer evening some eight years ago. I also wish to acknowledge the staff and students of the Department of History at Melbourne, and the Australian government, which financially supported my postgraduate study there.

Since my arrival in Cambridge, I have benefited from the advice and expertise of a great many. Correspondence and communication with my examiners, Professor Ian Breward and Dr Kevin Sharpe, initially prompted me to pursue the prospect of publication in some form, and assisted in the task of revising and developing the thesis in a number of important directions, as well as in filling some of the more glaring gaps.

I owe a particular debt to my current supervisor, Professor Patrick Collinson, for his invaluable comments on various versions, his unfailing support for this project, and above all, for indulging my periodic preoccupation with a topic so perversely peripheral to my PhD research. Mention must also be made of Dr John Morrill, who generously found time in his busy schedule to read the thesis, and who offered astute advice at a critical point.

Thanks are likewise due to the many fellow early modernists in Cambridge and Melbourne who have discussed the subject with me, given helpful suggestions, and answered questions on a range of issues: in particular, John Craig, Anthony Milton, and Amanda Whiting. I am especially grateful to two close friends, Anne Maxwell and Eileen Groth, who have successively endured more than their share of my obsession with a group of individuals and a set of ideas in a century distant to their own scholarly concerns.

I must equally record my appreciation of the assistance given by librarians and archivists on both sides of the world: the staff of the Baillieu Library, Melbourne; the State Library of Victoria; Monash University Library; the Joint Theological Library, Ormond College; Cambridge University Library; and the British Library. I am grateful to the Rector of St Mary's College, Oscott, for allowing me to cite from the important manuscript by I.G. in the archives of that institution; and to the Bodleian Library, Oxford, for granting permission to reproduce the illustration from Stephen Bateman's *A christall glasse of Christian reformation* (1569), which appears on the jacket and as the frontispiece.

Finally, I extend my sincerest thanks to the Royal Historical Society for stretching the rubrics of the Studies in History series and opening an entirely unexpected opportunity to publish such a slim volume; and to their executive editor, Christine Linehan, for her enthusiasm, efficiency and flexibility.

Alexandra Walsham
Trinity College, Cambridge
April 1992

A Note on Citation

All quotations from and citations of contemporary manuscript and printed works retain original punctuation, capitalisation and spelling, with the exception that i is transposed to j, and u to v. The false imprints in Catholic books are retained as a reflection of the sophistication of the propaganda campaign of the clerical exiles; corrections are inserted in square brackets. Mispagination and confusing repeated pagination in early printed books are indicated by [*sic*] following the page number. Short titles are used in the footnotes; fuller titles may be found in the bibliography, in which, for ease of reference, *STC*, *A&R* and *ERL* numbers have also been included. Dates are given in Old Style, except that the year is reckoned to begin on 1 January.

Biblical references in chs ii and iii are to the Douai–Rheims Bible:
The Holie Bible Translated into English (Old Testament), 2 vols, Douai 1609–10, *The New Testament of Jesus Christ Translated Faithfully into English*, Rheims 1582.

All other scriptural citations are from the Authorised Version: *The Holy Bible, Conteyning the Old Testament and the New: newly translated out of the originall tongues: & with the former translations diligently compared and revised, by his Majesties speciall commandement*, London 1611.

Abbreviations

APC	*Acts of the Privy Council of England*, 32 vols, ed. John Roche Dasent, London 1890–1907
A&R	A. F. Allison and D. M. Rogers, *A Catalogue of Catholic Books in English Printed Abroad or Secretly in England 1558–1640*, Bognor Regis 1956
ARG	*Archiv für Reformationsgeschichte*
BIHR	*Bulletin of the Institute of Historical Research*
BL	British Library
CRS	Catholic Record Society
CS	Camden Society
CSP Dom	*Calendar of State Papers, Domestic Series, of the Reigns of Edward VI, Mary I, Elizabeth I and James I*, 12 vols, ed. R. Lemon and M. A. E. Green, London 1856–72
CSP Spanish	*Calendar of Letters and State Papers Relating to English Affairs, Preserved Principally in the Archives of Simancas*, 4 vols, ed. Martin A. S. Hume, London 1892–9
DNB	*The Dictionary of National Biography*, 22 vols, ed. Sidney Lee and Leslie Stephen, London 1917
EHR	*English Historical Review*
ERL	*English Recusant Literature 1558–1640* (Facsimiles of works listed in A. F. Allison and D. M. Rogers's *A Catalogue of Catholic Books in English Printed Abroad or Secretly in England 1558–1640*), 394 vols, select. and ed. D. M. Rogers, London 1968–79
HMC	Historical Manuscripts Commission
JEH	*Journal of Ecclesiastical History*
HJ	*Historical Journal*
OED	*The Oxford English Dictionary on Historical Principles (Corrected Re-issue with Introduction, Supplement and Bibliography)*, 12 vols, ed. J. A. H. Murray *et al*, Oxford 1933; 2nd edn, 20 vols, ed. J. A. Simpson and E. S. C. Weiner, Oxford 1989
P&P	*Past and Present*
PRO, SP	Public Record Office, London, State Papers Domestic
RH	*Recusant History*
PS	Parker Society
SCH	Studies in Church History
SR	*The Statutes of the Realm*, ed. T. E. Tomlins *et al*, London 1819
STC	A. W. Pollard and G. R. Redgrave, *A Short Title Catalogue of Books Printed in England, Scotland and Ireland and of English*

Books Printed Abroad 1475–1640, London 1926; revised and enlarged by W. A. Jackson, F. S. Ferguson and Katherine F. Pantzer, 2 vols, London, vol. i, 1986, vol. ii, 1976

TRHS   *Transactions of the Royal Historical Society*
VCH   *Victoria County History*

Introduction:
The Discovery of the Church Papist

In 1582, a species of Christian was newly detected within Elizabethan society –
'church papist'. The chief features of this breed were vividly delineated in an
apocalyptic diatribe against Roman Catholicism, a vigorous piece of popular
propaganda devised by an Essex vicar, George Gifford. *A Dialogue between a
Papist and a Protestant* opens with an acrimonious exchange between the two
interlocutors in which 'Professor of the Gospel' slurs his fellow speaker with a
disparaging appellation, a nickname:

> Pa[pist]: Wherefore shoulde yee call me Papist, I am obedient to the lawes,
> and do not refuse to go to the Churche.
> Pro[fessor of the Gospel]: Then it seemeth you are a Church Papist?
> Pa[pist]: A Church Papist, what meane ye by that?
> Pro[fessor of the Gospel]: Doe not you knowe? I will tell ye, there are
> Papists which will not come at the Churche: and there are Papistes which
> can keepe their conscience to themselves, and yet goe to Church: of this
> latter sorte it seemeth you are: because yee goe to the Church.[1]

Gifford's tract unmasked and upbraided an apparently familiar figure on
the parochial landscape. It caricatured a category of individuals who had
responded prudently rather than enthusiastically to the official Protestant
Reformation restored by and enshrined in the parliamentary settlement of
1559. It embodied an energetic attack on people who obediently appeared at
the compulsory Sunday services of the re-established Church of England, but
nevertheless continued to adhere tenaciously and instinctively to the faith in
which they had been baptised, to the Catholicism of their ancestors.

Gifford's unease about such perfunctory 'Protestantism' was a typically
puritan preoccupation. Yet it strikingly parallels the pastoral concerns and
sensitivities of his polemical opposites. 'Church papists' also attracted the
attention and aroused the indignation of the authors of a growing collection of
illegally printed Catholic literature. In 1580, the Jesuit missionary Robert
Persons composed a *Brief Discours conteyning certayne reasons why Catholiques refuse
to goe to Church* (1580), in which he vociferously denounced 'schismatics',

> [that] sorte of Catholikes, that albeit they doe judge al other religions
> besides theire owne, false and erroneous, and damnable: yet doe they not
> thincke, but that for some worldly respecte they may at the least wise in

---

[1] George Gifford, *A Dialogue between a Papist and a Protestant, applied to the capacitie of the unlearned*,
London 1582, 1v.

goyng to Church shewe them selves conformable men to the proceedinges of them of the contrarie religion: and doe also thincke others too scrupulous which doe stand in refusall of the same.[2]

'Church papist' was a pejorative phrase coined in an era of unprecedented disorder and dislocation, a stinging insult invented during the unsettled half-century that followed the theological upheavals of the mid-1500s. It supplies us with a sensitive index to some critical contemporary tensions and apprehensions. This book attempts to analyse the shape and the significance of that set of ideological anxieties. It examines the cultural and ecclesiastical politics of defining religious deviance and of constructing confessional identities in Elizabethan and early Stuart England.

In the 1570s, recusancy, principled refusal to attend Common Prayer, emerged as the hallmark of post-Reformation English Catholicism. In the succeeding decades, Catholic clerics published much propaganda condemning compromise and conformity, and insisting on the inescapable obligation of adopting this bold and brave ritual of omission. Recurrently disseminated, such tracts betrayed the existence of a laity which manifestly fell short of the staunchly separatist community idealised by their priestly writers. They sought to reform temporisers whose behaviour was perceived to endanger the successful resistance of an outlawed religion against annihilation, and to deface its defiantly 'recusant' public image.

The issue of churchgoing, however, was increasingly acknowledged to be an intense moral and political predicament. It was recognised as a serious practical problem that confronted probably the majority of consciously 'Catholic' men and women with weekly regularity. As official hostility escalated, furthermore, the 'schismatic's' expedient line of conduct came to be regarded with ever more indulgence and compassion by the Jesuit and secular clergy. It progressively settled within a sphere of pastoral practice in which concession was a distinct possibility. By 1600, occasional conformity was in fact privately condoned and quietly countenanced by the leaders of the Counter Reformation mission as an alternative, albeit inferior, form of conscientious objection. The two central chapters of this book explore and offer an explanation for the apparent discrepancy between ideology and accepted observance, between the printed polemic of priests and their confidential casuistical treatment of the ethical dilemmas of the lay people under their charge.

Turning aside from clerical prescriptions and pragmatics, I then advance some preliminary suggestions about the character of non-recusant Catholicism, and consider the consequences of re-emphasising the role of 'schismatics' for our interpretation of late sixteenth- and early seventeenth-century Catholic culture. I aim thereby both to reopen scholarly discussion and debate on the subject, and to provide a framework for more detailed investigations of church papistry at the regional and village level – for those local studies that must form the backbone of historians' understanding of post-Reformation religion.

[2] [Robert Persons], *A Brief Discours contayning certayne reasons why Catholiques refuse to goe to Church*, Douai [London secret press] 1580, 5v–6r.

This book thus focuses on Roman Catholic efforts to grapple with and resolve the awkward question of 'conformity'. Yet, above all, it seeks to extract the 'church papist' from the confines of confessional historiography. This was a context in which meaningful religious distinctions were only gradually evolving, an age in which those deceptively neat denominational labels we are so tempted to employ were profoundly anachronistic. The term 'church papist' was one symptom of this state of flux. Identifying a sector of the populace that occupied a kind of confessional limbo, it was stretched to designate a bewildering variety of opinions and attitudes, a wide spectrum of positions and stances. It is intractably difficult to erect clear boundaries between conforming Catholics and those ingenuous, but too often inconspicuous practitioners of Christopher Haigh's 'parish Anglicanism' and Judith Maltby's 'Prayer Book Protestantism'.[3] Or, indeed, that anonymous and invisible mass of individuals who were spiritually indifferent, although politically and socially compliant. In the end, 'church papists' are perhaps best assessed as a congregational component of that inclusive and eclectic institution – that effective umbrella organisation – the Church of England. They numbered among the miscellaneous membership of a religious body which the Amsterdam separatist Henry Ainsworth scornfully described in 1608 as nothing more than a 'constreyned union of Papists & of Protestants.[4]

Church papists are a compelling but neglected presence in early modern society; a presence which may well subvert persisting notions of the 'Catholic community' – if not of the Protestant nation itself.

---

[3] Christopher Haigh, 'The Church of England, the Catholics and the people', in idem (ed.), *The Reign of Elizabeth I*, London–Houndmills 1984, 218–19; Judith Maltby, 'Approaches to the Study of Religious Conformity in late Elizabethan and early Stuart England: with special reference to Cheshire and the diocese of Lincoln', unpubl. PhD thesis, Cambridge 1991, passim esp. pp. 7, 14, 73; cf Patrick Collinson, *The Religion of Protestants: the Church in English society 1559–1625*, Oxford 1982, 192.

[4] Henry Ainsworth, *Counterpoyson*, [Amsterdam?] 1608, 228.

1

The Reformation and
the Rediscovery of the Church Papist

> At the first, and for some years after the said change made by Queen
> Elizabeth; the greatest part of those who in their judgements and affections
> had before bin Catholickes, did not well discern any great fault, novelty, or
> difference from the former religion, that was Catholick . . . And so easily
> digested the new religion and accommodated themselves to thereto. – J.
> McCann and H. Connolly (eds), *Memorials of Father Augustine Baker and Other
> Documents Relating to the English Benedictines* (CRS xxxiii, 1933), 16.

Prominent on the contemporary horizon, church papists have so far largely
evaded the historian's gaze.

Conformists have too often received token acknowledgement in narratives
and assessments of early modern English Catholicism: its post-Reformation
history is traditionally and unashamedly 'recusant history'. In a field
dominated by hagiographical, polemical and apologetic influences until the
mid-twentieth century, the schismatic's seemingly spiritless posture was
predictably, even deliberately overlooked. Church papists have been the
understudies of the priest martyrs and recusant gentry heroes who are the
critical actors in the drama of Catholicism's evolution from a position of
unrivalled hegemony to one of sectarian vulnerability. Formal, ritualistic
separation from the Church of England remains the key criterion in defining
and measuring the 'English Catholic community': in recent years, John Bossy
has been most influential in highlighting its markedly nonconformist and
sectarian character after 1570.[1] But Christopher Haigh is the most outspoken

---

[1] John Bossy, *The English Catholic Community 1570–1850*, London 1976, esp. pp. 6ff., 108, 121ff.,
144 (note, however, that church papists are statistically included: p. 192). See also idem. 'The
character of Elizabethan Catholicism', *P&P* xxi (1962), 39–59, and 'The English Catholic
community 1603–1625', in A. G. R. Smith (ed.), *The Reign of James VI and I*, London 1973,
91–105. For examples of 'recusant history', the continuing emphasis on nonconformist
Catholicism, and passing acknowledgement or summary dismissals of 'church papists', see
Richard Challoner, *Memoirs of Missionary Priests*, ed. J. H. Pollen, London 1924; John Morris
(ed.), *The Troubles of Our Catholic Forefathers Related by Themselves*, 3 vols, London 1872–7, esp. vol.
iii. p. ix; J. H. Pollen, *The English Catholics in the Reign of Queen Elizabeth: a study of their politics, civil
life and government*, London 1920, esp. pp. 94–7; A. O. Meyer, *England and the Catholic Church Under
Queen Elizabeth*, trans. J. R. McKee, London 1967 (first publ. Rome 1911), esp. pp. 61, 70; Brian
Magee, *The English Recusants: a study of the post-Reformation Catholic survival and the operation of the
recusancy laws*, London 1938; A. G. Dickens, 'The first stages of Romanist recusancy in Yorkshire
1560–1590' and 'The extent and character of recusancy in Yorkshire, 1604', *Yorkshire
Archaeological Journal* xxxv (1941), 157–81, and xxxvii (1948), 24–48; David Mathew, *Catholicism in
England: the portrait of a minority: its culture and tradition*, London 1948, esp. ch. ii; A. C. Southern,

advocate of a reinterpretation that calls for a broader and more flexible definition comprehending 'non recusant Catholicism'.[2] The rediscovery of the 'church papist' is a corollary of understanding Catholicism as 'a vague body of opinion' instead of a precisely countable phenomenon, and affiliation to that body as an idea rather than a public act.[3] Outward conformists none the less remain a 'shadowy aura', a 'penumbra' around 'the hard core of absolute recusants', which has not yet merited attention in its own right.[4]

The related transformation in Reformation studies has also fostered the historical rehabilitation of 'church papists'. Their embarrassing presence was dismissed in the enduring teleological version of Protestant history which presented the Reformation as a spontaneous, progressive movement swiftly grasping the minds and loyalties of a populace deeply disillusioned with the medieval Church. There was no logical place for merely acquiescing individuals in a process sustained by 'a positive evangel', already irreversible in Henry VIII's reign, and briefly and chiefly over by 1558.[5] The religious

Elizabethan Recusant Prose 1559–1582, London–Glasgow 1950; E. I. Watkin, *Roman Catholicism in England from the Reformation to 1950*, London 1957, esp. pp. 22–3; W. R. Trimble, *The Catholic Laity in Elizabethan England 1558–1603*, Cambridge, Mass. 1964; K. J. Lindley, 'The lay Catholics of England in the reign of Charles I', *JEH* xxii (1971), 199–221, esp. p. 209; J. C. H. Aveling, *The Handle and the Axe: the Catholic recusants in England from Reformation to Emancipation*, London 1976, chs ii, vi and passim, esp. pp. 21, 72–3, cf pp. 40–9, 162; Adrian Morey, *The Catholic Subjects of Elizabeth I*, Totowa, NJ 1978, 213; Arnold Pritchard, *Catholic Loyalism in Elizabethan England*, London 1979, esp. pp. 4–5; Edward Norman, *Roman Catholicism in England from the Elizabethan Settlement to the Second Vatican Council*, Oxford 1985, ch. ii, esp. pp. 27, 29. The edited volumes of primary source material and the monograph series published by the Catholic Record Society similarly manifest a 'recusant' bias, and its journal, which previously appeared as *Biographical Studies 1534–1829*, was renamed *Recusant History* in 1951. The persisting tendency to equate Catholicism and recusancy in this period is also reflected in the title of the series of facsimile editions of published Catholic writings between 1558 and 1640: *English Recusant Literature*, 394 vols, select. and ed. D. M. Rogers, London 1968–79.

[2] Christopher Haigh, *Reformation and Resistance in Tudor Lancashire*, Cambridge 1975, 276 and ch. xvii passim; see also idem. 'The Church of England, the Catholics and the people', 169–94. For his aggressive demolition of the Bossy thesis in particular, see 'The fall of a Church or the rise of a sect? Post-Reformation Catholicism in England', *HJ* xxi (1978), 181–6; 'From monopoly to minority: Catholicism in early modern England', *TRHS*, 5th ser. xxxi (1981), 129–47; 'The continuity of Catholicism in the English Reformation', *P&P* xciii (1981), repr. in Christopher Haigh (ed.), *The English Reformation Revised*, Cambridge 1987, 176–208. Haigh's views are substantially endorsed by A. D. Wright, 'Catholic history, north and south', *Northern History* xiv (1978), 126–51. Earlier revisionist interpretations include Roger B. Manning, *Religion and Society in Elizabethan Sussex: a study of the enforcement of the religious settlement 1558–1603*, Leicester 1969, esp. pp. xvi, 257; K. R. Wark, *Elizabethan Recusancy in Cheshire* (Chetham Society, 3rd ser. xix, 1971), esp. pp. vii, 26. More recently, see P. R. Newman, 'Roman Catholicism in pre-Civil War England: the problem of definition', *RH* xv (1979), 148–52; Caroline M. Hibbard, 'Early Stuart Catholicism: revisions and re-revisions', *Journal of Modern History* lii (1980), 1–34, esp. pp. 16–21; Patrick McGrath, 'Elizabethan Catholicism: a reconsideration', *JEH* xxxv (1984), 414–28; Alan Dures, *English Catholicism 1558–1642: continuity and change*, Harlow 1983, passim. esp. pp. 3, 6, 18, 33, 57; John Guy, *Tudor England*, Oxford 1988, 299–301; Diarmaid MacCulloch, *The Later Reformation in England 1547–1603*, Houndmills, Hants 1990, ch. ix, esp. p. 150.

[3] Haigh, 'The fall of a Church or the rise of a sect?', 184–5, cf Wright, 'Catholic history', 131.

[4] H. Aveling, 'Some aspects of Yorkshire Catholic recusant history 1558–1791', in G. J. Cuming (ed.), *The Province of York* (SCH iv, 1967), 110; Haigh, 'The continuity of English Catholicism', 207; idem. 'The Church of England, the Catholics and the people', 205 and *Reformation and Resistance*, 275.

[5] This historical interpretation was first enshrined in John Foxe's 'Book of Martyrs', *The Acts and*

revolution of the period is now seen, however, not as an inevitable event, but as a protracted and largely unwelcome development, far from complete at Elizabeth I's accession. The triumph of popular Protestantism is being perpetually postponed, chronologically divorced from the official Reformation, the series of statutes enacted between 1529 and 1559. English Calvinism, from this perspective, was a 'sickly child', in serious danger of expiring in its infancy. Indeed, its impact in some quarters has seemed so negligible as to warrant the opinion that it very nearly perished at birth. One result of this shift in thinking has been awareness of a reluctant and confused majority that yielded to political, ecclesiastical and social pressure rather than the magnetic appeal or ideological coherence of the 'new Gospel'.[6] In a reformation that generated, at least initially, not rapid conversion but grudging conformity, interest is converging on the 'immeasurable but certainly substantial number of so called "church papists" '.[7] Men and women adequately described as neither committed 'Catholics' nor convinced 'Protestants' shed light on the translation of a constitutional decision into a local and psychological reality.

The arguments and emphases of self-styled 'revisionist' scholars have thus contributed much to slowly dismantling the historiographical paradigms that combined to relegate church papists to the fringes of academic enquiry. They are rescuing from obscurity figures who were similarly caught between and marginalised by competing creeds in the sixteenth and seventeenth centuries.

Monuments of John Foxe with a life of the martyrologist and a vindication of the work, 8 vols, ed. S. R. Cattley, London 1837–41. The most authoritative and important modern version of the 'fast', 'popular' Reformation is undoubtedly A. G. Dickens, *The English Reformation*, 1st edn, London 1964, passim esp. p. 328. His second edition (London 1989) acknowledges, but largely resists the relentless march of 'revisionism'. See also Claire Cross, *Church and People 1450–1660: the triumph of the laity in the English Church*, paperback edn, [London] 1976.

[6] See, for example, Roger B. Manning, 'The spread of the popular Reformation in England', in Carl S. Meyer (ed.), *Sixteenth Century Essays and Studies* i, St Louis, Miss. 1970, 35–52; D. M. Palliser, 'Popular reactions to the Reformation during the years of uncertainty 1530–1570', in F. Heal and R. O'Day (eds), *Church and Society in England: Henry VIII to James I*, London 1977, 35–56; Penry Williams, *The Tudor Regime*, Oxford 1979, ch. viii; Ralph Houlbrooke, *Church Courts and the People During the English Reformation 1520–1570*, Oxford 1979, esp. p. 257; Paul Seaver, 'The English Reformation', in S. Ozment (ed.), *Reformation Europe: a guide to research*, St Louis, Miss. 1982, 271–96; Keith Wrightson, *English Society 1580–1680*, London 1982, 199ff.; Collinson, *The Religion of Protestants*, ch. v, and idem. 'The Elizabethan Church and the new religion', in Haigh, *The Reign of Elizabeth I*, 195–219; J. J. Scarisbrick, *The Reformation and the English People*, Oxford 1984; Rosemary O'Day, *The Debate on the English Reformation*, London–New York 1986, esp. ch. vi. For 'revisionism' *avant la lettre*, see H. N. Birt, *The Elizabethan Religious Settlement*, London 1907, esp. p. xi. For Haigh's forceful contribution to the revisionist enterprise, see: 'From monopoly to minority'; 'The Church of England, the Catholics and the people'; 'Puritan evangelism in the reign of Elizabeth I', *EHR* xcii (1977), 30–58; 'The recent historiography of the English Reformation', *HJ* xxv (1982), 995–1007; 'Revisionism, the Reformation and the history of English Catholicism', *JEH* xxxvi (1985), 394–406. Perhaps the most extreme statement of this prevailing position yet is to be found in Haigh's review article: 'The English Reformation: a premature birth, a difficult labour and a sickly child', *HJ* xxxiii (1990), 449–59. As recent surveys of the period reflect, the 'slow', 'unpopular' Reformation has attained the status of an orthodoxy: Guy, *Tudor England*, ch. x; MacCulloch, *Later Reformation*, ch. viii; and for a more cautious and qualified endorsement, W. J. Sheils, *The English Reformation 1530–1570*, London–New York 1989, 74–8.

[7] Patrick Collinson, *The Birthpangs of Protestant England: religious and cultural change in the sixteenth and seventeenth centuries*, London 1988, 27, 58.

These redirections in research suggest that the sharp polarities in Church and society indicated by labels like 'Catholic' and 'Protestant' are, in many respects, invalid in the early modern environment. In a period of cultural upheaval and protracted religious transition, the phrase 'church papist' is one element of a dynamic vocabulary that both reflects and generates doctrinal, moral, political and social tensions and tendencies. Indeed, the framers of the Royal Injunctions complementing and implementing the religious legislation of 1559 required subjects to refrain from uttering 'in despite or rebuke of any person these contentious words: papist, or papistical heretic, schismatic, or sacramentary, or any such like words of reproach'. Sir Nicholas Bacon spoke no less reprovingly in the early Elizabethan House of Lords of the pernicious contemporary habit of name-calling, of resorting captiously to 'contumelious or opprobrious' terms.[8] It was anticipated and acknowledged that the parochial politics of religion and reformation was, in large part, a politics of language.

Words, especially God's Word, were extraordinarily emotive objects in the early modern period, charged with potential conflict. The very use of 'Catholic' involved entering a sphere of theological contention and controversy. It was an act of arrogation, a bid for the title of the 'true church', endorsed by Scripture, descended directly from the purity of the apostolic congregations, and unarguably the only channel to salvation. Polemicists from both sides of the Reformation divide wrangled for much of Elizabeth's reign as to whom it should be righfully accorded: Robert Crowley's *Deliberate Answere made to a rash offer*, for example, 'plainly & substantially prooved, that the papists that doo nowe call themselves Catholiques are in deed AntiChristian schismaticks: and that the religious protestants, are in deed the right Catholiques'.[9] And John Foxe prefaced his classic propagandist history of Protestantism, the 'Book of Martyrs', with an address to 'all the professed friends and followers of the Pope's proceedings . . . *pretending* the name of Catholics, *commonly* termed Papists'.[10] 'Art thou a Papist, a Protestant, a Puritan or what Religion art thou of?', questioned the interrogators of one martyr. To his persecutors, his apparently modest claim to be but 'a poore Catholique' simply betrayed popish presumptuousness and pride.[11] Alternatively, the Injunctions insisted upon the legitimacy of the ecclesiastical structure they reinforced: 'You shall pray for Christ's holy Catholic church; that is, for the whole congregation of Christian people, dispersed

---

[8] P. L. Hughes and J. F. Larkin (eds), *Tudor Royal Proclamations*, 3 vols, New Haven–London 1969, ii. 128; T. E. Hartley (ed.), *Proceedings in the Parliaments of Elizabeth I, Volume I. 1558–1581*, Leicester 1981, 35.

[9] Robert Crowley, *A Deliberate Answere made to a rash offer, which a popish Antichristian Catholique, made to a learned protestant . . . Anno Do. 1575*, London 1588, title page. For an overview of these printed polemical disputes, see Peter Milward, *Religious Controversies of the Elizabethan Age: a survey of printed sources*, London 1977, 43, 45–6, 128.

[10] Foxe, *Acts and Monuments*, i. p. xxvii (my emphasis). The phrase was echoed by James I in a speech to his first parliament in 1604, referring to 'falsely called Catholics but truly Papists': J. R. Tanner (ed.), *Constitutional Documents of the Reign of James I AD 1603–1625*, Cambridge 1930, 27.

[11] Thomas Worthington, *A Relation of Sixtene Martyrs*, Douai 1601, 9–10. See also *SR*, 35 Eliz. c. 2 (1593), for the discovery and averting of traitorous conspiracies and attempts by those 'terming themselves Catholics'.

throughout the whole world, and specially for the Church of England and Ireland.'[12]

Parallelling the words 'papist' and 'puritan', 'church papist' originated as a term of abuse and opprobrium. Initially used to stigmatise people who shared a salient feature, it was later distorted and exploited for its derisive connotations, and applied indiscriminately to discredit and insult. 'Church papist' creates a dichotomy which has essentially a relative, polemical 'truth' and subjective significance, and which betrays as much about the labeller as the labelled. It was a nickname, as the Catholic exile, Richard Bristow, wrote of 'papist', 'put upon us by the Heretikes'.[13] Like its parent, 'church papist' was deployed to brand individuals as adherents of that popular target for satire and scorn, the pope, and to galvanise the ranks of the 'true professors', the 'godly', against those who no less aggressively slandered them as 'puritans'. Its Catholic synonym, 'schismatic', also aimed to belittle those deviating from a clerical model of conscientious and recalcitrant dissent, especially in the face of persecution. As Patrick Collinson has observed of the name 'puritan', the distinction and discord implied is sociological as well as theological. And it too infers partial, rather than full, alienation from the ecclesiastical establishment.[14]

A lasting and elastic epithet, 'papist' had a learned Lutheran heritage. 'Church papist', however, seems to register in the written English language only in the early 1580s.[15] Its advent marked an impulse to categorise degrees of 'popery', to distinguish between men and women who daringly revealed their adherence to the Church of Rome by boycotting attendance at Protestant services, and those who manifested their Catholicism in other, often less provocative ways. 'Some call them Churche-papistes, other Scismatiques', wrote a Carthusian monk, Thomas Wright, recording the proliferation of terms for conforming Catholics in use by 1596 – 'demi-catholickes, or catholique-like protestantes, or externall protestantes, and internall cath-olikes'. According to Bishop Thomas Cooper of Lincoln's classification scheme they were 'cunning papists'; the pursuivant Richard Topcliffe styled the same 'dissembling papists'.[16] But it was 'church papist' that acquired

---

[12] Hughes and Larkin, *Tudor Royal Proclamations*, ii. 131.

[13] Richard Bristow, *A Briefe Treatise of diverse plaine and sure wayes to finde out the truthe in this doubtful and dangerous time of Heresie*, Antwerp 1574, 11b.

[14] Patrick Collinson, *The Elizabethan Puritan Movement*, London 1967, 26; idem. 'A comment: concerning the name puritan', *JEH* xxxi (1980), 485. For further useful comments on religious terminology, see Christopher Hill, 'The definition of a puritan', in his *Society and Puritanism in Pre-Revolutionary England*, Harmondsworth 1964, 15–30; Thomas Clancy, 'Papist – Protestant – Puritan: English religious taxonomy 1565–1665', *RH* xiii (1975–6), 227–53; M. Van Beek, *An Enquiry into Puritan Vocabulary*, Groningen 1969, 12, 40.

[15] See *OED s.v.* 'papist', which cites John Fisher's 1521 sermon against Luther: 'The popes holynes & his favourers, whom he [Luther] calleth so often in derisyon papistas, papastros, & papanos, & papenses'. The earliest instance of 'church papist' I have encountered in print is in George Gifford's 1582 *Dialogue between a Papist and a Protestant*, although its oral currency probably predates its appearance on record, cf *OED s.v.* 'church papist', in which the first recorded instance is 1601. See also Clancy, 'Papist – Protestant – Puritan', 228–32; Elliot Rose, *Cases of Conscience: alternatives open to recusants and puritans under Elizabeth I and James I*, Cambridge 1975, 5.

[16] Thomas Wright, *The Disposition or Garnishmente of the Soule*, Antwerp [English secret press] 1596, sig. A3v; Thomas Cooper, *Certaine Sermons wherin is contained the Defense of the Gospell nowe preached*,

quasi-official status: by 1607, a derogatory word forged by a vigorous oral culture could be employed as bureaucratic jargon in a report to the Privy Council on the state of religion in Northumberland.[17]

The discovery of the church papist, signalled by the evolution of the phrase into the language, evidences the emergence of comment and concern about conformity in late sixteenth-century society. In a sense, this was a phenomenon that could not be discerned by contemporaries until *nonconformist* Catholic practice appeared on a wider scale – until the concept of recusancy was universally recognised. The word 'recusantes' was obviously still relatively unfamiliar in 1583, for when the divine, Gervase Babington, employed it in the catechetical treatise he published that year he felt compelled to add by way of clarification, 'that is, our refusing Papistes'. First utilised by ecclesiastical commissioners in 1561 to denote a group of Marian clergy who had rejected the new Protestant regime in its entirety, 'recusant' was ultimately applied more exclusively to identify members of the laity who absented themselves from Church of England services.[18] A Caroline commentator, memorialising the late Tudor period in 1641, traced the genesis of the term to 1570, noting that prior to that date, 'Catholiques were not more then Church Papists.' Sir Edward Coke too, saw the year of Pope Pius V's bull excommunicating and deposing the queen as a watershed in the transformation of post-Reformation Catholicism and in the expansion of existing religious terminology. Until then, he asserted, 'all Papists came to our Church and service without scruple', until then 'the name recusant was never heard of amongst us'.[19] Belated governmental recognition of these crystallising distinctions came in 1593, when statute law sharply differentiated between 'recusants' and 'papists': that all-purpose pejorative 'papist' now narrowly defined persons who had either thus far complied with the regulations, or had yet to be formally convicted of infringing them.[20] Central, therefore, to the question of church papistry is the development of that unacceptably public posture of Catholic religious resistance, recusancy.

London 1580, 192 [*sic*]; for Richard Topcliffe, see John Strype, *Annals of the Reformation and Establishment of Religion and Other Various Occurrences in the Church of England During Queen Elizabeth's Happy Reign*, 4 vols in 7, Oxford 1824, iv. 53.

[17] Claire Talbot (ed.), *Recusant Records* (CRS liii, 1961), 150ff. For other uses, see Arthur Dent, *The plaine Mans Path-way to heaven*, London 1610 (first publ. 1601), 125; William Harrison, *A Brief Discourse of the Christian Life and death, of Mistris Katherin Brettergh*, annexed with separate title page to *Deaths Advantage little regarded*, London 1602, 5; McCann and Connolly, *Memorials of Father Augustine Baker*, 74.

[18] Gervase Babington, *A Very Fruitful Exposition of the Commandements*, London 1596 (first publ. 1583), 77. Cf Robert Persons, who defined the term for the Rector of the English College in Rome in 1580: L. Hicks (ed.), *Letters and Memorials of Father Robert Person, S.J.: vol. I (to 1588)* (CRS xxxix, 1942), 46, 89. For the 1561 usage, see *CSP Dom 1547–1565 Addenda*, 521.

[19] Sir Robert Naunton, *Fragmenta Regalia*, [London] 1641, 18; for Coke (who was here speaking at Henry Garnet's trial for complicity in the Gunpowder Plot), see *A True and Perfect Relation of the Whole proceedings against the late most barbarous Traitors, Garnet a Jesuite, and his Confederats*, London 1605, sig. H2r, cf sigs P2r-v, Z1v; and Edward Coke, *The Lord Coke His Speech and Charge*, London 1607, sig. D1v.

[20] See M. M. C. Calthorp (ed.), *Recusant Roll No. I, 1592–3* (CRS xviii, 1916), p. xi; H. Bowler (ed.), *Recusant Roll No. 2 (1593–4)* (CRS lvii, 1965), p. viii; Wark, *Elizabethan Recusancy in Cheshire*, 81.

The principle of outward conformity was inherent in the Elizabethan settlement, the legal and political Reformation of 1559. The Act of Uniformity and the Royal Injunctions of that year made attendance at Sunday and feast day services at one's parish church the obligation of every individual, and truancy an offence punishable by the forfeiture of one shilling. All inhabitants of the realm were prohibited from performing or participating in Catholic rites. They were bound to consent, if only by their presence, to the liturgy of the revised Edwardian Book of Common Prayer, the reformed theology it somewhat ambiguously embodied, and the ecclesiastical supremacy of their monarch.[21] Churchgoing was the corner stone of Elizabethan religious policy, the minimum, minimal commitment the Church of England required of most laypeople. It was an enactment of orthodoxy. Church papists were thus obedient subjects – 'statute protestants', 'injunction men', 'such . . . as jumpe with the queenes lawes', as an Essex preacher, William Dike, scornfully labelled them in 1580.[22]

This was an axiom remaining intact in the increasingly draconian legislation devised to combat the 'popish' menace within and without the realm. Penal laws were designed to detect and discipline recusants, not church papists. The Acts of 1581, 1587 and 1593 aimed at eliminating obstinate upper-class nonconformity by exacting crippling monthly £20 fines and sequestrating land in default. But these harsh measures were qualified by unconditional provisos discharging all who 'come to some Parishe Churche on some Sondaye or other Festivall Daye, and then and there heare Devine Service, and at Service tyme before the Sermon or readinge of the Ghospell, make publike and open Submission and Declaracion of his and their Conformytie to her Majesties Lawes and Statutes'.[23]

Government policy was based on the premise that religious dissidence was to be punished only when it threatened national security and the established order, as propaganda like William Cecil's 1583 *The Execution of Justice* was at pains to emphasise on the Continental stage. Catholics were ostensibly persecuted not as heretics but as enemies of the state – not for their sinful opinions but for the potentially subversive consequences of holding them.[24] In the eyes of official spokesmen, public presence at worship could legitimately be commanded as a 'tollerable & convenient' means of distinguishing Christian men and women from 'brute beastes', the rationally religious from the senseless, heathen savage. Indexing a hesitancy to intervene in private matters, however, meddling with their specific beliefs was consistently upheld

---

[21] *SR*, 1 Eliz. c. 2. § III. Edward VI's 1552 Act of Uniformity was the first to make attendance at church compulsory, although punishment was by the censures of the Church alone: offenders were subject to no civil penalty. See 5 & 6 Edw. VI c. 1. § I and III.

[22] Quoted in Collinson, *The Religion of Protestants*, 200n.

[23] *SR*, 23 Eliz. c. 1. § VII, 29 Eliz. c. 6. § VI, 35 Eliz. c. 1. § III, 35 Eliz. c. 2. § X. The clause quoted is from the last act. Recusants were also exempted from general pardons except under the same conditions: see, for example, 29 Eliz. c. 9. § X, 31 Eliz. c. 6. § VIII. For more detailed discussions of recusancy legislation, see Williams, *The Tudor Regime*, 275ff., and Rose, *Cases of Conscience*, ch. i.

[24] William Cecil, *The Execution of Justice in England*, ed. R. M. Kingdon, Ithaca, NY 1965 (first publ. 1583), passim esp. pp. 11, 36. See also W. K. Jordan, *The Development of Religious Toleration in England from the Beginning of the English Reformation to the Death of Queen Elizabeth*, London 1932, 83.

to be untenable. 'Conscience', it was maintained, was 'internall, invisible, and not in the power of the greatest monarch in the worlde, in no lymittes to be streightened, in no bondes to be conteyned.'[25] The queen vetoed the efforts of her bishops and the parliaments of 1571, 1576 and 1581 to delve beyond 'the externall and outward shewe' to 'the very secretes of the harte in God's cause', and to make reception of communion rather than churchgoing 'the very touchstone of triall'. Qualms about terrorising consciences, and fears of the international implications of overtly appearing to do so, also prevented the inclusion of a similar clause in the anti-recusancy act of 1593.[26] Symbolic of Elizabeth's vaunted reluctance to molest consciences, to make windows into men's souls, the eucharist never became the legal standard for creedal consent in her reign. Churchgoing remained the sole test of what Catholic polemicists dubbed 'Parlimentarie Religion'.[27]

'If any man will but yield to go to Church all treasons are remitted.' This was the epigram and exaggeration recorded by an anonymous sixteenth-century editor in his notebook. The Jesuit president of Douai College Thomas Worthington likewise put the caveat 'become a good subject, and go to church' into the mouths of the caricatured heretical oppressors in his *Relation of Sixtene Martyrs* 'glorified' in 1600–1. Official offers of mercy, in return for attendance at Protestant services, were triumphant proof for such martyrologists that the priests and laypeople condemned to death after 1577 were executed for their religious convictions rather than for political crimes.[28] Yet churchgoing *was* a political act in an Erastian state, and the church a political arena in which ministers were expected to indoctrinate their parishioners in appropriate attitudes to authority and their social superiors, in the ideology of non-resistance embodied in Elizabethan homilies 'on obedience'. Frequently chained to lecterns, Foxe's 'Book of Martyrs' contained the elements of an apocalyptic nationalism chiefly characterised by virulent anti-Catholicism. The occasional prayers of public thanksgiving for deliverance composed following events such as the 1588 Spanish Armada similarly

[25] The words were Edward Aglionby's, in a speech delivered in response to a proposed bill of 1571 'for coming to comon prayer and for receavinge of the comunion': Hartley, *Proceedings in the Parliaments of Elizabeth I*, 240–1. For other official statements to this effect, see Cecil, *The Execution of Justice*, 6, 9–11; Jordan, *The Development of Religious Toleration*, 127, 199; Thomas Clancy, *Papist Pamphleteers: the Allen–Persons party and the political thought of the Counter Reformation in England 1572–1615*, Chicago 1964, 138; Hughes and Larkin, *Tudor Royal Proclamations*, iii. 94 (no. 739, 1591); *CSP Dom. 1547–1580*, 381 (15 June 1570).

[26] See Hartley, *Proceedings in the Parliaments of Elizabeth I*, 201–2, 205–6, 240–1; J. E. Neale, *Elizabeth I and her Parliaments*, 2 vols, London 1953–7, i. 192ff., 212ff.; F. X. Walker, 'The Implementation of the Elizabethan Statutes against Recusants 1581–1603', unpubl. PhD thesis, London 1961, 33–5, 80, 124–6; Talbot, *Recusant Records*, 120. Bishop John Aylmer argued for communion as a test of conformity in 1577: Patrick Ryan (ed.), 'Diocesan returns of recusants for England and Wales 1577', in *CRS Miscellanea XII* (CRS xii, 1921), 1–114, at p. 1.

[27] [Edmund] Thomas Hill, *A Quartron of Reasons of Catholike Religion*, Antwerp [English secret press] 1600, 14, cf Bristow, *Brief Treatise*, 156bff., esp. p. 158b.

[28] Morris, *Troubles of Our Catholic Forefathers*, iii. 21; Worthington, *A Relation of Sixtene Martyrs*, 17. See also Robert Southwell, *An Humble Supplication to Her Majestie*, [English secret press] 1595 [1600], 58; Morris, *Troubles of Our Catholic Forefathers*, i. 97; iii. 39, 43, 181; John Gerard, *John Gerard: the autobiography of an Elizabethan*, trans. P. Caraman, London 1956, 87ff.; Hicks, *Letters and Memorials*, 58; J. H. Pollen (ed.), *Unpublished Documents Relating to the English Martyrs: vol. I 1584–1603* (CRS v, 1908), 126.

cultivated a militant and chauvinistic patriotism.[29] And in buildings stripped of religious iconography, royal coats of arms usurped the traditional site of the crucifix. As David Cressy has demonstrated, the anniversary of Elizabeth's accession became a 'holyday', something of a substitute for the abolished festivals in the traditional ecclesiastical calendar; the cult of Gloriana almost literally replaced that of the Virgin Mary.[30] Presence at church was more than figuratively a mark of respect for monarchy and state: this was a setting in which refusal to say 'Amen' to collects for the queen took on a sinister signification.[31] Simply *to be* Catholic savoured of sedition in the context of the Northern Rebellion of 1569, the machinations of leading clerical exiles on the Continent, and especially of Pius V's bull *Regnans in Excelsis* – that clumsy, technically flawed document that decisively established, none the less, the fatal connection between deference to Rome and disloyalty to the queen. Most notably in times of crisis, conformity to the Church of England consequently became a stamp of national allegiance and civic responsibility, as well as respectable Protestantism. 'Such as do not come to church' were popularly pilloried as rebels, 'the enemies of God and of good order'.[32] And since Common Prayer was a secular as well as a spiritual gathering, refusal to attend amounted to ascetic withdrawal from the social, as well as the sacral community. In an age in which religion was perhaps still rooted more in habitual action than self-conscious belief, recusancy evolved as a counter-ritual, an heroic gesture of Catholic constancy and defiance – a meaningful token of rejection of the English Reformation.

But, as Christopher Haigh has pointed out, 'refusal to attend services at the parish church was not a natural reaction to the theological revolution of 1559'.[33] Clear-cut divisions between 'Catholicism' and 'Protestantism' did

---

[29] See William Haller, *Foxe's Book of Martyrs and the Elect Nation*, London 1963, for the influential thesis that the central theme of the *Acts and Monuments* is the identification of England as the 'elect nation', but cf Katharine R. Firth *The Apocalyptic Tradition in Reformation Britain 1530–1645*, Oxford 1979, 69–110, and V. Norskov Olsen, *John Foxe and the Elizabethan Church*, Berkeley 1973, passim esp. pp. 36–7; Paul Christianson, *Reformers and Babylon: English apocalyptic visions from the Reformation to the eve of the Civil War*, Toronto 1978, 39–45; Jane Facey, 'John Foxe and the defence of the English Church', in Peter Lake and Maria Dowling (eds), *Protestantism and the National Church in Sixteenth Century England*, London 1987, 162–92. For occasional prayers of thanksgiving, see W. K. Clay (ed.), *Liturgical Services: liturgies and occasional forms of prayer set forth in the reign of Queen Elizabeth* (PS, 1847), 524ff.

[30] David Cressy, *Bells and Bonfires: national memory and the Protestant calendar in Elizabethan and Stuart England*, London 1989, esp. ch. iv.

[31] For examples of reports to the central government, see *CSP Dom 1566–1579 Addenda*, 514 (1577); *CSP Dom 1595–1597*, 420 (May 1597); *CSP Dom 1598–1601*, 553 (12 Feb. 1601). Catholic writers made considerable mileage out of this Protestant political idolatry. The Jesuit Richard Holtby, for example, polemically described the official religion thus: 'the prince is made a god . . . What meaneth this precise exaction of conformity in matters of religion, as frequenting their churches, prayers, and sacraments, &c; the which in their laws and statutes they term a natural obedience due to the Queen, if they did not pretend thereby the prince to be more than a creature?': Morris, *Troubles of Our Catholic Forefathers*, iii. 130.

[32] *CSP Dom 1566–1579*, 435 (1572), cf 439 (1572?); *CSP Dom 1580–1625 Addenda*, 27 ([Dec. 1580]); Gerard, *Autobiography*, 4; Peter Clark, *English Provincial Society from the Reformation to the Revolution: religion, politics and society in Kent 1500–1640*, Hassocks 1977, 156ff.; Morris, *Troubles of Our Catholic Forefathers*, i. 77.

[33] Haigh, *Reformation and Resistance*, 247.

not pass into being in rural and urban localities as smoothly or rapidly as the legislation of that year: for several decades, continuity may well have been more marked than change. After the abrupt religious reversals under Henry VIII, Edward VI and Mary, Elizabeth's new reformation was widely anticipated to be an equally impermanent affair. Probably the majority instinctively temporised.

At the local level, transition was to be effected by ecclesiastical and civil officials no less perturbed by the confusion and turmoil of their time. Wedded to regional interests, a voluntary bureaucracy was far from the impersonal instrument of central government. As diocesan surveys ordered by the Privy Council in 1564 revealed, too many magistrates and unpaid Justices of the Peace were 'outwardly men conformable', 'only making a good face of Relligion'. Civic administration was widely controlled by 'popish' Marian office holders, including the mayor of Hereford, 'a maynteyner of supersticion and namely of abrogated holydaies'. Neither could the indifference of county magistrates, 'neuters' such as Sir Thomas Palmer of Sussex, 'a fainte furtherer', effectively promote the Gospel.[34] For humble, sometimes half-hearted constables and churchwardens, the enforcement of laws and directives was pre-eminently a personal decision. The detection of religious deviance, like public misconduct and crime, was a matter of perception – indeed, often selective perception. *Omnia bene*, that notoriously common answer at visitations and assizes, conceals the halting advance of the Reformation in numerous communities.

Although all but one of the Marian bishops proved to be unco-operative and were deprived after 1559, in the lower ecclesiastical ranks an army of timeservers survived, men who had passively and prudently submitted to the settlement. The backwardness of cathedral chapters was disconcerting: in 1564 Hereford's resident canons, for instance, were certified to be 'but dissemblers and rancke papists'.[35] Falling short of the Calvinist ideal of a preaching ministry that would powerfully entrench the religion of the Word in its congregations' minds, 'dumb dogs' and 'popish priests' were a perennial concern of the episcopal hierarchy, and an over-riding obsession of puritan agitators, as late as 1604.[36] Biconfessional incumbents who were prepared to

---

[34] Mary Bateson (ed.), 'A collection of original letters from the bishops to the Privy Council 1564 (with returns of J.P.s and others within their respective dioceses, classified according to their religious convictions)', *Camden Miscellany IX* (CS, n.s. liii, 1895), 57, 49, 14, 9 respectively. Of the civil officials classified by these surveys, 264 were recorded as 'indifferent', 157 'hinderers' or 'adversaries', and 431 'favourers'. On crypto-Catholicism in town corporations, see Manning, *Religion and Society in Elizabethan Sussex*, 81ff.

[35] Bateson, 'A collection of original letters', 20. See also Houlbrooke, *Church Courts and the People*, 207; Trimble, *The Catholic Laity in Elizabethan England*, 12.

[36] Numerous examples might be cited: see W. P. M. Kennedy (ed.), *Elizabethan Episcopal Administration: an essay in sociology and politics*, vols ii and iii (*Visitation Articles and Injunctions 1575–1582, 1583–1603*) (Alcuin Club Collections xxv–xxvii, 1924), ii. 113, 122 (Chester 1581); iii. 140, 146 (St Davids 1583); iii. 154 (Bath and Wells 1583); iii. 163 (Coventry and Lichfield 1584); Edward Cardwell (ed.), *Documentary Annals of the Reformed Church of England*, 2 vols, Oxford 1844, i. 403 (Canterbury Province 1576); Albert Peel (ed.), *The Seconde Parte of a Register being a calendar of manuscripts under that title intended for publication by the Puritans about 1593*, 2 vols, Cambridge 1915, ii. 88–174; idem. (ed.), 'A Puritan survey of the Church in Staffordshire in

say clandestine masses, prior to publicly administering communion according to the new rite, similarly troubled their Catholic counterparts.[37] Curates like William Shaw, of Badsley, in Warwickshire, 'a secreat perswader of the simple to poperie, one that praieth for the dead', connived with reactionary parishioners to ensure the persistence of traditional practices well into the reign.[38] John Pullyver of Writtle, in Essex, moreover, was energetically spreading rumours in 1580 that 'the mass was up in Lincolnshire very trim' – such clerics seemed the spearhead of a resurgent Rome rather than mainstays of a 'godly reformation'.[39] Indeed, recent work by Patrick McGrath and Joy Rowe has reminded us that it is unwise to draw too sharp a line between recusant and conservative clergy.[40] The presence of the proverbial Vicar of Bray must have eased the official break with inveterate tradition: it can only have encouraged placid conformity.

The structural adjustments to the parish churches decreed in 1559 were slow to take effect: in many districts, iconoclasm was paradoxically a gradual process. Episcopal visitation articles, the records of the archidiaconal courts and churchwardens' accounts, all bear ample witness to the resilience of the 'Old Religion', both in the 'dark corners of the land' and in regions closer to the nerve-centres of Protestantism. Demolition of stone altars and their replacement by bare communion tables often remained incomplete. While the largest of such monuments of 'idolatry', the six foot roods and their lofts, had yet to be dismantled in some outlying Lancashire parishes in the 1570s and 1580s, comparable delays were also occurring in Essex villages.[41] And Bishop Overton was still expecting to uncover considerable evidence of Catholic

---

1604', *EHR* xxvi (1911), 338–52; F. G. Emmison, *Elizabethan Life: morals and the Church courts, mainly from Essex archiadiaconal records* (Essex Record Office lxiii, 1973), 200ff.

[37] See Edward Rishton's continuation of Nicholas Sander, *The Rise and Growth of the Anglican Schism*, ed. and trans. David Lewis, London 1877 (first publ. in Latin 1585), 267. John Murren similarly condemned the practice in a manuscript disseminated in Chester in the early 1560s, printed in James Pilkington, *The Works of James Pilkington B.D. Bishop of Durham*, ed. James Scholefield (PS, 1842), 621ff., 633. See also T. F. Knox (ed.), *The First and Second Diaries of the English College Douay and an Appendix of Unpublished Documents* (Records of the English Catholics Under the Penal Laws i), London 1878, p. xxiii.

[38] Peel, *Seconde Parte of a Register*, ii. 169. In addition, see Haigh, 'The Church of England, the Catholics and the people', 198ff.; Williams, *The Tudor Regime*, 266.

[39] F. G. Emmison, *Elizabethan Life: disorder, mainly from Essex sessions and assize records* (Essex Record Office lvi, 1970), 49.

[40] Haigh, *Reformation and Resistance*, 257; Patrick McGrath and Joy Rowe, 'The Marian priests under Elizabeth I', *RH* xvii (1984), 103–20, esp. pp. 111ff., 117. Many of these time-serving clergy moved into full-blown recusancy in later years.

[41] Haigh, *Reformation and Resistance*, 219ff.; Emmison, *Morals and the Church courts*, 177–89. See also J. S. Purvis (ed.), *Tudor Parish Documents of the Diocese of York*, Cambridge 1948, 15ff. Still useful as an introduction to churchwardens' accounts is J. Charles Cox's *Churchwardens Accounts from the Fourteenth Century to the Close of the Seventeenth Century*, London 1913, esp. ch. xiii. Ronald Hutton's important study of two hundred sets of accounts shows that churchwardens obediently complied with official orders to suppress Catholic worship, but argues that these documents none the less attest to the widespread reluctance of parishioners to do so: 'The local impact of the Tudor Reformations', in Haigh, *The English Reformation Revised*, 114–38. Evidence derived from the same source suggests evasion of government pressure and command was common enough elsewhere: Scarisbrick, *The Reformation and the English People*, 99ff.; Christopher Haigh, 'Introduction' to idem. *The English Reformation Revised*, 12.

survivalism in the diocese of Coventry and Lichfield in 1584 – images, relics and the entire paraphernalia of pre-Reformation worship, 'vain popish trish-trash'.[42] Even in London in 1601, Richard Bancroft was enquiring about persons who had appropriated and secreted such equipment for private use, 'which it is to be conjectured they do keep for a day, as they call it'.[43]

Neither did ritualistic customs immediately conform to the rubrics of the Book of Common Prayer. Services in which the eucharist was consecrated after the old fashion constituted Protestant 'masses', blurring and obscuring the liturgy's already vague repudiation of transubstantiation. Tell-tale gestures like 'crossing or breathing over the sacramental bread and wine, or shewing the same to the people to be worshipped and adored' worried Archbishop Grindal in 1576.[44] Other aspects of popular Catholicism continued to be disclosed twenty and more years after Elizabeth's accession: superstitious bell ringing and intercessions for the dead, christenings and burials celebrated with popish trappings, and a variety of dubious para-liturgical practices. Customarily the hub of communal and festive life, churches persisted as the venues for the village wakes and ales, interludes and seasonal revelry frowned upon by zealous reformers.[45] The parish of Weaverham in Cheshire seemed a positive den of 'popery' in 1578, scarcely altered since Marian times:

They want a Communion booke a Bible of the largest volume the first tome of the homilies. Ther is in the church an altare standing undefaced. There lacketh a lynnon clothe and a coveringe for the Communyon table a chest for the poore and keping of the Register in. The parishioners refuse the peramabulacion. The people will not be staied from ringinge the bells on All Saints daie. They frequent alehowses in service tyme. Great talkinge used in the churche. No levyinge for the poore of thabsents from the churche. Morres Daunces and rishe bearings used in the Churche. Jane . . . an old noonne [nun] is an evell woman and teacheth false doctrine. They refuse to communicate with usuall breade. None come to the Communion iii tymes a yeare. They refuse to bringe in ther yowth to be catechised. Crosses ar standinge in the churche yeard. The Vicar weareth not the surplesse . . . There is a pece of an altare standing in Mr. Irelands quier.[46]

[42] Kennedy, *Elizabethan Episcopal Administration*, iii. 163. See also ii. 98–9 (York Province 1578); ii. 111–12 (Chester 1581); iii. 140–2, 152–3 (St Davids 1583); iii. 210 (Chichester 1586); iii. 261–2 (York Province 1589); Cardwell, *Documentary Annals*, i. 357 (Canterbury Province 1569); i. 370–1 (York Province 1571); Emmison, *Morals and the Church courts*, 136ff., 179ff., 188ff.; Purvis, *Tudor Parish Documents*, 2ff., 15ff.

[43] Kennedy, *Elizabethan Episcopal Administration*, iii. 346.

[44] Cardwell, *Documentary Annals*, i. 399 (Canterbury Province 1576). See also Houlbrooke, *Church Courts and the People*, 248ff.

[45] For examples, see Emmison, *Morals and the Church courts*, 136ff.; Purvis, *Tudor Parish Documents*, 174ff.; Wark, *Elizabethan Recusancy in Cheshire*, 7ff.; Haigh, *Reformation and Resistance*, 218ff.; F. R. Raines (ed.), 'A description of the state, civil and ecclesiastical of the county of Lancaster about the year 1590', *Chetham Miscellanies V* (Chetham Society, o.s. xcvi, 1875), 4–5.

[46] Purvis, *Tudor Parish Documents*, 64–5, cf Wark, *Elizabethan Recusancy in Cheshire*, 16 and 80–1 where this presentment is also cited, and the vicar's refusal to wear the surplice noted to be a further symptom of neglect, rather than a mark of puritan nonconformity.

Such localities sheltered, in a sense, whole congregations of 'church papists'; conditions were far from conducive to the internalisation of the Protestant message.

Overlap with the Catholic past was not just the consequence of entrusting religious change to an imperfect administrative machinery. The official strategy for the institutionalisation of the Reformation was deliberately fabian – unacceptably so in the eyes of those nicknamed 'puritans'. Preserving unchanged the ecclesiastical superstructure of the medieval Church, the Elizabethan settlement was characterised by calculation, compromise and the comprehension of a latitude of belief. The authorised liturgy had seemingly little to offend, and much in which it commended itself to the sympathisers of the Church of Rome. Pope Pius IV actually offered to confirm it in the early 1560s, should Elizabeth deign to acknowledge his jurisdiction.[47] As William Harrison recorded in his *Description of Britain* in 1577, stained glass in religious buildings was allowed to decay rather than ordered to be ritualistically destroyed.[48] Even ceremonies with suspiciously 'superstitious' origins, such as the churching of women and annual rogation perambulations, found approval in 1559. And since the Injunctions enjoined the use of the familiar unleavened wafers, in contradiction with the Prayer Book rubrics which endorsed the 'common fine bread' favoured by Continental reformed Churches for communion, eucharistic practice must have varied as widely as the whims of individual vicars. In an incident in Cheshire in 1580, the regional bishop was advised by the Privy Council 'charitabley to tollerate them (that esteem wafer bread), as children, with milke'. The Church of England was to be a nursery in which the masses were gently weaned, not roughly snatched, from popery.[49] This tentative, indulgent, but eminently pragmatic policy was similarly embodied in the homilies commanded to be read regularly from every pulpit. Intended as an interim measure until the natural extinction of the Marian clergy and the expansion of a trustworthy preaching pastorate, they delivered Protestantism's central tenets and resounding condemnations of Catholic errors to an audience assumed to have not yet fully forsaken its 'popish' convictions. The 'Homily of the Place and Time of Prayer' openly admonished a large body of individuals who merely outwardly conformed: 'But see that yee come thither with your holyday garment, not like hypocrites, not of a custome and for manners sake, not with lothsomenesse, as though ye had rather not come then come, if ye were at your liberty.'[50]

---

[47] See Laurence Vaux, *A Catechisme or Christian Doctrine*, ed. T. G. Law (Chetham Society, n.s. iv, 1885) (first publ. Louvain 1568), introduction, p. xvii. Significantly, the Elizabethan Prayer Book omitted the petition in Edward VI's litany against the 'tyranny of the Bishop of Rome', as well as the 'Black Rubric' which unmistakably upheld Protestant eucharistic theory.

[48] William Harrison, *Harrison's Description of England in Shakspere's Youth*, 2 vols, ed. F. J. Furnivall, London 1877 (first publ. 1577), i. 28.

[49] For the Injunctions, see Hughes and Larkin, *Tudor Royal Proclamations*, ii. 131; for the Prayer Book rubrics, Clay, *Liturgical Services*, 198; for the incident in Cheshire, Wark, *Elizabethan Recusancy in Cheshire*, 18n. For useful comments on Elizabethan Protestantism and comparison with the Continental, especially Lutheran reformations, see William Monter, *Ritual, Myth and Magic in Early Modern Europe*, Brighton 1983, ch. ii.

[50] 'The second part of the Homilie of the place and time of Prayer', in *Certaine Sermons or Homilies*

Concessions to tradition like the surplice and the sign of the cross in baptism certainly made 'statute Protestantism' more palatable to that sector of society reluctant to discard time-honoured ways. But to those seeking to purify the Church, such undisguised reminders of old mysteries retarded rather than spurred the spiritual regeneration of a populace whose cultural heritage was intensely visual. In the words of a 1572 parliamentary bill on the subject, they occasioned 'the backslidynge of the people from true religion to supersticion'. A Church that retained the external manifestations of popery – ceremonies, vestments and structures tainted with a 'shewe of evyll' – could not hope to succeed in refashioning individual mentalities, in winning over the weaker brethren.[51] The disputes over *adiaphora* that erupted during the Vestiarian controversy of the 1560s and the revived assault on 'popish remnants' prior to the Hampton Court Conference in 1604 thus constituted a fundamental critique of the sluggish attitude and approach to the pastoral task of religious rehabilitation inaugurated by Elizabeth's accession. It was a 'patch and peece' reformation that left the members, as well as the institutional framework of the Church of England, 'but halflie forward and more then halflie backward'.[52] According to Thomas Cartwright, the architects of the settlement brazenly accommodated crypto-Catholics at the expense of puritans: 'Some of them have saide, that conformable Papists were more tollerable then these precisions and godlye men that seeke for reformation.'[53]

Whether an establishment which espoused pure doctrine, but whose unsatisfactory discipline inadequately restrained the ungodly, could be termed a 'true Church' at all, was a recurrently disputed theological question amongst the advocates of further religious reform. Separatists believed the Church of England to be malignant and false, not least because it promiscuously enrolled in its membership 'a misceline multitude of believers and infidels, holy and profane'. Radically dissociating themselves from this 'unlawful comixture of the children of God and children of the Divil', they formed their own 'gathered' congregations comprised solely of the elect.[54] For puritans who remained loyal to the establishment, however, the presence of church papists and 'statute protestants' was not quite sufficient reason to invalidate its privileged status, to warrant secession or merit its vehement condemnation as the creature of AntiChrist. Their preparedness to tarry within an incompletely reformed institution revolved around the fine rhetorical point that 'there be many *in* the Church that are not *of* the Church'. It rested on an ambivalent distinction between superficial and impermanent professors of the Gospel and

Appointed to be Read in Churches in the Time of Queen Elizabeth I (1547–1571), 2 vols in 1, intro. Mary Ellen Rickey and Thomas B. Stroup, Gainesville, Florida 1968, 132.

[51] W. H. Frere and C. E. Douglas (eds), *Puritan Manifestoes: a study of the origin of the Puritan revolt* (The Church Historical Society lxxii, 1907), 149, 35 respectively.

[52] Ibid. 19 and Peel, *Seconde Parte of a Register*, ii. 60. On the Hampton Court Conference, see HMC, *Lord Montagu of Beaulieu*, i, London 1900, 32–40 passim esp. p. 37.

[53] Frere and Douglas, *Puritan Manifestoes*, 105.

[54] Ainsworth, *Counterpoyson*, sig. ***3v and p. 245 respectively, cf pp. 131, 206, 228. See also Leland H. Carlson (ed.), *The Writings of John Greenwood 1587–1590* (Elizabethan Nonconformist Texts iv, 1962), 129ff.; G. R. Elton (ed.), *The Tudor Constitution: documents and commentary*, Cambridge 1982, 447–8, 456–61; B. R. White, *The English Separatist Tradition: from the Marian martyrs to the pilgrim fathers*, London 1971, passim esp. p. 33.

those inwardly and effectually 'called', on an acceptance that drawing any final temporal line between them was highly problematic.[55]

By contrast, for the champion of that other significant strand of sixteenth-century Calvinist divinity, John Whitgift, there was no such ambiguity about the relationship between the visible and invisible Churches of Christ. It was the place of God, not God's people to divide the faithful and the reprobate, the saved and the damned: human organisations ought to be content with exterior observance alone as the criterion for inclusion within the earthly edifice.[56] As Richard Hooker's 1596 *Lawes of Ecclesiastical Polity* definitively declared, the Church in this world embraced not only saints, but 'hypocrites and dissemblers whose profession at the first was but only from the teeth outward' – unequivocally, therefore, it comprehended the 'church papists' of Elizabethan England. Of pivotal importance in Hooker's retrospective philosophical justification of the English Reformation was his defence of its candid commitment to fostering, rather than smothering the 'feeble smoke of conformity'.[57]

As early as 1558, the unknown official who composed the comprehensive paper advising royal councillors on the 'alteratione' of religion in the realm anticipated that adopting a compromising, cautious Protestantism would find little favour with those of more 'precise' opinions. His prediction that it would be defamed as 'a Cloked papestrye or a mingle mangle' was disarmingly accurate, for the phrase was echoed by the early seventeenth-century Bedfordshire clergyman, Thomas Brightman, in an inflammatory biblical commentary he claimed to have written under divine inspiration. In his eyes, the Church of England's 'mingle mangle of the Popish Government with pure doctrine' made it the typological 'Counterpaine' of the Church of Laodicea, definitively denounced in Revelation iii. 16: 'because thou art lukewarme, and neither cold nor hot, I wil spew thee out of my mouth'. Its reprehensible lack of zeal for reformation, its 'mungrell', 'hotch-potch' 'mediocritie', merely reflected and reinforced the disturbing indifference of its numerous nominally Protestant members.[58] Censure of the ecclesiastical status quo in these uncomplimentary terms was apparently also circulating in provincial towns such as Bury St Edmunds in the 1580s. Urban elites who intended to

---

[55] Quotation from Dent, *The plaine Mans Path-way to heaven*, 261 (my emphasis), cf Ainsworth, *Counterpoyson*, 123, and Thomas Cartwright, in John Whitgift, *The Works of John Whitgift*, 3 vols, ed. John Ayre (PS, 1851–3), iii. 102–4. On Puritanism, consult Collinson, *The Elizabethan Puritan Movement*, passim esp. pp. 25ff.

[56] See Whitgift, *Works*, i. 385–6; Peter Lake, *Anglicans and Puritans? Presbyterianism and English conformist thought from Whitgift to Hooker*, London 1988, 36ff.; D. J. McGinn, *The Admonition Controversy*, New Brunswick 1949, 132.

[57] Richard Hooker, *The Works of that Learned and Judicious Divine Mr. Richard Hooker with an account of his life and death by Isaac Walton*, 2 vols, ed. J. Keble, Oxford 1850, ii. 98, 96ff., 102 respectively.

[58] The 1558 'Device for Alteration of Religion' can be found in British Library, London, Cotton MS Julius F. VI, fos 167–9, at fo. 167v. Thomas Brightman, *A Revelation of the Revelation*, Amsterdam 1615, 123–65, quotations at pp. 137, 124, 132, 133 respectively. See also Christianson, *Reformers and Babylon*, 100ff., esp. p. 101. For other uses of this phrase, see Peel, *Seconde Parte of a Register*, i. 150 ('Articles sent to the Bishops and Cleargye in the convocation house . . . From the Marshalsye by John Nasshe the Lordes prisoner 1580 Januarye') and ii. 49ff., esp. p. 52 ('A copie of Mr. Fullers booke to the Queene', 1586).

have this scriptural text painted beneath the royal coat of arms in their local church were 'stayed by advyce', and inscribed a slightly less controversial quotation instead. In the context of Elizabeth's known distaste for clerical marriages and the tale-bearing silver crucifix in her chapel, such graffiti was tacitly too treasonous – an imputation, perhaps, that the queen herself was a church papist.[59]

As the growing genre of local studies is revealing, until the 1570s at least, the Church of England largely proved a tolerable substitute for, if an inferior version of, its medieval predecessor.[60] The apparent increase in recusancy in the second decade of the reign may be partly the product of spiralling governmental concern – a misleading impression generated by a sudden upsurge in legislative and administrative activity against 'popery'. But conformity did become gradually less attractive to committed Catholics as religious positions polarised, the Calvinist temper of the Elizabethan Church stiffened, and its puritan vanguard resolved itself into a political movement agitating for progressive liturgical reform and ecclesiastical reconstruction on presbyterian lines, and advocating a more aggressive approach to the task of evangelism. If the onset of the Catholic counterblast trumpeted by the excommunicating bull of 1570 was less of a landmark for conservative individuals in rural localities than their rulers, the threat of foreign intervention it precipitated was critical in shaping the course of the subsequent statutory onslaught against Catholicism. And the parochial consequences of the eventual attrition of time-serving 'popeling' priests and the rise of inflexibly Protestant, university-educated clergy can hardly be overestimated.

---

[59] On the Bury incident, see J. S. Craig, 'The Bury Stirs revisited: an analysis of the townsmen', *Proceedings of the Suffolk Institute of Archaeology and History* xxxvii (1991), 208, 221 n.7; cf Diarmaid MacCulloch, 'Catholic and Puritan in Elizabethan Suffolk: a county community polarizes', *ARG* lxxii (1981), 274–5; idem. *Suffolk and the Tudors: politics and religion in an English county 1500–1600*, Oxford 1986, 204 (I am grateful to John Craig for clarifying this episode for me). On Elizabeth's silver crucifix, see John Jewel's letter to Peter Martyr, 16 Nov. 1559, in Hastings Robinson (ed.), *The Zurich Letters 1558–1579* (PS, 1842–5), i. 54–5.

[60] See, for example, on Lancashire, Haigh, *Reformation and Resistance*, esp. pp. 247–8, 276. On Cheshire, Wark, *Elizabethan Recusancy in Cheshire*, esp. pp. 9, 128ff. On Yorkshire, Dickens, 'The first stages of Romanist recusancy', esp. p. 163. For Essex refer to Michael O'Dwyer, 'Catholic recusants in Essex c.1580 to c.1600', unpubl. MA thesis, London 1960; M. S. Byford, 'The Price of Protestantism: assessing the impact of religious change on Elizabethan Essex: the cases of Heydon and Colchester', unpubl. DPhil thesis, Oxford 1988; and the forthcoming Cambridge PhD thesis of Michael O'Boy. On the dioceses of Norwich and Winchester, see Houlbrooke, *Church Courts and the People*, ch. viii, esp. pp. 256–7. On Sussex, Manning, *Religion and Society*, esp. p. 44. On Hampshire, John E. Paul, 'Hampshire recusants in the time of Elizabeth I, with special reference to Winchester', *Proceedings of the Hampshire Field Club* xxi (1959), 61–81, esp. pp. 67ff. On Durham, Northumberland and Cumberland, see respectively J. A. Hilton, 'Catholicism in Elizabethan Durham', *RH* xiv (1977); idem. 'Catholicism in Elizabethan Northumberland', *Northern History* xiii (1977), esp. pp. 46ff; and 'The Cumbrian Catholics', *Northern History* xvi (1980). On Suffolk, MacCulloch, *Suffolk and the Tudors*, esp. pp. 192ff., and J. S. Craig, 'Reformation, Politics and Polemics in Sixteenth Century East Anglian Market Towns', unpubl. PhD thesis, Cambridge 1992. For York, see D. M. Palliser, *Tudor York*, Oxford 1979, ch. ix, esp. pp. 246–8, 254–6. On Devon and Cornwall, Robert Whiting, *The Blind Devotion of the People: popular religion and the English Reformation*, Cambridge 1989, esp. p. 146. Haigh's 'Recent historiography' and 'Revisionism' provide helpful summaries and syntheses of regional and local studies up to the early 1980s.

Recollecting the first decades of the reign, contemporaries as ideologically opposed as Robert Persons and Sir Edward Coke agreed that recusancy was a belated development as the mark of Catholic dissent.[61] Writing to Claude Aquaviva, general of the Jesuit order in Rome in 1590, Henry Garnet, their superior in England, reflected ruefully on the 'days of darkness' at the beginning of the queen's reign. 'Multitudes nominally Catholics', he said, were then 'in fact traitors to their holy religion and deserters from it'. They had offered their presence at heretical services senselessly supposing that it was a satisfactory sign of their dissent to enter first and leave last, and furthermore imagining they might 'atone for these great evils' by proceeding on to the mass, that 'most august sacrifice of the Church'.[62] Nor were these merely considered opinions derived with the benefit of hindsight. Conservative Lancashire gentlemen rejoicing over rumours of a Spanish invasion to restore Catholicism in 1567, solemnly vowed not to cease attending church, but to avoid the reformed eucharist.[63] And in reply to Privy Council requests for a census of recusants in 1577, Bishop Scambler of Peterborough remarked that returns of those refusing to receive the Lord's Supper would have been vastly more informative. Refraining from the Protestant communion, that obvious theological sticking-point, was evidently the most prevalent form of spontaneous religious resistance in his diocese and elsewhere.[64] As the silenced Northamptonshire preacher, that notable urban apostle of Genevan Calvinism, Perceval Wiburn observed in 1581, recusancy was but a recent phenomenon. He confidently charged the 'papists' that it was 'but a late taken up scrupulositie among the moste of you'.[65] Full or partial compliance with, rather than separatist disaffection from, the Church of England epitomised lay response to the Elizabethan settlement for at least a generation.

Indeed, it was in the 1570s that the clerical agents of the Counter Reformation intensified their assault on conformity – on the 'schismatic' behaviour of a troublesome sector of their flock. Their public propaganda against church papists is the subject of the next chapter.

---

[61] Hicks, *Letters and Memorials of Father Robert Persons*, 58; *A True and Perfect Relation*, sigs H2r, P2r-v, Z1v; Coke, *The Lord Coke His Speech and Charge*, sigs D1r-v. For similar statements, see Edward Rishton's continuation of Sander, *Rise and Growth of the Anglican Schism*, 267; McCann and Connolly, *Memorials of Father Augustine Baker*, 16.

[62] Quoted from papers in the Jesuit Archives, Rome, in Philip Caraman, *Henry Garnet 1555–1606 and the Gunpowder Plot*, London 1964, 110.

[63] *CSP Dom 1547–80*, 303 (20 Dec. 1567). Cf the Worcester visitation returns of 1569, which specifically called for enquiry into the annual reception of communion, but made no mention of attendance at church, cited in Walker, 'Implementation', 16.

[64] *CSP Dom 1547–1580*, 561 (Oct. 1577), cf Emmison, *Morals and the Church courts*, 75.

[65] Perceval Wiburn, *A checke or reproofe of M. Howlets untimely shreeching [sic] in her Majesties eares*, London 1581, 84r, 143r.

2

'Reasons of Refusall'

Manye at this day will aske, whether their resorte to the material churche of heretikes, can make them cease to be of the Catholike churche? – H. B., *A Consolatory Letter to all the Afflicted Catholikes of England*, Rouen [London secret press] [1587–8], 27.

'Who knoweth not how often the question of going to hereticall Churches hath bene tossed in our countrey?' queried the Jesuit Henry Garnet in 1593.[1] Garnet addressed an issue arising from the Elizabethan settlement of persisting and far from peripheral concern to the clerical opponents of Protestantism thirty-five years later. In the context of efforts to entrench recusancy as the inescapable religious duty of the Catholic laity, church papistry represented a formidable pastoral challenge. Commanding the attention of the Counter Reformation's leading advocates and international diplomats, as well as the rank and file of its missionary corps, 'schismatics' were targeted for a sustained offensive at the level of public discourse.

I

Conformity with Protestantism immediately raised misgivings in the minds of a minority of committed and conscientious Catholics. 'Whether it is lawful for the laity to receive the communion as is now used?' was a vexing question as early as 1561, when John Murren, former chaplain to Bishop Edmund Bonner, distributed in the streets of Chester a manuscript treatise condemning such compromising conduct.[2] A year later, the scruples of a group of noblemen prompted requests mediated by the Portuguese and Spanish ambassadors to the Council of Trent and the pope for an authoritative statement on the legality of attendance at Common Prayer itself. The evils of partaking in 'Calvin's supper' were apparently already undisputed. Favourable and indulgent replies were anticipated by the initiators of these appeals, but Pius IV's categorical negative was independently endorsed by the secret committee appointed at Trent: church papistry was a mortal sin *omnino non licere*, in no case lawful.[3] Surprisingly, neither formal decrees nor canons

---

[1] [Henry Garnet], *A Treatise of Christian Renunciation . . . Whereunto is added a shorte discourse against going to Hereticall Churches with a Protestation*, [London secret press] [1593], 13.
[2] Printed in Pilkington, *Works*, 617–39, at p. 634. See also *CSP Dom 1547–1565 Addenda*, 524 (1561?).
[3] See C. G. Bayne, *Anglo-Roman Relations 1558–1565*, Oxford 1913, 163–81; Pollen, *The English Catholics in the Reign of Queen Elizabeth*, 99ff.; Meyer, *England and the Catholic Church Under Queen Elizabeth*, 68; Phillip Hughes, *The Reformation in England*, iii, London 1954, 250–1; F. W.

followed: indeed, both decisions were deliberately suppressed. Politic considerations concerning the foreseeably bitter consequences for lay Catholics justified their lapse into oblivion: 'it will not stand with our safety', it was said, 'that the question be propounded publickly in the Counsell: least it being divulged, may provoke the mindes of our Protestants, and hasten the daunger of diverse'.[4] The matter continued to be conveniently regarded as unsettled.

Throughout the 1560s, localised and sporadic endeavours were made by surviving and refugee Marian clergy to enforce these poorly publicised rulings. William Allen laboured to eliminate the 'pernicious opinion' that presence at reformed assemblies was excusable during his visit to Lancashire between 1562 and 1565.[5] Armed with a renewed papal prohibition, Laurence Vaux, ex-warden of Manchester College, undertook the task of disseminating this 'defynytyve sentence' in 1566. Pastoral letters stressing the heinous spiritual offence involved were surreptitiously circulated in the north-west, and by 1568 a trickle of other deprived priests were acquiring faculties to reconcile schismatics and joining the offensive against conformity.[6] Vaux expected his message to 'appeare hard sharpe bytter and sower' to a majority apt to deride recusants as 'found folysshe men'.[7]

Maitland, 'Pius IV and the English Church service', *EHR* v (1900), 330-2. The Spanish ambassador, Bishop de Quadra's appeal to Rome was accompanied by a letter that exaggerated Catholic woes under the early Elizabethan regime, implying that non-attendance at church was a capital crime, and claimed that the Book of Common Prayer contained 'no impiety or false doctrine'. It set forth arguments in favour of permission for churchgoing. See, in addition to the above, *CSP Spanish 1558-1567*, p. 258 (7 Aug. 1562). On the Trent decision, see T. G. Law's introduction to Vaux, *Catechisme*, p. xxx; Joseph Gillow, *A Literary and Biographical History or Bibliographical Dictionary of the English Catholics from the Breach with Rome in 1534 to the Present Time*, 5 vols, London 1885-1903, iv. 117. (Bayne, *Anglo-Roman Relations*, appendix 44, pp. 290-1, prints extracts from the petition). The decision remained shrouded in mystery until the 1590s, and subtly differing versions were reported by key Catholic propagandists in the preceding years. See the manuscript treatise written by I. G., 'An answere to a comfortable advertisement, with it addition written of late to afflicted catholykes concerning goinge to churche with protestantes' (*c*.1593), St Mary's College, Oscott, Birmingham, MS E. 5. 16, chs iv, vi, and postscript; Gregory Martin, *A Treatise of Schisme*, Douai [English secret press] 1578, sig. C6v; *The Declaration of the Fathers of the Councell of Trent, concerning the going unto Churches, at such time as hereticall sevice is saied, or heresy preached*, [London secret press] [1593], (bound with Garnet, *Treatise of Christian Renunciation*, cited above), a 'reprint' in Latin and English of the decision; and [Henry Garnet], *An Apology against the Defence of schisme*, [London secret press] [1593], 14-15; Robert Southwell, *An Epistle of Comfort*, Paris [London] 1587-8, 171v-2r; Robert Persons, *Quaestiones Duae de sacris alienis non adeundis*, [St Omer] 1607, extracted in Bayne, *Anglo-Roman Relations*, appendix 45, pp. 291-2. Garnet's views on the decision were also voiced during his trial for treason in 1606: *A True and Perfect Relation*, sigs X1r-v.

[4] *Declaration of the Fathers*, 25.

[5] *DNB s.v.* Allen; Vaux, *Catechisme*, pp. xxix-xxx; T. F. Knox (ed.), *The Letters and Memorials of William Cardinal Allen 1532-1594* (Records of the English Catholics under the Penal Laws ii), London 1882, pp. xxiii, 21.

[6] Knox, *Letters and Memorials*, 21ff. Four priests were noted in this royal writ sent to the sheriff of Lancashire in 1567-8: John Murren; Dr Richard Marshall, the Dean of Christ Church, Oxford; James Hargreaves, vicar of Blackburn; and one 'Norreys'. Only Nicholas Sander, Thomas Harding, Thomas Wilson, and Thomas Peacock had formally acquired these faculties by 1567: see Meyer, *England and the Catholic Church*, 475-8. For Vaux, see, Hughes, *The Reformation in England*, iii. 249-50; Vaux, *Catechisme*, pp. xxxiiff.; Wark, *Elizabethan Recusancy in Cheshire*, 9; Haigh, *Reformation and Resistance*, 248-51, 259, 266.

[7] Vaux, *Catechisme*, pp. xxxviii-xxxix.

The impact of these initial clerical exertions, however, seems to have been severely limited. In 1567, the exiled divine Nicholas Sander was lamenting that 'it hath not ben more earnestly opened and looked unto'. But his own stern exhortation on the subject prefacing a learned counter-attack on the Protestant theology of idolatry may have had no more that a restricted academic readership.[8] Similarly, *De Schismate*, a Latin treatise against churchgoing written in 1573 by John Young, the ousted Master of Pembroke Hall, Cambridge, possibly travelled no further than Louvain, that safe haven for conservative scholars. 'Certaine considerations and causes, movyng me not to bee presente at, nor to receive, neither use the service of . . . the Common boke of praiers', the manuscript originally released at court by the Marian abbot of Westminster had a distinctly personal tone and pertinence too. It was chiefly an explanation of John Feckenham's own obstinacy for the private satisfaction of Protestant friends.[9]

Tridentine apologists vehemently maintained that innocent English lay-people had been scandalously misguided by their ecclesiastical predecessors *en bloc*.[10] The 'wonderful harvest' that had been gathered into 'the barn of the Church' in recent years, declared Garnet in 1590, had been 'sown by the seminaries established and maintained by the Holy See'. These 'splendid and illustrious triumphs' were exclusively the work of the 'pontifical priests'. Single-handed, they had awakened their inert and languid precursors from 'the lethargy of schism'.[11] Yet, as Christopher Haigh has repeatedly emphasised, the concept of a separated Catholic Church existed prior to the arrival of the first seminarists from the Low Countries in 1577: some Marian clergy were already schooling their followers in comprehensive nonconformity a decade earlier. The crusade against church papists was not launched, but appropriated and accelerated by the Douai missionaries and, after 1580, from the Jesuit College in Rome.[12] Nevertheless, the doctrine of recusancy did not become the *public* ideology of post-Reformation Catholicism until the middle years of the reign when Protestantism began to consolidate a more substantial grasp on the religious establishment.

Systematic printed propaganda against conformity dates from 1578, when Gregory Martin published his *Treatise of Schisme*. Robert Persons's *Brief*

---

[8] Nicholas Sander, *A Treatise of the Images of Christ, and of his Saints*, Louvain 1567, preface, and sig. A2v. This was a contribution to the theological controversy sparked by John Jewel's 'Challenge' sermon preached at Paul's Cross in Nov. 1559.

[9] John Young's *De Schismate* was republished in Douai in 1603: *DNB s.v.* Young. Feckenham's text was printed for refutation in William Fulke, *A Confutation of a Popishe and sclaunderous libelle, in forme of an apologie*, London 1571, 1v–17r. HMC, *First Report*, London 1870, 90, dates the manuscript tract to 1563. See also Peter Holmes, *Resistance and Compromise: the political thought of the Elizabethan Catholics*, Cambridge 1982, 85, 236n.

[10] See, for example, Martin, *Treatise of Schisme*, sig. C6v; Garnet, *Treatise of Christian Renunciation*, 16–18, 167; I. G. 'An answere to a comfortable advertisement', ch. iv; J. H. Pollen, 'The memoirs of Father Robert Persons', in *CRS Miscellanea II* (CRS ii, 1906), 61–2.

[11] Quoted from papers in the Jesuit Archives, Rome, in Caraman, *Henry Garnet*, 109.

[12] Haigh, 'The continuity of English Catholicism', 187, 197 and passim; idem. *Reformation and Resistance*, 255, 267. See also Manning, *Religion and Society*, 44ff.; Dures, *English Catholicism*, 87; Holmes, *Resistance and Compromise*, 85; Scarisbrick, *The Reformation and the English People*, 142; McGrath and Rowe, 'The Marian priests under Elizabeth I', 104–5, 114.

Discourse contayning certayne reasons why Catholiques refuse to goe to Church was hastily prepared and rushed through a secret London press two years later. In subsequent decades, 'dissuasives against frequenting Protestant Churches' appeared from the pens of Catholic activists and evangelists as eminent as William Allen, Robert Southwell, Henry Garnet and perhaps John Gerard. While Elizabethan examples were primarily directed towards an upper-class audience, after James I's accession in 1603 experienced seminary priests like John Radford and Ralph Buckland determined to indoctrinate plebeian as well as aristocratic Catholics in the principles of dissent and composed similar tracts 'accommodating' themselves to the understanding of the 'unlearned' and 'poore simple soules'.[13] Separatist tenets, moreover, were firmly embedded in the annotations prepared by influential figures for the Douai-Rheims English Bible, that crowning co-operative achievement of intellectual exiles in this period.[14] Coinciding with the critical legislative stages of

---

[13] This chapter is based on a detailed study of the tracts listed below. In examining them as a homogeneous whole, I concentrate on their thematic similarities, rather than their individual peculiarities, generic differences, or the contributions of particular authors. Gregory Martin, *Treatise of Schisme* (1578), and idem. *The Love of the Soule Whereunto are annexed certaine Catholike Questions to the Protestants*, [Lancs, Birchley Hall press] 1619 (first publ. 1597). Robert Persons, *Brief Discours* (1580) was reprinted in 1599, 1601, 1621. Persons further addressed the question in 1580 in a manuscript reply to the author of an anonymous tract in favour of the lawfulness of churchgoing: 'Against going to Churche', BL, Add. MS 39830; and in *Quaestiones Duae* (1607). Thomas Hide, *A Consolatorie Epistle to the afflicted Catholikes*, Louvain [London] 1580 (first publ. Louvain 1579). William Allen addressed the subject more briefly in *An Apologie and True Declaration of the institution and endevours of the two English colleges*, Henault [Rheims] 1581, ch. vii ('An admonition and comfort to the afflicted Catholikes'), 104v–22v; and in 'The satisfaction of Mr James Bosgrave', in *A true report of the late apprehension and imprisonment of John Nicols Minister*, Rheims 1583, 32v–4v, and the unpaginated 'An admonition to the reader'. Robert Southwell, *Epistle of Comfort* (1587–8), and, in passing, in his *Humble Supplication* (1595 [1600]), 79ff. H. B., *Consolatory Letter* (1587–8). The manuscript treatise, 'An answere to a comfortable advertisement', written *c*.1593 by I. G. (who describes himself as a 'preest in the southe'), and now at St Mary's College, Oscott, has been persuasively attributed to John Gerard by Peter Holmes, *Resistance and Compromise*, 238n., but cf Southern, *Elizabethan Recusant Prose*, 139–40, who suggests George Cotton as a possible alternative author. Henry Garnet, *Treatise of Christian Renunciation* ([1593]) and *Apology* ([1593]); *Declaration of the Fathers* ([1593]). [Edmund] Thomas Hill, *Quartron of Reasons* (1600). N. C., *The Pigeons Flight From Out of Noes Arke, over the floud, into the Arke againe*, [English secret press] [1602–5]. John Radford, *A Directorie Teaching the Way to the Truth in a Briefe and plaine discourse against the heresies of this time*, [English secret press] 1605, esp. pp. 495–517. Ralph Buckland, *An Embassage from Heaven*, [English secret press] 1611. (Gillow, *Bibliographical Dictionary*, i. 332 also attributes to Buckland, *A Persuasive against Frequenting Protestant Churches*, but as this tract does not appear in *STC* or in *A&R* it may now be lost.) See also Richard Broughton, *The First Part of Protestants Proofes, for Catholikes Religion and Recusancy*, [English secret press] 1607, and *Protestants Demonstrations for Catholiks Recusance*, Douai 1615, two tracts which employed the innovative method of refuting one's opponents by their own words. Briefer discussions are in Richard Bristow, *Briefe Treatise* (1574), 129bff.; Thomas Worthington, 'The maner of proceding against M. John Rigbie, a Catholique gentleman put to death in London, this present yeare, 1600', in *A Relation of Sixtene Martyrs* (1601), 3–45; Thomas Wright, *The Disposition or Garnishmente of the Soule* (1596), 'To the Catholique-lyke Protestantes', sigs C8v–D2v. Martyrology and anti-apostate literature often emphasised and reiterated the duty of recusancy. In addition to Allen, *A true report*, 32vff. and Worthington, *A Relation of Sixtene Martyrs*, see Challoner, *Memoirs of Missionary Priests*, 118ff.; 'The fall of Anthony Tyrell', in Morris, *Troubles of Our Catholic Forefathers*, ii. 287–501.

[14] *The New Testament of Jesus Christ Translated Faithfully into English*, Rheims 1582, and *The Holie Bible Faithfully Translated into English* [Old Testament], 2 vols, Douai 1609–10. See the annotations to Matt x. 32–4, Mark iii. 13, viii. 36, Acts iv. 19, 1 Cor viii. 10, 2 Cor vi. 14, 2 Tim ii. 17, Titus

government persecution, the recurrent dissemination of such literature suggests 'schismatics' were not quickly harried out of existence by the envoys of a renascent Rome, nor bullied into docility by their bid to harness the resources of a mass medium to mould and regularise popular opinion.

Why did the spokesmen of the Counter Reformation choose the permanence, indelibility – and illegality – of print to expound the ideology of recusancy? Why did they select the forum of vernacular, public discourse to parade a stance which could only exacerbate official suspicion and enmity towards their afflicted countrymen and women? In an age of steadily advancing literacy, print was a crucial, if imperfect, instrument of control for a religion insisting on the hegemony of the Church and its agents in questions of belief and practice, and yet dispossessed of the parochial structure and ecclesiastical manpower indispensable to its effective exercise. It was a potential surrogate for the personal pastoral discipline which was so accentuated a feature of Tridentine Catholicism on the Continent.[15] This, however, is but a partial answer: recusancy propaganda, I would argue, collapses any uneasy distinction between 'devotional' and 'polemical' writings.[16]

II

These tracts were framed as the private religious literature of a community banished in its own land and struggling to prevent and postpone its progressive decline into a sect. They addressed persons whose very possession and perusal of prohibited reading matter was perhaps an act of defiance, an assertion of identity, and a self-consciously pious gesture. 'Reasons of Refusall' proceeded from a 'Catholicke in minde', 'throughly perswaded that onelye the Catholycke Romaine Relygion is truth, and that al other new doctrines, and religions, are false religions, as all new gods are false gods'.[17] Grounded on the premise that Protestantism and its worship were heretical and execrable, this literature aimed to stiffen those faint-hearted not in their

---

iii. 10, 2 John x, Rev iii. 22, Numbers xvi. 23–6, Daniel iii. 6, 4 Kings v. 19, Psalms xxv. 5, cxviii. 164, 124. Richard Bristow, William Allen and Thomas Worthington were among those involved in preparing the annotations.

[15] Jean Delumeau, *Catholicism Between Luther and Voltaire: a new view of the Counter Reformation*, London 1977, 190–201, and idem. 'Prescription and reality', in Edmund Leites (ed.), *Conscience and Casuistry in Early Modern Europe*, Cambridge–Paris 1988, 146–9; John Bossy, 'The Counter Reformation and the people of Catholic Europe', *P&P* xlvii (1970), 51–70.

[16] There has been relatively little scrutiny of printed Catholic literature, but for some attention to the tracts under consideration here, see: Holmes, *Resistance and Compromise*, ch. vi; Perez Zagorin, *Ways of Lying: dissimulation, persecution, and conformity in early modern Europe*, Cambridge, Mass. 1990, ch. vii; Clancy, *Papist Pamphleteers*, esp. pp. 142–91; Southern, *Elizabethan Recusant Prose*, 136–43; Rose, *Cases of Conscience*, 74ff.; Helen C. White, *English Devotional Literature [Prose] 1600–1640* (University of Wisconsin Studies in Language and Literature xxix), Madison, Wisc. 1931, chs v, vi. See also the introduction to John R. Roberts, *A Critical Anthology of English Recusant Devotional Prose, 1558–1603*, Pittsburgh 1966, 1–49.

[17] Persons, *Brief Discours*, 6r, 3v. Cf Southwell, *Epistle of Comfort*, 170r; Hill, *Quartron of Reasons*, 167.

fidelity to the habitual, hereditary faith of their forefathers, but in their inner resolve to suffer for it. Its intended audience was composed of church papists who mentally substituted 'Catholic' for the abusive labels with which they were christened by belligerent Protestants, but carelessly dismissed the possibility that temporising might contradict their confessional orthodoxy and imperil their spiritual redemption. Such books were one manifestation of that seemingly misnamed enterprise, the English 'mission': heading its pastoral agenda was not the conversion of heretics, but the reconciliation of schismatics.[18] Gregory Martin typically echoed and reprehended 'colde Catholikes' who rashly snubbed recusants: 'Why are you so scrupulous? is it so great a matter to come to Churche? am not I Catholike as wel as you?'[19] As penitential pastors rather than proselytisers, therefore, these authors clarified for the anxious and doubtful 'the qualitie of this sinne' of conformity. That it was sin was unquestioned. Robert Persons instead sought to recover thousands from the 'desperate presumption' and 'perilous perswasion, builded only on their owne phantasie', that churchgoing was no mortal and damnable deed, but venial and pardonable, extenuated by the dangers of 'these troublesome tymes'.[20]

In assailing an outlook characterised by moral laxity rather than doctrinal error, recusancy propaganda embodied a reassertion of clerical mastery over individuals who 'flattered' themselves to be 'Devines' – over a dispersed, hitherto neglected and recalcitrant flock who impertinently supposed they could better assess their spiritual health than the official custodians of their souls.[21] As much as an idealistic push for religious perfectionism, the onslaught on church papistry was the protest of the Counter Reformation priesthood against an ascendent and increasingly autonomous laity and its seemingly studied evasion of sacerdotal supervision. It symptomised an angry reaction on the part of the proponents of a neo-clerical ideology against an Erastian shift in the balance of power – that slow but irreversible passage of authority from priests to aristocratic laypeople that was occurring on a European-wide scale.[22]

Clerical writers supplied an impressive litany of 'Reasons of Refusall' – a string of relevant papal edicts, conciliar canons and examples from biblical and ecclesiastical history, and a catalogue of other practical, patristic and scriptural arguments against attendance at Protestant services. Later tracts routinely rehearsed well-established proofs that outward conformity was unforgivable, fundamentally contrary to divine, natural and church law.

Presence at reformed worship was invariably alleged to be intellectually and psychologically hazardous. Recalling St Paul's counsels to Timothy and the Romans, recusancy propagandists warned the unwary that to participate in

---

[18] As Haigh has pointed out: 'The continuity of English Catholicism', 195.

[19] Martin, *Treatise of Schisme*, sig. C7v, cf H. B., *Consolatory Letter*, 27 and Persons, *Brief Discours*, 6r.

[20] Ibid. 67v, 37v, 6r, 23r, cf Garnet, *Treatise of Christian Renunciation*, 165–7, and Martin, *Treatise of Schisme*, sig. C2v.

[21] Garnet, *Treatise of Christian Renunciation*, 14; *Declaration of the Fathers*, 5.

[22] Bossy, *The English Catholic Community*, esp. p. 31; idem. 'The character of Elizabethan Catholicism', esp. pp. 50ff.; and 'The English Catholic community 1603–1625', passim.

the enemy's 'noughty service' was to risk 'infection' with the disease of heresy: 'Because ther speche crepeth lyke a canker and they have subverted the faith of certayne', 'By sweete words and gaye blessings they seduce the harts of the Innocent.'[23] Conscious of the Church of England's superficial 'brotherly affinitie' with its Roman counterpart and sensitive to the draw of a vernacular liturgy, they emphasised human vulnerability to Protestantism's lures.[24] Since the mere company and carnal conversation of heretics was contagious, exposure to their sacred rites and invocations, to the almost physical and sacramental efficacy of the unvarnished Word, even more acutely endangered one's soul. Preachers had 'a popular way of talke whereby the unlearned, and specially women loden with sinne, are easily beguiled'. Garnet advised Catholics to take precautions against their diabolical cunning, and to 'tremble at the lively voice of your blasphemous ghospellers, as from whose mouth undoubtedly the Prince of heresy him selfe, belcheth out the smoaky doctrine of his filthy kingdome'.[25] Others demonstrated in detail 'by what meanes Schismatikes grow to be Heretikes'. Listless conformity was liable to lead to complete assimilation of Calvinist belief and the antinomianism immoderately attached to it by generations of popery's more ferocious defenders. It was a high road to 'flat' heresy, but an 'easie leape', the veritable origins of the mass apostasy of the Reformation: by Thomas Hill's hypothesis 'if no Catholicke would have heard Luth[er] to have preached . . . there had beene at this day neyther Lutheran, Zwinglian, Protestant, Puritane, nor any such late sprung up fellowes'.[26]

Appearance at Common Prayer was equally strenuously denounced as a voluntary act of idolatry, an unpardonable offence against the first table of the Decalogue. Compelling Old Testament precedents for recusancy included Tobias's refusal to revere Jerusalem's golden calves; the three young Hebrews in Daniel who chose to be cast into a burning furnace rather than adore the statue of King Nebuchadnezzar; and the 'famous history' of Eleazarus from Macabees, who selected death in preference to eating even a substitute for meat forbidden by Jewish ceremonial law. The punishment of Jeroboam and the ten tribes for bowing to false gods only too plainly prefigured the dire penalties for acquiescing in heresy.[27] To be publicly seated in a pew itself

[23] Persons, Brief Discours, 6rff., at 7r. Cf Martin, Treatise of Schisme, sigs **5v, A1v–2rff.; H. B., Consolatory Letter, 45; Bristow, Briefe Treatise, 140b; Southwell, Epistle of Comfort, 171v; Declaration of the Fathers, 33; Hill, Quartron of Reasons, 175; Radford, Directorie Teaching the Way to the Truth, 501, 507; I. G., 'An answere to a comfortable advertisement', ch. ix.

[24] Martin, Treatise of Schisme, sig. G5v. Cf Hide, Consolatorie Epistle, sigs B6r–v; Garnet, Apology, 50ff.; Bristow, Briefe Treatise, 143a–4b; Buckland, Embassage from Heaven, 31–2, 35–6.

[25] See respectively the New Testament annotations to Rom xvi.18 and 2 Tim ii.17; and Garnet, Apology, 119.

[26] Buckland, Embassage from Heaven, 62ff.; Hide, Consolatorie Epistle, sigs C4vff., at C5r, cf Hill, Quartron of Reasons, 90–1; Hill, Quartron of Reasons, 175. Cf Garnet, Apology, 91, 94; Declaration of the Fathers, 32–4; Persons, Brief Discours, 8v; Martin, Treatise of Schisme, sig. **4v.

[27] For Tobias, the Hebrew youths and Jeroboam, see ibid. ch. ii, sigs C7r–C8r, D2r–3r, and the annotations to Tobias i. 5–6, Daniel iii. 6, 2 Paralipomenon xi. 14 respectively. Cf Worthington, A Relation of Sixtene Martyrs, 43; H. B., Consolatory Letter, 106; Buckland, Embassage from Heaven, 41. On Eleazarus, 2 Maccabees vi. See also Buckland, Embassage from Heaven, 42; Martin, Treatise of Schisme, sig. A8r; Worthington, A Relation of Sixtene Martyrs, 43; Radford, Directorie Teaching the Way to the Truth, 510.

constituted an endorsement of Protestant errors. No less heinously than the fully seduced did church papists condescend 'to honour Calvins bread, and Cranmers communion booke by the assistance of their bodylye presence'.[28] Accomplices to a crime warranted no mercy, John Radford informed conniving Catholics: 'you see if one be drawne in amongst theeves, perhaps partly against his will to be at a robbery, as to hold the horses, he shal be hanged for his paines'.[29] Participating in or approving of another's sin made one 'a fellowe or cooperatour with the principall agent, and they both are worthye of deathe'. 'Exteriour' or 'half' heretics would be disciplined as heretics indeed.[30]

These treatises sought to reclaim their readers from the wilderness of 'schism', rather than the abyss of heresy. Conformists could not be chastised for forsaking their essential convictions or disputing doctrinal certainties. But as 'peacebreakers' severing themselves from the visible Church of Christ, they were guilty of a 'monstrous vice' against Catholic charity, of the grievous sin of undermining its intrinsic unity and thereby jeopardising the solidarity and salvation of the entire body of the faithful.[31] Elizabethan and Jacobean schismatics could thus expect the fate Numbers recorded for the rebels Korah, Dathan and Abiram who conspired against Moses and Aaron – to be swallowed up alive.[32] Simply by frequenting the familiar parish church of their childhood and youth, inconspicuous individuals committed an awesome ecclesiastical crime.

Tapping a pervasive distrust of duplicity and disguise in contemporary culture, recusancy propagandists also reviled outward conformity as a disturbing exhibition of dissimulation or 'feigning'. Pretended assent to Elizabeth's religious revolution would be construed and censured as genuine assent: as Persons alleged, 'al dissemblinge of our faith [is] taken, for denying our faith: and al seeminge, to be condemned, for doinge'. It was nothing less than perjury or 'detestable lying', treacherous deception of God and one's neighbours.[33] To prove that any form of double-dealing was abominable, Garnet singled out 'those which having secrett Pewes or closettes looking into the Church, cause some other to go thither, that them selves may be deemed present'.[34] The literal divorce between a Catholic's mental resistance and his deputy's physical submission mirrored the schizophrenic contradiction

---

[28] H. B., *Consolatory Letter*, 107.

[29] Radford, *Directorie Teaching the Way to the Truth*, 498. Cf Martin, *Treatise of Schisme*, sigs A3rff. and B6v; Hill, *Quartron of Reasons*, 176.

[30] I. G., 'An answere to a comfortable advertisement', ch. ii; Garnet, *Apology*, 69–82, 96–7. See also Wright, *The Disposition or Garnishmente of the Soule*, sig. D1r; *Declaration of the Fathers*, 6, 28; Martin, *Treatise of Schisme*, sigs C1r–v; Hill, *Quartron of Reasons*, 171; H. B., *Consolatory Letter*, 30.

[31] Garnet, *Apology*, 84–96; Martin, *Treatise of Schisme*, sigs **4r–v; Persons, *Brief Discours*, 18r–29v; Hill, *Quartron of Reasons*, 173; I. G. 'An answere to a comfortable advertisement', ch. viii.

[32] See the annotation to Numbers xvi. 23–6. Cf Hide, *Consolatorie Epistle*, sig. E7r; Worthington, *A Relation of Sixtene Martyrs*, 41; Garnet, *Apology*, 86; Allen, *Apologie and True Declaration*, 106.

[33] Persons, *Brief Discours*, 35r; H. B., *Consolatory Letter*, 32–5, at p. 33. For similar imputations, see Martin, *Treatise of Schisme*, sigs **2v, A6v, A7r–v, B2r; Buckland, *Embassage from Heaven*, 53–5; Hill, *Quartron of Reasons*, 174; Sander, *Treatise of the Images of Christ*, sig. A1v.

[34] Garnet, *Apology*, 62, cf Persons, *Brief Discours*, 66r.

inherent in outward conformity itself. Temporising, Sander argued, 'divideth one man into twain, setting the hart in one cumpanie, and the bodie in an other: as though anie man could go to the church, except his hart and mind caried his bodie thither'.[35] Indeed, because false religions were 'counterfeit' and hypocritical by definition, to don the 'visard of heresy' and masquerade as a Protestant was effectively to be one.[36]

Representative of Counter Reformation literature designed to cultivate rigorous habits of moral scrutiny and inculcate an interiorised piety, these tracts deplored churchgoing as an act in contempt of 'conscience', of that inviolable absolute, self. 'Conscience' was not to be lightly dismissed as effeminate whim, remonstrated Hill, 'the common aunswere, which . . . women, and such sillie soules are accustomed to make'.[37] Behaviour that patently negated a personally acknowledged truth constituted an active renunciation of God the Father and a willful transgression against the Holy Ghost. Deserving both temporal and internal punishment, it promised internal as well as eternal torment. 'Nothing can be looked for', said I. G., 'but the verifynge of godes threats spoken to this end.' Thomas Wright wondered that 'the verye hell you feele in your soules, the horrible torture of your consciences, enforcethe you not to leave that hellish Sinagog?'[38] Such writings ostensibly disclose remarkably developed notions of intellectual freedom and the limits of an individual's answerability to imperatives outside the self. Persons, for instance, parallelled the iniquity of a Catholic attending Protestant services with the wickedness of a Jew sacrilegiously swearing to the blessed Trinity, or a Calvinist counterfeiting adoration of transubstantiated bread and wine. More topically and tellingly, Martin compared church papistry with the base conduct of puritan ministers who in despite of their reformist objections wore the 'fryers weede'. Transcending ingrained sixteenth-century religious prejudices, they contended 'how good so ever the action in it selfe were . . . yet unto the doer, it should be a damnable sinne, because it seemed nought in his judgment and conscience'.[39] While recusancy's exponents urged respect for the dictates of even an erroneous conscience, they none the less assumed unreservedly the right to prescribe and superintend the principles motivating that inner voice. 'Conscience' was less an autonomous faculty, than an interior machine to be harnessed to clerical ideology.

Church papists additionally failed to fulfil the scriptural obligation of open avowal and public profession of one's faith. To conform was to display a callous disregard for Christ's warnings in the Gospels: 'He that shal denie me

---

[35] Sander, *Treatise of the Images of Christ*, sig. A2r.

[36] H. B., *Consolatory Letter*, 32–5, esp. p. 33, cf Sander, *Treatise of the Images of Christ*, sig. A3r.

[37] Hill, *Quartron of Reasons*, 181, cf 167. Cf the Protestant writer John Dove, *A Perswasion to the English Recusants, to Reconcile themselves to the Church of England*, London 1602, 9. He scoffed at recusants who claimed they refused to conform for reasons of 'conscience': 'So then what is their proofe, but a womans reason, it is so, because it is so; I will have it so, because I thinke so'.

[38] I. G., 'An answere to a comfortable advertisement', ch. ix; Wright, *The Disposition or Garnishmente of the Soule*, sigs D1v–D2r.

[39] Persons, *Brief Discours*, 5v, sig. + + 3r; Martin, *Treatise of Schisme*, sigs C3r, A6r–v. Cf N. C., *Pigeons Flight*, 58.

before men, I also wil denie him before my father which is in heaven.'[40]
Richard Bristow reminded the complacent that secret espousal of the true
religion was grossly inadequate: silent presence at heretical worship was as
flagrant a gesture of repudiation as disowning the Messiah and the Church of
Rome from one's own mouth.[41] Both 'in mans reason, and Gods censure',
Southwell stressed, deeds in fact outweighed words. Buckland inferred that a
schismatic's overt, deliberate action was therefore far more disgraceful than
the apostle Peter's three rash but private utterances: 'waded he not so farre, as
by any other external signe, to beare shew of an enimy'.[42] It was a form of
spiritual defection akin to the betrayal of Judas or Elizabethan and early
Stuart apostates.

Clerical authors consequently conceived of recusancy as a confessional act.
They asserted that to recoil from this aggressively negative posture of religious
protest was to eschew an essential exercise in externally affirming one's
orthodoxy and the validity of a prescribed system of belief. Indeed, Persons's
Brief Discours and Hill's *Quartron of Reasons* seem as determined to provide
persuasive inducements to nonconformity, as a convenient and concise
compendium of justifications for those summoned at diocesan visitations for
absence from church and ordered to explain 'for what cause they have refused
so to do?'[43] Like the manuscripts circulating that advised how best to answer
this question, these manuals drilled confirmed recusants in lucid replies to
Protestant demands for a declaration of the motives behind their
delinquency.[44] The struggle against conformity epitomised the growing
parochial emphasis on individual catechetical instruction that twinned an
unprecedented impulse for the production of formalised national creeds – the
emerging confessionalism of the post-Reformation age.[45]

In admonishing church papists to become 'confessant catholikes', tract
writers claimed that an activity traditionally regarded as the sole responsibility
of martyrs was now the foremost duty of every layperson.[46] In the spirit of Sir

---

[40] See the annotation to Matt x. 32–4. Cf Persons, *Brief Discours*, 34v, 35v–6v; Hide, *Consolatorie Epistle*, sig. B4r; Martin, *Treatise of Schisme*, sigs A5r–vff.; Southwell, *Epistle of Comfort*, 176v; Hill, *Quatron of Reasons*, 181–2; Radford, *Directorie Teaching the Way to the Truth*, 509. This was also a common theme in catechisms, see for example, Vaux, *Catechisme*, 29; St Peter Canisius, *Certayne Necessarie Principles of Religion which may be entituled, A Catechisme conteyning all the partes of the Christian and Catholique Fayth*, trans. T. I., Douai [London] 1578–9, passim.

[41] Bristow, *Briefe Treatise*, sig. xx3v.

[42] Southwell, *Epistle of Comfort*, 170r, cf Garnet, *Apology*, 60; Persons, *Brief Discours*, 61v; Buckland, *Embassage from Heaven*, 8–10, at p. 9.

[43] See, for example, Bishop Aylmer's articles for London diocese, 1580: Kennedy, *Elizabethan Episcopal Administration*, ii. 108.

[44] PRO, SP 12/136/15 (1580), cf 12/279/90 (1601). See especially, Persons, *Brief Discours*, 6r ('I have put doune here thes reasons that folowe, which may serve for the justifiing of thone parties conscience, and for the dewe reforming of the other'); Hill, *Quartron of Reasons*, 161, 167 (Hill's discussion of 'schism' was framed as the reply to a letter of two London citizens requesting 'what Scripture, authority or reason can you shew, or pretend for refusing so to doe?'). Cf Rose, *Cases of Conscience*, 81.

[45] See Delumeau, *Catholicism Between Luther and Voltaire*, 199ff. and Bossy, 'The Counter Reformation and the people of Catholic Europe', 66ff.

[46] Hide, *Consolatorie Epistle*, sigs A5r, A7v, D7r–v; H.B., *Consolatory Letter*, 3, 5; Martin, *Treatise of Schisme*, sigs A5rff.; Southwell, *Epistle of Comfort*, 178v; Allen, *Apologie and True Declaration*, 107.

Thomas More's *Dialogue of Comfort against Tribulation* a generation earlier, they sought to stimulate otherworldly zeal for a stance that could legally entail embracing pecuniary loss, if not imprisonment. Ordinary individuals should jubilantly endure the daily trials and sacrifices accompanying dissidence, cheerfully surrender their earthly wealth for the holy state of poverty, and ultimately brace themselves to relinquish their lives. By a paradoxical providential logic, such adversities were God's 'gift' to his 'special friends'.[47] Intractable recusants were thus scarcely less glorious than dead Counter Reformation saints; predictably, unflinching scorn of the Protestant taunt, 'Wil you not go to the Church?', was a prominent motif in contemporary martyrology.[48] Nor was forsaking kin, acquaintances and 'all other worldly creatures' simply a voluntary vow of the cloistered 'religious', as Garnet's *Treatise of Christian Renunciation* laboured to establish at length. Demanding obsessional courage as a matter of course, he enjoined English Catholics to emulate the legendary woman of Edessa who 'most speedely' repaired to the site of a planned massacre, dragging her infant son behind her, that he too might partake of the rewards of dying for the cause of truth.[49] Thomas Hide equally melodramatically urged his readers to harden their hearts towards those who hindered their abandonment of 'schism':

> Though thy nephew a litle ladde and playing boye hang about thy necke, though thy mourning mother with rent heares and blubbered cheekes shewe thee her pappes wherewith she gave thee sucke, though thy feble father lye at thy thresholde, passe by thy father, passe by thy mother with drie eyes, and hasten to the crosse of Christ: crueltie in this case, is the onelye kinde of pietie, and pietie for God, is no crueltie.[50]

Rather more pragmatically, H. B.'s 1587–8 tract presented itself as a 'cordiall' against the 'thirten monthes mulct' – the monthly £20 fine instituted by the anti-recusant legislation of that decade. It balanced chapters detailing the material and monetary burdens proceeding from existing laws and the superlative spiritual benefits of suffering for a religion based on an economy of merit and sin.[51] Hide also assigned space to trivialising the less tangible

---

[47] Hide, *Consolatorie Epistle*, sigs A7v, F4r. Thomas More's *A dialogue of Cumfort against tribulacion*, first published in 1553, was republished in Antwerp in 1573.

[48] See, for example, Worthington, *A Relation of Sixtene Martyrs*, 3–45, esp. pp. 14, 44–5, which exploited the ostentatious remorse, triumphant reconciliation and edifying death of John Rigby, a temporiser in his youth, to teach a lesson in the doctrine of recusancy; Allen, *A true report*, 'The satisfaction of Mr James Bosgrave', 32v–4v, and cf the unpaginated 'Admonition to the reader'; Challoner, *Memoirs of Missionary Priests*, 42–3, 188ff.; Morris, *Troubles of Our Catholic Forefathers*, i. 69; Hicks, *Letters and Memorials*, 58, where among the notable cases Robert Persons recorded for his Jesuit superiors in Rome was that of 'a certain matron of gentle birth' who had opted to remain in prison rather than merely 'to pass through the middle of the church, whilst the heretics were holding service there, making no stay and giving no sign of reverence'.

[49] Garnet, *Treatise of Christian Renunciation*, passim, esp. p. 5, and *Apology*, 171.

[50] Hide, *Consolatorie Epistle*, sig. B2r. For an almost identical passage, see Martin, *Treatise of Schisme*, sigs K8rff., esp. sig. L1r; Buckland, *Embassage from Heaven*, 91–3; Radford, *Directorie Teaching the Way to the Truth*, 522.

[51] H. B., *Consolatory Letter*, 8ff., 58ff. ('what Recusants shall lose'), 86ff., 104ff. ('Rewarde for

hardships that attended refusal to go to church: harassment and ostracism by family, friends and neighbours, and the injuries inflicted by language – the persecution of 'wordes' as well as 'swordes'. 'What if the professed enemies of the Church nickname you?', he challenged, 'What if they revile you?' Conforming to elude that odious epithet 'papist', 'a fewe syllables, and them not of yll sound nother', was singularly cowardly. To be slighted and slandered by one's peers in effect entitled one to that universally envied designation, 'Catholic'.[52] Recusants might be ridiculed and 'esteemed for very fools' by their time-serving co-religionists, but according to Martin, it was schismatics who would 'howle and cry out for very anguish and confusion' in God's final analysis. Those who ignored the onerous and distasteful directives of their priests, deeming 'the way of salvation to straite', could hope for no pity in the afterlife. Opting for the discomforts of dissent under a Protestant regime was foresight rather than caprice, the compulsory code of the 'heavenly wise' not the unnecessary stoicism of the pretentiously pious.[53]

Clerical hostility towards conformity was enhanced by an awareness that securing every subject's public presence at Common Prayer was the linchpin of the 1559 Settlement. To appear at heretical services in deference to the Act of Uniformity, reasoned Robert Southwell, was to collaborate with the Elizabethan government in its chosen strategy for the eventual extermination of the 'Old Religion':

> Was not the lawe of goinge to churche, and of beinge there present at that which they call divine service, made and published purposelye to the abolyshinge of the Catholique Faythe, to the contempte, reproofe, and overthrow of the true Churche, to the establishing of theyre untrue doctrine? And can any Catholicke knowing this, (as none can be ignorant therof), imagyne, but that in obeyinge this lawe he consenteth unto it, and to the accomplyshing of that, which the lawe intendeth, that is the impugning of the true and the setting upp of a false faythe . . . Moreover was not thys lawe made, to force men to shewe and professe a conformablenesse in external behaviour to this new faith? Is it not required as a signe of renouncinge the true church, and approvinge this newe forme of service, sacraments, and religion?[54]

'I lessen therby the number of Catholikes, and encrease the number of Protestantes, at the least in open show', headed Hill's list or *Quartron of Reasons* for refusing to conform, responses to be memorised and staunchly recited under cross-examination.[55] Since ecclesiastical authorities appar-

Recusantes') and passim. Cf Southwell, *Epistle of Comfort*, 175rff, and Hide, *Consolatorie Epistle*, sigs A7r–v and passim.

[52] Ibid. sigs D6v, C8r–v, D3r. See also Sander, *Treatise of the Images of Christ*, sig. ****5v; Southwell, *Humble Supplication*, 76–8; and on the 'name of Catholikes', Richard Bristow, *Demaundes to be Proponed of Catholiques to the Heretikes*, Antwerp 1576, 24–5, and his *Briefe Treatise*, 5a–8b; Hill, *Quartron of Reasons*, 7–10.

[53] Martin, *Love of the Soule*, 68, and Garnet, *Apology*, 62.

[54] Southwell, *Epistle of Comfort*, 168v–9r. Cf H. B., *Consolatory Letter*, 20, and the annotation to Daniel iii. 6.

[55] Hill, *Quartron of Reasons*, 168.

ently accounted passive compliance with statute Protestantism as much a victory as enthusiastic conversion, church papistry perceptibly, if unintentionally, bolstered the rival camp: 'You goe thither as one of them, you sit there as one of them, you behave your selfe reverently as one of them. The Calvinist taketh you for Proselites, and as either converted or conformed; not altogether abhorring their pretended religion, not over resolute in the old faith, and finally as persons not farre from their Kingdome.'[56] It perversely promoted instead of passionately obstructed heresy's bid for hegemony.

Such texts endeavoured to breed a contentious spirit in timid schismatics, to nurture insolence towards the 'newe no gospell' and its devotees.[57] They represented a confident conviction that Catholicism's very survival demanded resistance and reprisal, that its post-Reformation identity could only be generated by disdainful opposition and tireless antagonism towards the ecclesiastical status quo. Recusancy, Persons maintained, ought to be adopted with alacrity not least because it was officially appointed and popularly accepted by Protestants as the 'signe distinctive betwixt religion and religion'. According to his theory of subjectivity, what in heretics' prejudiced perception was the earmark of a 'papist' naturally and necessarily became the 'proper and peculier signe of a true Cathol[i]que': 'For what doth make a thing to be a proper and peculier signe, but the judgment and opinion of men?'[58] And since those who adhered to the old faith themselves had come to 'accompte the recusantes to be sound catholykes, & the goers to be ether flatt protestantes or dissemblinge & halfe catholykes', I. G. stated, the case was closed. It was as obvious as if the orthodox and 'conformable' had been branded on their foreheads with the letter 'O'.[59]

Spurning the services of the Church of England was to be the keystone of an extensive system of conspicuous and contemptuous separation from Protestants in secular, as well as religious affairs. Sixteenth- and seventeenth-century Catholics, like the early Christians, were to conscientiously heed and apply St Paul's counsels to 'shunne the man that is an heretike and avoyde him': 'Bear not the yoke with infidels. For what participation hath justice with infidels. For what participation hath justice with iniquitie? or what societie is there betwene light and darknes? And what agreement with Christ and Belial? or what part hath the faithful with the infidel?'[60] Mimicking the 'childish piety' of the boy from ecclesiastical history who fanatically burnt a ball 'polluted' by rolling under the hooves of a heretic's mule, they should unsqueamishly adhere to a doctrine whose strict observance meant drastic estrangement from family and community, and austere dissociation from

---

[56] Buckland, *Embassage from Heaven*, 21.

[57] Hide, *Consolatorie Epistle*, sigs C1r–v; H. B., *Consolatory Letter*, 43.

[58] Persons, *Brief Discours*, 15r–18r passim, quotations at 15v, 16v, 17r . See also Garnet, *Apology*, 131ff.; idem. *Treatise of Christian Renunciation*, 160; *Declaration of the Fathers*, 28; Martin, *Treatise of Schisme*, sig. C3r.

[59] I. G., 'An answere to a comfortable advertisement', ch. vii.

[60] 2 Titus iii. 10, 2 Cor vi. 14–15, 2 John x. See Persons, *Brief Discours*, 7r; Martin, *Treatise of Schisme*, sigs A1r–2r; Worthington, *A Relation of Sixtene Martyrs*, 42; Bristow, *Briefe Treatise*, 134b; H. B., *Consolatory Letter*, 44–5; Hill, *Quartron of Reasons*, 175–6.

habitual ways and accustomed observances.[61] Martin ridiculed the 'fonde reasons' commonly tendered by Catholics who too readily yielded to the persuasions of their local minister or bishop 'because he is a gentle person forsoothe, and his wife a verye honest woman', or foolishly imitated the shabby example of the time-serving vicar of their youth.[62] Although Garnet acknowledged that in regions where the faithful were reduced to an oppressed and subjugated minority, conciliar law permitted daily, domestic interaction with the enemy, he incited his readers to exercise spontaneously a more comprehensive segregation from Protestants none the less: 'yet ever in worldly conversation and seculer actes of our life we must avoide them as much as we may, because their familiarity is many waies contagious and noisome to good men, namely [especially] to the simple'.[63]

'Schismatics' themselves were to be victims of this sweeping spiritual apartheid. Dissemblers, Radford warned, were 'as dangerous as heretikes them selves in some respects worse'.[64] The truly pious would as coldly repel conformist as convinced Protestants, for it 'hath alwaies bene an inviolable custome, that aswell the Schismaticke hath avoided the Catholicke, as the Catholicke hath shunned the spirituall communication with the Schismaticke'.[65] A number of writers spelt out some of the more awkward implications of these severe precepts, deducing that not only were men compelled to divorce unresisting spouses, but – at odds with traditional patriarchal injunctions on female obedience – that wives were likewise constrained to mutiny against and flee unmanly, capitulating husbands.[66]

Ironically, if not somewhat inconsistently, Counter Reformation propagandists envisaged a militant resurgence of Catholicism chiefly fostered by energetic paternalism. Their published works may indeed appear unduly concerned with instilling in upper-class males the stamina for dissent.[67] But

---

[61] Garnet, *Apology*, 176; Radford, *Directorie Teaching the Way to the Truth*, 508–9. See Martin, *Treatise of Schisme*, sigs D6v–F4v, for other examples from Scripture and patristic sources.

[62] Ibid. sigs E4v and I5r.

[63] Garnet, *Apology*, sig. *2r, who quotes from New Testament annotation to 2 John x, cf H. B., *Consolatory Letter*, 50. Sander and Martin specified that marriages contracted with Protestants were explicitly forbidden, see respectively *Treatise of the Images of Christ*, sig. A6v, and *Treatise of Schisme*, sigs B6v–7v (cf the marginal comment to 2 Cor vi. 14–15).

[64] Radford, *Directorie Teaching the Way to the Truth*, 496. Cf Southwell, *Epistle of Comfort*, 178v–9r; Martin, *Treatise of Schisme*, sigs G3rf, G6v; Canisius, *Certayne Necessarie Principles*, sig. B2r.

[65] Garnet, *Apology*, 189, cf Martin, *Treatise of Schisme*, sigs E5v–6r.

[66] Radford, *Directorie Teaching the Way to the Truth*, 522; Hide, *Consolatorie Epistle*, sig. B2r; Martin, *Treatise of Schisme*, sigs K3rff.; Buckland, *Embassage from Heaven*, 91. Wives were urged to leave their husbands by Garnet, *Treatise of Christian Renunciation*, 144ff.

[67] Gregory Martin, for example, posed as the private chaplain of a socially superior Catholic patron in 'A letter sent to a gentleman of authoritie, touching his following the world, and dissembling in religion against his conscience and knowledge', included in his *Love of the Soule*, 35ff. Robert Persons's *Brief Discours* was also framed as 'The answer of a vertuous and lerned man to a gentleman in England, towching the late imprisonment of Catholiques ther', 1r. On this point, see Haigh, 'From monopoly to minority', 138. As I have noted above, however, later tracts, particularly those by Buckland and Radford, were allegedly intended for the 'simpler sort': see Radford, *Directorie Teaching the Way to the Truth*, 'The preface to the reader', sigs A2r–A4r; Buckland, *Embassage to Heaven*, sigs *2r–v.

tutoring the socially and sexually elite in the seigneurial duty of exemplary recusancy was considered paramount in a coherent clerical strategy for the successful reconciliation of a nation of lapsed Catholics. Its champions recurrently underlined the grave sin of 'scandal' incurred by churchgoing aristocrats and gentry whose disgraceful deportment encouraged their wives, children and servants to follow suit. Church papists were guilty of 'paricidiall impiety', the soul murderers of sons, daughters and dependents whose attendance at common prayer they condoned or coerced.[68] The wider hierarchical consequences of such negligence, Gregory Martin surmised, were equally costly:

If a weakling see thee (a man of accompt and estimation) present in the Churche of heretikes, or at their sermons, their conscience being not fullye setled to detect heresie, is he not easily induced to frequent their conventicles with daunger of dayly corruption, and either to like the better, or to mislike the lesse of their sayinges and doinges[?][69]

Rather more far-fetched and extravagant were suggestions that co-operative Catholics 'disedified' Protestants themselves because their presence in the parish church provoked in heretics 'doting insolency and ranticke triumph'. Those who came making a 'protestation' of their disapproval of the service, sacraments and sermons, I. G. posited, generally caused 'greater realinge [railing] in the preacher'.[70] In Garnet's view, schismatics offended all sense of propriety actively as well as passively. Too many 'private persons' not merely refused to amend their conformist ways and bow to the directives of their spiritual mentors – 'which were a crime more tolerable' – 'but that which is more heinous & a most high degree of pride', defended their wickedness and sought by 'all possible meanes [to] allure their frendes & subjectes to the same iniquitie'. Far from stopping at unseemly disrespect for their priestly superiors, they arrogantly trespassed on their pastoral and advisory role.[71]

Casting such stumbling blocks in the path of the innocent and weaker brethren guaranteed intolerable miseries in the next world, and a lifelong burden of blame, for 'may not the simple and ignorant people impute their damnation to such as are their Rulers in the case of heresie?'[72] It furthermore diminished hope of and hampered schemes for an institutional return to Rome. Buckland's chastening charge to his refractory readers was: 'Is your continuance in Schisme to further the conversion of England?' Compromising in the interval 'til time serve our turne', protested Cardinal Allen, was no way

[68] On scandal generally, see ibid. 70ff.; Hill, *Quartron of Reasons*, 174–5; Radford, *Directorie Teaching the Way to the Truth*, 510; H. B., *Consolatory Letter*, 14–17; Persons, *Brief Discours*, 9r–15r, esp. p. 14r. On parents and children in particular, Garnet, *Apology*, 127ff.; Martin, *Treatise of Schisme*, sigs B5rff., cf B2vf.; Southwell, *Epistle of Comfort*, 173vff.
[69] Martin, *Treatise of Schisme*, sig. B3v; idem. *Love of the Soule*, 47ff.
[70] *Declaration of the Fathers*, 29; I. G., 'An answere to a comfortable advertisement', ch. ix. Cf Southwell, *Epistle of Comfort*, 171v–2r and Persons, *Brief Discours*, 14v.
[71] Garnet, *Treatise of Christian Renunciation*, 13–14.
[72] Martin, *Love of the Soule*, 49–50.

to either 'deliver our soules, or ever recover the Realme to the unity of Gods Church againe'.[73]

In these respects, Jesuit and seminarist writers admitted, church papists were even put to shame by their spiritual enemies. Implicitly acknowledging as authentic the arguments of Catholicism's adversaries, they pronounced the nonconformist principles and practice of infidels and Continental heretics, Marian Protestants and present-day puritans and separatists to be edifying, albeit mortifying models for schismatics. Southwell, for instance, cited with nothing less than approval Calvin's invective against French 'Nicodemites' and the teachings of other leading Swiss and German reformers on the subject.[74] Persons, furthermore, exploited these parallels to expose the Church of England's villainous inconsistency: in compelling Catholics to resort to church against their consciences, its defenders 'goe quit against their own doctrine and example'.[75] Indeed, polemicists who attempted to undermine recusancy tracts in print frequently found it difficult to deny that church papistry and 'dastardlie dissimulation' *was* utterly unethical. Thomas Sanderson's 'countermaund' to Ralph Buckland's 'counterfeit Embassage', for instance, had to agree that his opponent's general 'scope' or 'drift' was irrefutable; the assumptions underlying recusancy theory were sound, said Perceval Wiburn, but 'verye badlye applied'.[76] Undoubtedly, this was due in large part to the comparable conflicts of conscience experienced by their clerical colleagues and, progressively their congregations, as to the morality of remaining loyally within an unsatisfactorily reformed Church – dilemmas that were giving rise to a literature echoing much of the reasoning rehearsed by their 'popish' rivals. It was a tender point. How could upright Protestants press Catholics to conform, and insist, moreover, on the prerogative of public ecclesiastical authorities to force them to do so, while upholding in another context the defensibility – not to say responsibility – of liturgical dissent, non-subscription, and civil or social separatism? Frequently they deflected the question, directing energy and attention to that old battleground – the debate about the identity of the true Church. For while it was taken for granted that the faithful were bound to separate from and shun heretics, if Protestants were in fact disproved to be God's enemies, the syllogism would shatter and Catholic arguments for recusancy automatically fall apart. On the other hand, admitted John Field, had Persons satisfactorily shown Rome to hold the uniquely privileged status of the universal Church of Christ, 'they had wonne

---

[73] Buckland, *Embassage from Heaven*, 76; Allen, *Apologie and True Declaration*, 112v. Cf Sander, *Treatise of the Images of Christ*, sig. A5v.

[74] Southwell, *Epistle of Comfort*, 172v–3r, where he specifically referred to Calvin's tract *De vitandis superstionibus . . . Eiusdem excusatio, ad Pseudonicodemus*, Geneva 1549, and to Phillip Melanchthon, Peter Martyr and Martin Bucer. For Continental parallels, see also Southwell, *Humble Supplication*, 80; Persons, *Brief Discours*, 52rff. ('Example of infidels and heretics', esp. p. 52v, and H. B., *Consolatory Letter*, 53–5. On Marian Protestants, ibid. 53, 55; Hill, *Quartron of Reasons*, 177. For parallels with puritans and separatists: Persons, *Brief Discours*, 39v–40r, 52v–3r; Martin, *Treatise of Schisme*, C3r; N. C., *Pigeons Flight*, 58.

[75] Persons, *Brief Discours*, 52v–3r. He cited as further proof a passage from a catechism by 'John Gardiner' [Jean Garnier], *A briefe and cleare Confession of the Christian fayth*, London 1579.

[76] Thomas Sanderson, *Of Romanizing Recusants and Dissembling Catholicks*, London 1611, sig. ***v and p. 3, cf sig. A4r; Wiburn, *Checke or reproofe*, sig. Yy4r.

their cause'.[77] Rarely did either side of the Reformation divide concede as much, but abhorrence of conformity constituted a region of ideological common ground.

Unable to disregard the conflicting demands of Church and State facing the contemporaries of an Erastian age, Catholic propagandists appreciated that outward conformity was a predicament of political as well as moral proportions. Garnet believed 'feare of being esteemed a hollow and dissembling subject' was in fact the 'greatest motive' for the schism of the laity.[78] He and his associates confronted law-abiding citizens for whom consistent defiance of civil authority was unthinkable, and whose external

[77] John Field, *A Caveat for Parsons Howlet, concerning his untimely fliughte, and scriching in the cleare day lighte of the Gospell*, London 1581, sig. A5v. Cf Wiburn, *Checke or reproofe*, sigs Yy1r–v. William Perkins drew similar conclusions when he considered the directly parallel question: 'Whether it be lawfull for a man being urged, to go to idol-service, and heare masse, so as he keepe his heart to God?', in his *The whole treatise of the cases of conscience*, London 1608 (first publ. 1606), 163–7. Indeed, much past and present Continental writing on the subject was translated and printed in England or exported from the European mainland in the mid-sixteenth century, often explicitly intended for the benefit of Marian Protestants. Elizabethan editions were more implicitly pertinent to puritan ministers experiencing governmental pressure to conform. See Jean Calvin, *The Mynde of the Godly and excellent lerned man . . . what a Faithfull man, whiche is instructe in the Worde of God, ought to do, dwellinge amongest the Papistes*, [Ipswich] 1548; idem. *A sermon of the Famous and godly learned man . . . conteining an exhortation to suffer persecution for followinge Jesus Christe*, London 1581. Henry Bullinger, *Two Epystles One of Henry Bullynger . . . another of Jhon Calvyn . . . whether it be lawfull for a Chrysten man to communycate or be pertaker of the Masse of the Papystes*, [Antwerp 1544?]. Peter Martyr Vermigli, *A Treatise of the Cohabitacyon of the faithfull with the unfaithfull. Wherunto is added. A Sermon made [by Henry Bullinger] of the confessing of Christe and his gospell*, [Strassburg] 1555 (Martyr's treatise was later incorporated in his *Common places*, London 1583, pt ii, ch. iv). Pierre Viret, *Of the principal points which are at this daye in controversie, concerning the holy supper of Jesus Christ, and of the masse of the Romish Church*, London 1579; idem. *An Epistle to the Faithfull, necessary for all the children of God: especially in these dangerous dayes*, London 1582. Wolfgang Musculus, *The Temporysour (that is to saye the observer of tyme, or he that chaungeth with the tyme.)*, [Zurich?] 1555. Johann Wigand, *De Neutralibus & Mediis. Grosly Englished, Jacke of both sides*, London 1591 (first publ. 1562, republ. 1626). John Foxe's *Acts and Monuments* also recorded and compiled the relevant teachings of Marian martyrs such as John Bradford, John Philpot, William Tyms, John Hooper and others: see vol. vi. 662–4, 670ff. (Hooper), vii. 196ff. (Bradford), vii. 686ff. (Philpot), vii. 63 (George Marsh), vii. 567, 'A treatise of Bishop Ridley' (1555), viii. 113f, 762ff. (Tyms). See also John Hooper, *Later Writings of Bishop Hooper (together with his Letters and other pieces)*, ed. Charles Nevinson (PS, 1852), 570–8, for a reprint of *Whether Christian faith maye be kepte secret in the heart, without confession therof openly to the worlde as occasion shal serve*, Rouen [London?] 1553; John Bradford, *The Writings of John Bradford*, ed. Aubrey Townsend (PS, 1848–53), i. 379ff., 385f, 389; ii. 297–340 (a reprint of *The Hurte of Hering Masse*, London [1561?], republ. 1580); *An answer to a certain godly mannes lettres, desiring his frendes judgement, whether it be lawfull for a christian man to be present at the popishe Masse and other supersticious church service*, [Strassburg] 1557 (sometimes attributed to Thomas Becon). For historians' assessments of such writings and the practices they prompted and reinforced, see White, *The English Separatist Tradition*, esp. ch. i; Joy Shakespeare, 'Plague and punishment', in Lake and Dowling, *Protestantism and the National Church*, 119–20. On Nicodemism in Europe, especially in Italy and France, see Carlo Ginzburg, *Il Nicodemismo: simulazione e dissimulzione religiosa nell' Europe del' 500*, Turin 1970; who is criticised by Carlos M. N. Eire, 'Calvin and Nicodemism: a reappraisal', *Sixteenth Century Journal* x (1979), 45–69; idem. *War Against the Idols: the reformation of worship from Erasmus to Calvin*, Cambridge 1986, ch.vii; and Zagorin, *Ways of Lying*, passim esp. chs iv–vi. For Elizabethan puritan parallels, ibid. ch. x; Patrick Collinson, 'The cohabitation of the faithful with the unfaithful', in Ole Peter Grell, Jonathan I. Israel, and Nicholas Tyacke (eds), *From Persecution to Toleration: the Glorious Revolution in England*, Oxford 1991, passim esp. pp. 51, 65; Elliot Rose, *Cases of Conscience*, passim.

[78] Garnet, *Apology*, 143.

religious affiliation seemed dictated less by celestial considerations or the distant decisions of an Italian pope, than by the palpable presence and pressure of the village constable, churchwarden, or 'the Beadle of Bridewell come behind you with his staffe, fearcely and barbarously threatning you'.[79]

Sixteenth- and seventeenth-century theories of religious resistance rested on the assumption that since human decrees were by definition conditional on divine law, Christians not only possessed the right, but were encumbered with an obligation to defy edicts contravening that law.[80] Bent on re-educating readers anxious to sidestep the unpleasant practical implications of an ideology based on an imperative scriptural command to obey God above man, they presented refusal to attend church as a line of conduct wholly compatible with the political theology of non-resistance. Scrupulous recusancy, not conscienceless conformity, was the surest indication of the reliability of one's 'secondary faythe and allegiance' to a temporal Prince. So these tracts told Catholics and eavesdropping Protestants. For, asked Buckland, who could expect 'that he wil be loyal to man, who hath violated fidelity to his maker'?[81] Those who imagined inward convictions might be subordinated legitimately to the unchristian ordinances of an earthly ruler unmasked themselves as despicably Machiavellian, *politiques* who considered their religion but an adjunct of their politics. Volunteering one's presence at heretical services could never shake off suspicion of treachery against the queen: 'whom you should rather delude then obey by fained conformitye, wheras now you performe the true obedience of good subjects by suffering patiently whatsoever the lawe of your countrye shal laye uppon you'.[82] As 'John Howlet's' respectful dedicatory epistle to Persons's *Brief Discours* similarly reminded the Privy Council, it was recusants' peaceful submission to the penalties attached to their high principles rather than conformists' opportunist compliance that should inspire official clemency towards Catholics.[83] Repairing to church under the pretext and 'vayne pretence' of intending solely to demonstrate one's political probity was thus seriously misguided.[84]

Yet the writers of these tracts could not completely harmonise the notion of conscientious objection with that of meek obedience to the commands of a secular power. The inherent, explosive ambivalence of the doctrine of recusancy came sharply to the fore as early as 1578, when the government took exception to one of the prototypes for nonconformity Gregory Martin selected from the Apocrypha in his *Treatise of Schism*. Recalling Judith's assassination of the tyrannical general Holofernes to avoid eating the idolatrous meat he commanded her to consume, Martin exhorted Catholic gentlewomen to imitate her 'godlye and constant wisdome', that they too 'might destroye Holofernes, the master heretike, and amase al his retine, and

---

[79] Ibid. 44.
[80] Holmes, *Resistance and Compromise*, 81–2.
[81] Persons, *Brief Discours*, 2r, cf sig. + + 8v, pp. 55rff.; Buckland, *Embassage from Heaven*, 109. See also Martin, *Treatise of Schisme*, sig. **2rff.; Bristow, *Briefe Treatise*, 134a; Hill, *Quartron of Reasons*, 181; Southwell, *Epistle of Comfort*, 169r.
[82] H. B., *Consolatory Letter*, 39.
[83] Persons, *Brief Discours*, sig. + + 8v, pp. 2r, 67r.
[84] Ibid. 59v; Buckland, *Embassage from Heaven*, 82–3; Martin, *Treatise of Schisme*, sigs **3rff.

never defile their religion by communicating with them in anye smal poynt'. Reading remarkably like an incitement to ladies at court to commit regicide, this offending passage led to the summary execution of its London printer, William Carter.[85] In recommending recusancy as a politically acceptable alternative to church papistry, its theorists were clearly up against insurmountable obstacles.

Especial effort was expended by clerical propagandists in controverting the dangerously plain precedent for conformity afforded by the biblical figure Naaman Syrus, the courtier permitted by the prophet Elisha to physically assist his King at worship in the temple of Rimmon – to yield merely temporal service to his master. This was a favourite text, 'a great place with noble men', Martin complained, 'that gladly would yeelde a litle to please their prince, so they might doo it by example of scripture, and the authoritie of a prophet'.[86] In vain did tract writers attempt to argue it exegetically out of existence, by objecting that the case was almost entirely irrelevant to and inconsistent with the circumstances pertaining in late Tudor and early Stuart England. The situation was 'noe whit lyke'. Elisha's licence was a concession to one newly converted from idolatry, they asserted, 'pappe for infantes and yonge Catholikes', not 'strong meate' for the 'perfect' – those born, brought up, and long since confirmed in the faith. Contemporaries could scarcely claim 'childrens priviledge', or plea the infirmity of a 'milksopp' or 'very babe'.[87] 'Naaman', none the less, remained a major impediment in the struggle to discredit church papistry as a dishonest and dishonourable personal solution to the problem of reconciling 'popery' with patriotism. This campaign against political atheism registers the Counter Reformation's hostility to what Thomas Clancy has termed early modern society's 'schism of public and private morality'.[88]

Indeed, in a period in which the coexistence of differing versions of Christianity was still philosophically inconceivable and the concept of toleration at least theoretically anathema, it is hardly astonishing that outward conformity aroused profound unease. It appeared to perpetuate an unhealthy biconfessionalism in post-Reformation society. Echoing Elijah, these sixteenth-century prophets inveighed: 'How long halt you on two sides ? If our Lord be God, folow him: But if Baal, folow him.'[89] Martin supposed that many schismatics 'mislike of certaine things in the Catholike Religion, which . . . [they] would wish to bee otherwise, and conceive a mixt Religion, compounded of that which is best in both'. Individuals who

---

[85] For the passage citing Judith xi–xii, see ibid., sigs D2r–v. See also William Allen, *A True, Sincere, and Modest Defence of English Catholics*, ed. R. M. Kingdon, Ithaca, NY 1965 (first publ. 1584), 69; Holmes, *Resistance and Compromise*, 86; Southern, *Elizabethan Recusant Prose*, 350–3, 452–3.

[86] Martin, *Treatise of Schisme*, sig. F5r.

[87] I. G., 'An answere to a comfortable advertisement', ch. vi; Martin, *Treatise of Schisme*, sigs F4vff. and **3rff., quotations at F5v and 6r. Cf Persons, *Brief Discours*, 62rff.; Garnet, *Apology*, 28ff.; Radford, *Directorie Teaching the Way to the Truth*, 502ff.; and the extended annotation to 4 Kings xix. Elliot Rose discusses this case at length: *Cases of Conscience*, 74ff. and appendix A.

[88] Clancy, *Papist Pamphleteers*, 159ff. (esp. pp. 167ff.), 143.

[89] 3 Kings xviii. 21 and annotation. See Buckland, *Embassage from Heaven*, 77; Hill, *Quartron of Reasons*, 183; Allen, *Apologie and True Declaration*, 112v.

made 'a hodge podge of altogither', flippantly adapting the elements of two irreconcilable faiths to suit their personal tastes, unwittingly triggered further fragmentation of the Christian world.[90] Catholics who frequented church with a 'Protestation' were the butt of a bitter joke: there was 'no fitter name for these new heretickes', Garnet proposed, than 'Protesting Protestants'.[91] In Radford's experience, church papists too often became 'such as say they may be saved in any sect, or religion': adiaphorists who overlooked the generic distinction between matters of faith and things indifferent and so blurred the boundaries between Catholicism and Protestantism. Buckland's *Embassage from Heaven* ruthlessly reconstructed the excuses of those who rendered redundant denominational polemic:

> they are to precise, which either make them Heretikes, or thinke that Heretike must needes miscarry. What? we be al Christians, beleeve in one Saviour, expect one heaven, and enjoy our redemption. Have not al men soules to save: little differences make no great square, in the foundation we agree. At leastwise, whatsoever their lives be wicked, and doctrine false, their praiers and Churches must needs be of God, because they be good, and needes be good, because they honour God.[92]

Heresy was the antithesis of true religion, its logical opposite. Escaping this pattern of polarity and contrariety, church papistry, however, seemed subversive of prevailing assumptions about Christian 'order' itself. It struck at the heart of a universal principle of intelligibility, that predisposition to think in terms of binary opposition so central to sixteenth- and seventeenth-century intellectual culture.[93] These tracts betrayed precisely such a rationality. Overt hostility to orthodox Christianity was conflated and starkly equated with 'deviant' Catholicism, considered conformity with blind conformity. They assimilated schism with the ingrained impiety of the profane, an innate lack of enthusiasm for religious duty. As Persons lamented, 'Catholiques in hartes by goinge to Pro- testantes Churches, must needes bee brought . . . to flat atheisme, that is, to leave of all conscience, and to care for no relygion at all.'[94] The 'atheism' alarming the Counter Reformation clergy, like their Protestant counter- parts, therefore, was not philosophical scepticism but practical godlessness – superficial religiosity born of a sensual attachment to the world rather than a moment of rational rejection. It was a 'secret kind of Atheisme, or denying God; which is to deny him, not in wordes, but in life and

---

[90] Martin, *Love of the Soule*, 38; Radford, *Directorie Teaching the Way to the Truth*, 583.

[91] Garnet, *Treatise of Christian Renunciation*, 154.

[92] Radford, *Directorie Teaching the Way to the Truth*, 537; Buckland, *Embassage from Heaven*, 24–5.

[93] Stuart Clark, 'Inversion, misrule and the meaning of witchcraft', *P&P* lxxxi (1980), 98–127, esp. pp. 105, 110. See also Peter Burke, *Popular Culture in Early Modern Europe*, Aldershot, Hants 1978, 185–91.

[94] Persons, *Brief Discours*, 44v–5r. Cf Martin, *Treatise of Schisme*, sigs A5v–6r; Southwell, *Epistle of Comfort*, 170v–1r; Hill, *Quartron of Reasons*, 183–4. See also PRO, SP 12/279/90, calendared in *CSP Dom 1601-3*, 45 (1601): 'Directions [for Catholics] as to the lawful manner of anwering certain questions as to going to church or doing other religious actions' which included the equivocation, 'Think you that I will live like an Atheist?'

behaviour'.[95] In Garnet's judgement, those too lily-livered to accept the ethical and practical rigours of commitment to an unconventional position and unauthorised opinions effectively made 'Gods either of their belly and ease, or of the wicked mammon'.[96] To shirk from paying the price of dissent, from forfeiting temporal dignities and riches for a principle, amounted to weighing Creator and creation dispassionately in the balance, and unblushingly selecting the latter:

> before the care of God and conscience, I wil quietly enjoy my wealth, and live in estimation among al men to my power: Shal I be in danger of want, or seeke a straungers table, who am now able to entertaine others? Shal my enimies have advantage over me, and treade me under feete? Shal varlets and ribauldes possesse themselves of my substance, which I have so painefully gotten together, and so carefully kept? Shal I live in prison, and be used I know not how, who now may goe where I list, and sport at my pleasure?[97]

Such hedonism inexorably bred spiritual lethargy and moral insensibility. Minds overgrown with 'the rancke weedes of Carnalitye' were incapable of transcending the base impulses of their bodies and rising to higher contemplations: there was 'noe difference betwixte them, and a brute bullocke'.[98] By the stringent standards of Persons's *Book of Christian Exercise* (1582) too, temporisers were little more than pagans:

> These who can apply themselves to any company, to any time, to any Princes pleasure, for matters of the soule which is their least care. These men forbid all talke of spirit, religion or devotion in their presence; only they will have men eate, drinke, and be merie with them; tell newes of the Court and affaires abroad; sing, daunce, laugh, and play at cardes; and so passe over this life in lesse consideration of God or godlinesse, then doe the very Heathens.[99]

---

[95] As defined by Robert Persons in his devotional guide, *The Christian Directory Guiding men to eternall salvation*, Rouen 1607, 664 (first published as *The First Booke of the Christian Exercise*, 1582). He included chapters outlining proofs for the existence of God and the truth of the Christian religion in the first and second editions. On 'atheism' and anti-atheistical literature (which, in general, reflects a similar confusion of theoretical irreligion and bad behaviour), see G. E. Aylmer, 'Unbelief in seventeenth century England', in D. Pennington and K. Thomas (eds), *Puritans and Revolutionaries: essays in seventeenth century history presented to Christopher Hill*, Oxford 1978, 22–46; Michael Hunter, 'The problem of "atheism" in early modern England', *TRHS*, 5th ser. xxxv (1985), 135–57, esp. pp. 139, 154; Keith Thomas, *Religion and the Decline of Magic: studies in popular beliefs in sixteenth and seventeenth century England*, Harmondsworth 1971, 198–206; David Wootton, 'Unbelief in early modern Europe', *History Workshop* xx (1985), 82–100; and, more briefly, Collinson, *The Religion of Protestants*, 200.

[96] Garnet, *Treatise of Christian Renunciation*, 13, cf Bristow, *Briefe Treatise*, 135a, 141a.

[97] Buckland, *Embassage from Heaven*, 106–7, cf Southwell, *Epistle of Comfort*, 181r.

[98] Persons, *Brief Discours*, 50v, cf Buckland, *Embassage from Heaven*, 94, and N. C., *Pigeons Flight*, 58 (who declared church papists and their Protestant counterparts were like 'apes').

[99] Persons, *Christian Directory*, 665, cf 462ff. On Persons's *Directory* or 'Book of Resolution', see Bossy, 'The English Catholic community 1603–1625', 104; White, *English Devotional Literature*, 131; and for a survey of the literature generated by this book, Milward, *Religious Controversies of the Elizabethan Age*, 73–6.

In their round condemnation of lip-service to heretics as lip-service to God, recusancy tracts index an acute anxiety about the rise of a faithless generation and an approaching era of unbelief: an unsettling sense of the incipient stages of secularisation.[100] To Tridentine zealots, time-serving was a disquieting symptom of the 'keycold demeanour' of a 'dull age and dead season', of an apathy engulfing English society that augured apocalyptic catastrophe.[101] Repeatedly invoking that potent phrase and divine threat from Revelation iii. 15-16, 'I know thy workes, that thou art neither colde, nor hote. I would thou were colde, or hote. But because thou art lukewarme, and neither cold nor hot, I wil begin to vomite thee out of my mouth', they denounced schismatics as 'neuters', patently more wicked than Protestants themselves.[102] In H. B.'s perspective, God undoubtedly preferred 'a flat heretike'.[103]

Church papists then, evolved into a clerical *bête noire* not merely because compromise was deemed fatal to the collective cause of an proscribed faith. Outward conformity aggravated a broader impulse to eliminate attitudes and acts at odds with advancing ideals and lagging behind a semantic revolution. To Hide's mind, to embrace recusancy was 'religious . . . that is to say a matter of conscience'; through Garnet's lens it was 'morall vertue'.[104] Prescriptive propaganda against 'schism' reflects a progressive redefinition of religion less as a *state* than a *degree* of piety, as a self-conscious code of practice based on the internalisation of theological dogma, rather than what Keith Thomas has called 'a ritual method of living'.[105] It suggests that the gap between the 'godly' and the 'ungodly' in early modern England cut across ideological barriers. As a cantankerous Protestant preacher with 'precise' proclivities himself confessed, recusants were in fact 'Puritan Catholikes of the

---

[100] Cf Carlos Eire's discussion of this phenomenon in the sixteenth-century French context: 'Calvin and Nicodemism', 51. He argues that outward conformity and indifference to moral imperatives were separate issues.

[101] Sander, *Treatise of the Images of Christ*, sig. A4v, and H. B., *Consolatory Letter*, 4, cf 52; Hill, *Quartron of Reasons*, 184; Buckland, *Embassage from Heaven*, 94, 98; Radford, *Directorie Teaching the Way to the Truth*, 513-14.

[102] See the annotation to Rev iii. 15-16. Also, Martin, *Love of the Soule*, 38; Hill, *Quartron of Reasons*, 183; Wright, *The Dispostion or Garnishmente of the Soule*, sig. D1v.

[103] H. B., *Consolatory Letter*, 39; Buckland, *Embassage from Heaven*, 77; Martin, *Treatise of Schisme*, sig. A6r; Hill, *Quartron of Reasons*, 183.

[104] Hide, *Consolatorie Epistle*, sig. A6r; Garnet, *Apology*, 108.

[105] Thomas, *Religion and the Decline of Magic*, 88 and ch. iii passim; Wrightson, *English Society*, 181-221 passim, at p. 200. See also Bossy, *Christianity and the West 1400-1700*, Oxford 1985, passim; idem. 'The Counter Reformation and the people of Catholic Europe', passim esp. p. 54; Christina Larner, 'Pre-industrial Europe: the age of faith', in A. Macfarlane (ed.), *Witchcraft and Religion: the politics of popular belief*, Oxford 1984, 113-26 passim esp. p. 121; Delumeau, *Catholicism between Luther and Voltaire*, passim; and idem. 'Prescription and reality', esp. pp. 143ff.; A. D. Wright, 'The people of Catholic Europe and the people of Anglican England', *HJ* xviii (1975), 451-66; Haigh, 'Revisionism', 396. Indeed, in the late fifteenth and sixteenth centuries humanists revived an alternative to the accepted meaning of the word 'religion'. Until then chiefly used to denote a 'religious' rule or order and its members, it was increasingly employed to indicate 'a worshipful attitude to God or a respect for holy things'. No longer applied exclusively to clerical culture, it came to represent a model and obligation for the laity as a whole: see Bossy, *Christianity and the West*, 170-1.

hotter and better sort'.[106] Unsatisfactory adherents of any 'religion', schismatics numbered among the presumptuous multitude Martin reproved, who 'name themselves Christians, and usurpe the name'.[107]

The inevitable conclusion and grim verdict of printed tracts against conformity was hence the ejection, without exception, of church papists from the Catholic communion and community. 'Who are severed from the Churche?', questioned a catechism published in the late 1570s. The answer 'little ones and younglings' were to parrot back bracketed 'schismatics' with Jews and infidels, 'runagates' and heretics.[108] 'Calvins excrements' were beyond redemption, the personal enemies of Christ, to be denied by the Father on the Day of Judgement, deduced Hill in overwhelming unison with his fellow priests.[109] Consenting to attend Protestant services meant utter disqualification from the corporate benefits of fellowship in the true religion: confiscation of the accumulated merits of one's good works and philanthropic deeds, ineligiblity for indulgences which lessened the pains of purgatory, divine withdrawal of sacramental grace, and rude expulsion from the mass.[110] 'Schism' was a species of spiritual suicide, a ghastly form of living death: Southwell's gloomy caveat was 'you cary aboute you your owne funerall . . . your body is a filthy tombe of a more filthy soule, not only dead, but almoste rotten in sinne'.[111] The unforgiving, jealous 'God' who narrated Buckland's *Embassage from Heaven* vehemently voiced his 'just indignation against al such, as being Catholikely minded, dare yeelde their presence to the rites and publike praier, of the malignant Church'. 'Out of my sight, whom to behold is my griefe, the view of your ugly deformity I cannot abide.' 'Passe this life as merrily as you can but hope not for the life to come.'[112] Coupling unremitting threats of hell-fire for conformists with unequivocal assurances of places in Paradise for stubborn dissenters, the Counter Reformation clergy declared that the eschatalogical separation of the sheep from the goats would correspond with the secular and sociological distinction between recusants and church papists.

III

Tracts inveighing against outward conformity allegedly constituted a 'devotional' literature written to reclaim 'Catholics in mind'. Yet this propaganda destined for a public stage equally deserves consideration as polemic directed against a second, Protestant audience. Among the 'seditious

---

[106] Wiburn, *Checke or reproofe*, 117r, cf sig. A2r. See also Field, *A Caveat for Parsons Howlet*, sigs A6rff.

[107] Martin, *Treatise of Schisme*, sig. I6r.

[108] Canisius, *Certayne Necessarie Principles*, sig. B1v.

[109] Hill, *Quartron of Reasons*, 184, cf Garnet, *Apology*, 95.

[110] Persons, *Brief Discours*, 44v–52r; Martin, *Treatise of Schisme*, sigs **7v–8r; Hide, *Consolatorie Epistle*, sigs C6vff.; Hill, *Quartron of Reasons*, 180; Buckland, *Embassage from Heaven*, 19–21. Also the annotation to Esdras iv. 2.

[111] Southwell, *Epistle of Comfort*, 176r, cf Persons, *Brief Discours*, 50v.

[112] Buckland, *Embassage from Heaven*, title, 15, 115, cf Southwell, *Epistle of Comfort*, 178v–9r.

books' 'defacing' true religion suppressed by a continuing stream of royal proclamations, 'Reasons of Refusall' solicited immediate and vigorous confutation by controversialists of the highest calibre including William Fulke, Francis Dillingham and George Abbot.[113] Church papistry was a pivotal political, as well as pastoral, issue.

Indirectly, castigation and condemnation of 'schismatics' involved a withering critique of the Elizabethan Church. Temporising was interpreted as the logical, loathsome consequence of a religion 'framed only to serve turnes, and times'. According to Thomas Hill, for instance, the ethos of the 'new invented Churche of England' was as perfidious and unprincipled as that of conformists themselves.[114] An institution that 'apishly' imitated Catholicism, shamelessly and haphazardly borrowing its ceremonial customs, hierarchical structure and even doctrinal precepts, wantonly 'choosinge and refusing out of the whole', merited no less censure for dissimulation than the individuals whose duplicitous conduct it encouraged and endorsed.[115] Deftly turning hackneyed Reformation insults back against the heretics themselves, these propagandists slated English Protestantism as a spurious and synthetic system of belief and practice. Like 'Woolves . . . in sheeps cloathing . . . wormes . . . in a new cloath', N. C. accused his adversaries, they assumed 'a glittering of godlinesse . . . without the substance and trueth thereof indeede'.[116] One of Buckland's sideswipes at the religious opposition alluded adroitly to persisting infighting over the surplice: having broken from Rome, he scoffed, its clergy continued to 'jet up and downe, cladde in her robes. Can the veile of a Virgin, make a strumpet honest, or stolen attire beautifie heresie?'[117] Garnet likewise announced that the evangelising strategy of this ecclesiastical impostor was itself rooted in deception since it endeavoured 'with shew of piety, to darken true piety: and with maintaining some outward shewe of reverend antiquitye, to blotte out of peoples memory the auncient truth itselfe'.[118] An Erastian ecclesiastical establishment content with mere conformity, moreover, evinced an amoral attachment to the philosophy of 'plaine Macchiavellians', who

---

[113] See, for example, Hughes and Larkin, *Tudor Royal Proclamations*, ii, nos 567 (1567), 577 (1570), 580 (1570), 672 (1584). This was also an episcopal concern manifested in visitation articles, see, for example, Kennedy, *Elizabethan Episcopal Administration*, ii. 51 (1577), ii. 99 (1578); iii. 163 (1584), iii. 261 (1589). Robert Persons's *Brief Discours* was answered by William Fulke, *A briefe Confutation, of a Popish Discourse*, London 1581; John Field, *A Caveat for Parsons Howlet* (1581) and Perceval Wiburn, *A checke or reproofe* (1581). Henry Garnet's *Apology* and *Treatise of Christian Renunciation* were countered by Francis Bunny, *Truth and Falshood . . . Hereunto is added an Answere to such reasons as the popish Recusants alledge, why they will not come to our Churches*, London 1595. Thomas Hill's *Quartron of Reasons* provoked replies by Francis Dillingham, *A Quartron of Reasons, composed by Doctor Hill, unquartered and prooved a quartron of follies*, London 1603, and George Abbot, *The Reasons which Doctour Hill hath brought . . . Unmasked*, Oxford 1604. Ralph Buckland's *Embassage from Heaven* was answered by Thomas Sanderson in *Of Romanizing Recusants and Dissembling Catholicks* (1611). These tracts were part of a much broader literary assault on popery, for which see Milward, *Religious Controversies of the Elizabethan Age*, esp. ch. vi; and his *Religious Controversies of the Jacobean Age: a survey of printed sources*, London 1978, ch. iv.

[114] Hill, *Quartron of Reasons*, 98, 14; Bristow, *Briefe Treatise*, 158a, cf 143a–144b, 156b–158a.

[115] Ibid. 143b; N. C., *Pigeons Flight*, 47. Cf Buckland, *Embassage from Heaven*, 31.

[116] N. C., *Pigeons Flight*, 48, 49 respectively.

[117] Buckland, *Embassage from Heaven*, 36, cf 31–2, 35.

[118] Garnet, *Apology*, 50, cf Hide, *Consolatorie Epistle*, sig. B6v.

maintained 'in publike speaches, that man hath free libertie to dissemble his Religion': could a hypocritical Church do other than embrace and engender hypocrites?[119] Elizabeth's *ad hoc* indulgence and boasted refusal to pry into private opinions by exacting only external compliance was nothing, in Hide's view, but 'killing of souls with kindnes'. If it was heinous sin to coerce a person to act against his or her conscience, a government that enforced Catholics to attend heretical services assuredly damned itself as well as them.[120]

Such insinuations were more systematically stated by John Radford in 1605, in the context of a separate but related debate with the Protestant preacher Edmund Bunny, over the 'Treatise tending to Pacification' annexed to his pirated and 'perused' version of Persons's comprehensive and influential devotional manual, the *Book of Christian Exercise*.[121] In attacking Bunny's charitable inducements to conformity, Radford sarcastically expressed his Elizabethan colleagues' latent contempt for a Church that openly professed its readiness to 'beare Catholikes in hand' – for the pragmatism and adaptability that marked the 1559 Settlement: 'our politik courtly parlamentary religion heere in England to dazle simple mens eyes, will have such wordes as of Trinity still used to content the vulgar sort though they jump with their Apostles Zwinglius and Calvin in conceipt and opinion in the deepest degree'.[122] This was an institution with an emerging body of apologists, he revealed, who appeared to be coming round to the view that the pope was not actually AntiChrist and that Rome, although intolerably and inexcusably in error, was nevertheless the mother Church of English Protestants. Apologists like Bunny outrageously implied that the controversy at the core of the Reformation was less a dispute about the identification of the *true* members of the body of Christ, alone deserving the name 'Catholic', than a quarrel over the matter of assessing who were the '*truer* members' and '*better* Catholiks'.[123] Such an outlook dismissed as 'by matters' the crucial points of contention between two religions 'as farre as heaven and hell asunder' and as different as 'chalke' and 'cheese'; by underscoring their areas of agreement it was dangerously close to 'making of many divers sects one Church'.[124]

---

[119] According to the author of the *A Treatise of Treasons against Q. Elizabeth, and the Croune of England*, [Louvain] 1572, 97v.

[120] Hide, *Consolatorie Epistle*, sig. B6v; Persons, *Brief Discours*, 57v, sigs + + 3vff. Persons did not however, deny the prerogative of the 'true Church' to compel heretics to join its congregations for the conservation of 'catholic' unity: sig. + + 4r. See also the annotation to Luke xiv. 23.

[121] Radford, 'A short treatise against adiaphorists, neuters, and such as say they may be saved in any sect or religion, and would make of many divers sects one Church', appended to his *Directorie Teaching the Way to the Truth*, a reply to Edmund Bunny, *A Booke of Christian exercise*, London 1584. The *Treatise* is separately paginated.

[122] Radford, *Directorie Teaching the Way to the Truth*, 537, 557.

[123] Bunny, *Treatise tending to Pacification*, 112–13, cf Dove, *Perswasion to the English Recusants*, 31. Dove anticipated that his treatise might be thought to deal 'too favourably with the Papists' – a charge to which Bunny's work was equally vulnerable. A similarly irenical line is taken by William Bedel, in *An Examination of Certaine Motives to Recusansie*, Cambridge 1628. It is important to note, however, that the strikingly moderate stance adopted by these writers was tactical, the product of a particular polemical context. In their other writings, all three were markedly less conciliatory. I am indebted to Anthony Milton for this insight, and for drawing Bedel's tract to my attention.

[124] Radford, *Directorie Teaching the Way to the Truth*, 564, 560, 583, 537 respectively, and Bunny,

In taking up a task of refutation neglected since the 1580s, Radford was astutely exploiting an increasingly conspicuous rift inside the early seventeenth-century ecclesiastical establishment – exacerbating the divisive potential of diverging tendencies within the Calvinist camp. For Bunny was a proponent and precursor of opinions that were as distasteful to the Catholic clergy as to his more rigid co-religionists. Indeed, Radford could only side with puritans in scourging ill-grounded benevolence towards 'poore Papistes': ministers who remorselessly ejected Catholics from the communion of the self-styled 'true Church' should be commended for debarring nominal Prot-estants, not rebuked as 'rash' or 'inconsiderate'.[125] It was little wonder that the congregations of a Church so inattentive to the radical distinction between the righteous and the reprobate were composed of persons of 'no conscience, no fervour, no faith, no religion', in short of 'Neuter Nullifidian sots'. This was a religious establishment 'compacted of excrements'.[126] Its members were unholy half-breeds, mongrels – 'Calvin papists', according to common Catholic usage.[127] In the scathing evaluation of the mission's spokesmen, the Church of England was a direct descendent of the accursed lukewarm Church of Laodicea. Statute Protestantism was little more than institutionalised church papistry.

Above all, recusancy tracts seem designed to project a public image for the English Catholic community which no less than the symbolic act of refusing to attend church itself, was to daunt and defy Protestants. The inflexible ideology of nonconformity and non-cooperation they outlined was surely intended to unnerve the adversary, as much as to reanimate and rescue a flagging faith. Henry Garnet's publication of the purportedly unaltered and authoritative, but perhaps partially fabricated text of the Council of Trent's 1562 declaration against schism, for example, was more than an attempt to sway the spineless with the grave and sobering words of the Roman hierarchy. Suppressed thirty years earlier to protect the laity from further molestation, by 1593 this resolution of the mouthpiece of the Counter Reformation sold itself as a bald statement of repudiation and retaliation – ammunition for an imaginative exercise in intimidation at the level of discourse. It was occasioned, he claimed, not by 'any necessity to instruct devoute Catholickes in their dewty concerning this pointe', but rather his desire to construct for a hostile generation and preserve for posterity a 'wonderfull spectacle' and a towering 'monument of Catholicke piety'.[128]

Duplicating the themes of the apostolic letters of the New Testament, these tracts were frequently fashioned as 'consolatory epistles', succouring and celebrating an indomitable spiritual elite. H. B. typically milked this analogy, juxtaposing the dogged resistance of recusants with the fearless stance of

---

Treatise tending to Pacification, 102. Cf Dove, *Perswasion to the English Recusants*, 29: 'We contend about white and blacke, round and square, but in matters of religion, we agree'.

[125] Radford, *Directorie Teaching the Way to the Truth*, 563.

[126] Ibid. 586–7, and Garnet, *Apology*, 95 respectively. See also Hill, *Quartron of Reasons*, 184.

[127] As noted by the author of *A Survey of the Booke of Common Prayer*, [Middelburg] 1606, 10, citing Roman Catholic views of Puritanism: 'they call Protestants Calvin papists, as having their church government from them, and maintaining ceremonies retained, only by their grounds'.

[128] *Declaration of the Fathers*, 3ff.

afflicted Christian congregations in the 'Noone dayes of the Church'. He flattered and congratulated 'all ye' terrorised 'under the name of wilfull and obstinate Recusants, but in verye deed because you be true and constant Catholickes' at the expense of the schismatics he mercilessly excoriated and disgraced:

I speake of the base minded multitude who hardlye be perswaded in hope of felicitie in the life to come to live here with patience in penury or willingly to endure a paynfull death: who ar ether with holden by feare of penall lawes agaynst their consciences, from the harbour of salvation: or if they be yet in the Church, they stagger and ar ready to fall at the terror and blast of every new statute that commeth forth, behaving themselves in the meane time so coldly in their profession, that scarcely shall you perceive them by any outward acte to be Catholickes.[129]

And flaunting the survival of the Catholic race against the odds, Hide similarly proclaimed as 'rather miraculous than marvellous' its perseverance in the face of proscription and victimisation:

Notwithstanding all this, Gods Churche hath her faythfull flocke that confesseth the catholike trueth openly, mauger the divell, heresie, and tyrannie. And notwithstanding all worldly disgraces, overthwarts injuries, persecution, and execution, yet is there left some good number that never bowed their knees to Baal, never received the breaded Communion, neither went to the schismaticall service. Yea some number that be ready to render their goods to the world, and their soules to God, as willing in this quarrell to dye as to live . . . It is the blessed wil of God that the glory of his militant church should multiply in persecution, should increase under oppression.[130]

Intimately addressed to a chosen handful, the conscientious and uncompromising, these published 'private' communications inspirited a cohesive body not only undismayed by the swelling tide of savage legislation, but perversely thriving upon it.

In 1581, William Fulke, by then a seasoned disputant with the Louvain theologians, discerned a dramatic alteration in the objectives and tactics of his rivals. The 'papists', he noted triumphantly, but suspiciously, had apparently abandoned their ambitious project to prove 'popery' to be the true faith, in favour of a narrower aim – 'to cover the infirmitie of their cause, and to reteine such as they have seduced in obstinacie of errour'.[131] Recusancy tracts, on the contrary, imply that they had simply reorientated their apologetic

---

[129] H. B., *Consolatory Letter*, 4, 3, 6–7 respectively.

[130] Hide, *Consolatorie Epistle*, sigs C2r–v, B7vff. (mauger (maugre), in spite of), cf Persons, *Brief Discours*, 1v. Other tracts adopting this generic framework include: Southwell, *Epistle of Comfort*; Martin, *Love of the Soule*; Allen, 'Admonition and comfort to the afflicted Catholickes' in *Apologie and True Declaration*.

[131] Fulke, *A briefe Confutation*, 1r. See Milward, *Religious Controversies of the Elizabethan Age*, esp. ch. iii, and Southern, *Elizabethan Recusant Prose*, 60ff., for details of the Catholic/Protestant controversy which marked the early years of the reign.

energies and creatively refined their polemical technique. Dogmatic and unqualified denunciation of 'schismatics' was crucial to the characterisation of Catholicism as a religion supremely unstained by compromise and undiluted by indifference – a flawless Church that neither required the conditional membership of church papists to bolster its numbers, nor was prepared to accommodate in its privileged and pristine ranks the merely half-committed.

Does printed propaganda against conformity consequently contain the seeds of a contemporary, as well as an historiographical mistake – an irresistible illusion that the history of the Catholicism after 1559 is predominantly and disproportionately one of overt dissent and heroic resistance? This is an impression that the very virulence of the Protestant response and the vast bulk of subsequent Catholic scholarship have only served to perpetuate. Artificially 'inventing' a tradition, deliberately developing a resilient, recusant profile and rhetorically constructing a nonconformist front for the surviving supporters of the pope and Church of Rome, was evidently a priestly priority in the polemical circumstances of the early modern period.

Yet, such books simultaneously delineated an audience that was far from uniformly 'recusant'. Their authors were obliged to recognise and strive to salvage scores of individuals who attended the services of the Church of England, but none the less designated themselves 'Catholic', and were denigrated and defamed as 'papists' by Protestants. 'How many are there thinke you', enquired Gregory Martin in 1597, 'of secret Catholikes, that wish for the Old Religion againe with al their heart, and follow the new only for feare?'.[132] Perceval Wiburn's 'checke' and 'reproofe' of Robert Persons's 'untimely screeching' estimated that clerical writers who condemned conformists thereby damned the majority of 'Catholics': he provocatively proposed 'ye send the most of them quicke to Hell without all hope of recovery'.[133]

Were schismatics the victims of a relentless drive for recusancy, or does this prescriptive literature document its own pedagogic failure? Has the effectiveness of a propaganda campaign to erect recusancy as an ideological facade been confused with its pastoral accomplishment as a parochial reality? Church papists, perhaps, were scapegoats in the politics of post-Reformation Catholic confessionalism.

---

[132] Martin, *Love of the Soule*, 8.
[133] Wiburn, *Checke or reproofe*, 115v, cf 116r.

3

'Comfortable Advertisements'

These actions do not show that a man is a heretic, but that he is either a
heretic or a careful Catholic . . . to do these things is not to deny the faith,
but to conceal it as time and place require. – 'The resolution of the cases of
the English nation', *c.* 1582, in P. J. Holmes (ed.), *Elizabethan Casuistry*
(CRS lxvii, 1981), 71.

According to the doctrine of recusancy regularly restated in printed literature
from the late 1570s, the church papist was irredeemable, a lost soul. By
attending Protestant services, Catholics automatically and irrevocably
forfeited their religious identity and the spiritual grace promised to the faithful
adherents of the single true Church. The advocates of this public and priestly
ideology presented it as the unanimous opinion of the post-Reformation
clergy.

Yet there was not complete consensus in clerical circles regarding the
question of churchgoing. The extent to which such forbidding counsels might
be relaxed or qualified in the prevailing circumstances of persecution triggered
continuing uncertainty and dispute – it was one source of Catholicism's
contemporary 'domesticall difficulties'.[1] The suppression of the papal and
conciliar decisions of the early 1560s predictably produced a situation in which
much of the badly briefed Marian priesthood adopted the attitude that
outward conformity was permissible. Rumours remained rife, in Nicholas
Sander's opinion at the end of that decade, that 'this going to schismatical
Service is, or may be wincked at, or dispensed in the Catholikes'. As late as
1593, however, a prominent Jesuit was still bemoaning the 'many
schismaticall old preestes' who persisted in affirming that 'it was not onlye
lawfull in these extremityes to goe to churche without protestation but alsoe to
receave the supper of the lorde'. Since Counter Reformation missionaries
themselves were apparently often obliged to rely 'upon some other mans
credite' for the details of the Trent resolution, such confusion was far from
perplexing.[2]

Obtaining an official concession from Rome was still of over-riding concern
to the influential clerics and their lay patrons who vigorously prosecuted this
cause at the Synod of Southwark, which met immediately after the arrival of
Persons and Campion in England in 1580. But the ensuing debate concluded
in a stern reaffirmation by the Jesuits that recusancy was to be 'the sum of that

---

[1] Pollen, 'Memoirs', 49ff., 176ff.
[2] See Sander, *Treatise of the Images of Christ*, sig. A4v; I. G., 'An answere to a comfortable
advertisement', ch. iv and postscript respectively. See also Rishton's continuation of Sander, *Rise
and Growth of the Anglican Schism*, 265–6; Pollen, 'Memoirs', 61.

which all priests should teach and insinuate into Catholics in all places'.[3] Revived discussion of the issue was conducted in a charged atmosphere: its negative outcome only intensified the dilemma of a group of notable nonconforming laymen, imprisoned and subjected to considerable Privy Council pressure to submit. The circulation in various gaols of an anonymous manuscript suggesting, that, under duress, it was *not* mortal sin to go to heretical churches, was a key factor in the sensationalised capitulation of Thomas, Lord Paget, and a wealthy Londoner, Ralph Sheldon.[4]

Copied and disseminated by a legal clerk, William Clithero, the paper was widely attributed to Dr Alban Langdale, the deprived archdeacon of Chichester, then resident chaplain to Anthony Browne, Lord Montagu of Sussex. Articulating a view tacitly shared by other displaced priests, its eloquent defence of outward conformity was markedly consonant with the concerns of the gentlemen and noblemen who had sheltered the dissenting clergy since the 1559 Settlement. Indeed, in procuring what one commentator reproved as a 'shewe to redeme ther vexations . . . under a lerned mans warrantye', they clearly had a vested interest.[5]

Seminary-trained spokesmen who sought to counteract its appealing message denounced the pamphlet as a blatant contradiction of the 'cheefest purpose' of Persons's recent 'Reasons of Refusall'.[6] In spite of the exaggerated allegations of its decriers, this tract was by no means a confident justification of churchgoing as a legitimate practice for *all* Catholics. It offered instead a more tentative resolution applicable to the single unprecedented situation it examined – that of incarcerated upper-class individuals. Its author was no energetic 'opponent' of recusancy, but a casuist, conscious that 'circumstances do alter cases' and 'reddy to yelde to

---

[3] Hicks, *Letters and Memorials*, pp. xviiiff., esp. p. xx; Pollen, 'Memoirs', 178.

[4] J. H. Pollen, (ed.), 'Father Persons' Memoirs', in *CRS Miscellanea IV* (CRS iv, 1907), 4ff.; Pollen, 'Memoirs', 27–8, 178–81. On Sheldon's capitulation, see *APC*, xii. 301–2; Morey, *The Catholic Subjects of Elizabeth I*, 142. The others imprisoned were Sir John Arundell, Thomas Tresham, Sir William Catesby, Sir Thomas Frogmorton, Lord Compton, Lord Vaux of Harrowden.

[5] This paper is calendared as 'A discourse delivered to Mr Sheldon to persuade him to conform. Arguments to prove it lawful for a Roman Catholic to attend the Protestant service': *CSP Dom 1547–1580*, 691 (Dec. 1580). There is some doubt as to the authorship: it was attributed to Alban Langdale on the basis of the annotations to key passages employed in the tract which Robert Persons found in books in Langdale's library in London. See Pollen, 'Father Persons' Memoirs', 3–6; idem. 'Memoirs', ii. 28, 179–81; I. G., 'An answere to a comfortable advertisement', ch. iv (from which I quote). Holmes, *Resistance and Compromise*, 90–4, accepts this attribution, but Rose, *Cases of Conscience*, 75ff., discusses the tract as the work of an anonymous author. It may have been written by Clithero himself, who was subsequently ordained priest in 1582 and died in France. Edward Chambers believed it had been given out '*under*' the name of of learned Catholic man: Pollen, 'Memoirs', 179. Gillow argued that Alban Langdale had been confused with his nephew Thomas Langdale, a Jesuit (for whom, see below), but it seems unlikely, as he did not arrive in England until 1583: *Bibliographical Dictionary*, iv. 117–18. Persons suggested that it was partly written for Mr Johnson, a priest living with one Mr Hare, a prominent man, who favoured the opinion that it was lawful to go to church: Pollen, 'Memoirs', 180. On Alban Langdale, see *DNB* s.v. Langdale; Gillow, *Bibliographical Dictionary*, iv. 115–8; *CSP Dom 1547–1565 Addenda*, 523 (1561), where he is described in a list of 'recusants who are at large' as 'Learned, and very earnest in papistry'. The possibility that Langdale was a scapegoat cannot be entirely dismissed.

[6] Pollen, 'Memoirs', 179.

the better Judgment' of a higher authority.[7] His coherent arguments nevertheless acquired distorted significance in later years.

Langdale centrally asserted that 'the bare goinge and naked corporall presence' in Protestant churches was in its 'owen nature' faultless, a thing indifferent – an activity neither explicitly endorsed nor condemned by divine law. The exercise of Christian liberty in this respect could, however, be ruled out if doing so in a particular context violated the considerations of 'expedience', 'convenience' and 'edification' laid down in Scripture. His discourse therefore aimed to demonstrate that, even in Protestant England, attendance at Common Prayer was not entirely incompatible with or invalidated by this acknowledged duty to avoid offending the moral sensitivities of one's neighbours. Just as St Paul had rebuked the Corinthians for eating idolatrous meats *solely* because they neglected to consider the infirmities of the spiritually feeble, so too the evils of churchgoing might be eliminated by due regard for the 'weaker brethren'.[8] Because 'the bare act of yt selfe wanteth blame', outward conformity remained a legitimate option: the risks of disedification could be minimised by openly declaring one's contrary intentions and convictions, and by declining to participate verbally in heretical devotions or to adopt the physical postures of prayer.

In the light of puritan nonconformity, he objected furthermore, recusancy did not unambiguously betoken Catholicism. A church papist sufficiently identified and separated himself by refusing to repeat the required liturgical responses and receive their communion, and by sitting when they knelt: 'be not these *signa distincta* and do not these factes shewe a dissent as well as express woordes [?]'. And Langdale's shrewdly practical reply to the assertion that Christ had charged Christians to eschew heretics was a telling comment on the progress of the Reformation by 1580: 'many parisshes in E[ngland] ther be where nether the curate nor the parishionars are open professors of P[rotestantism] nor knowen P[rotestants] but dissemblinge catholickes'. There was no need to part company with the right-minded.

Although martyrdom and open profession of the faith was incumbent on bishops, priests and magistrates by virtue of their vocation, it was, by contrast, a work of supererogation in the laity. Such behaviour proceeded from a laudable and saintly impulse, but it was a course of action to be chosen with caution. In Langdale's eyes, the spiritual responsibility of public 'confession' still lay primarily with a clerical and monastic elite. Other Catholics should 'take out a lesson not to be bussye in exasperatinge our adversaries'. Recusancy was a counsel of perfection: it was neither mandatory for secular persons to follow it – nor was it perhaps very wise:

---

[7] PRO, SP 12/144/69. The manuscript is unfoliated and the first page or pages are missing. Gillow, however, who may have seen another surviving copy, gives the following title: 'A treatise to prove that attendance at the Protestant church was in itself no sin, and therefore might be lawfully submitted to for the purpose of avoiding a persecution so intolerable at present, and threatening to grow much more so': *Bibliographical Dictionary*, iv. 117. For an alternative discussion of this paper, see Holmes, *Resistance and Compromise*, 90–4, part of his chapter on 'Opponents of Recusancy'.
[8] 1 Cor viii.

for seing the owtward face of religion &c is throughe goddes permission for our synns taken away by the Civill magistrate, folly yt were for a man to seeke to exulcerat that which he cannot heale, and yt is not every manns lott to purge the Churche of chaffe: And for a matter which might be made indifferent, to sterr troble is not the best corse to quietnes. A man which dwellethe amonge the wicked muste lament the state and providently avoyde the perill of tentacion, and as muche as he may muste withdraw hym selfe from troble as a peaceable childe of the churche, not sekinge unnecessarily to provoke Ire.

Turning to answer other 'reasons of refusall', Langdale claimed that even if an apostolic canon expressly prohibiting churchgoing existed, according to the precepts of orthodox Catholic theology, human law was not in any event always or absolutely binding. An individual overwhelmed by 'juste feare' might licitly ignore men's directives. And *justu metu*, 'juste feare', by his definition, comprehended dread of death and imprisonment, as well as loss of fortune and patrimony, especially in the old, impotent and those supporting dependent families.

Among the biblical precedents he cited for outward compliance in straitened circumstances were Christ's timid and secret disciple, Nicodemus, and Joseph of Arimathea, the 'honourable' counsellor who quietly concealed his faith to circumvent detection while he awaited the advent of the Kingdom of God. Langdale's scriptural examples were particularly directed to proving that royal servants and aristocratic advisors might go to church without reprehension: appropriate parallels to the case he assessed included Obadiah, household steward to the Old Testament tyrant, King Ahab, who yielded his nominal presence to idolatrous rites although he was privately active in hiding the prophets, and Gamaliel, a companion of the Apostles who had continued to consult with the Pharisees in matters of civil and ecclesiastical policy, 'to the [e]nd he might pacify theire fury'. High-ranking Elizabethan gentlemen, he alleged, could likewise be excused in this respect, since they 'only geve theire bare presence for avoydynge farther mischeffe to qualify the indidnacion of the adversarye, and thereby to be a meane for the people to purchase a calme to the multitude'.[9]

Not unexpectedly, Langdale's most critical and compelling analogy was Naaman Syrus, that classic example of conformity motivated by political obedience. Adducing Elisha's licence for a courtier to perform an accustomed duty to his king as positive proof that church papistry was not mortal sin, he tendered that it was thus admissible for the conspicuous Catholics whose welfare he had at heart to serve their sovereign in like manner. In contending, moreover, that Elizabethan legislation against churchgoing was designed to distinguish between 'a trew subject and a rebbell', rather than a Protestant and a Catholic, Langdale was in fact implicitly acknowledging a sphere of

---

[9] Luke xxiii. 50–3 and Mark xv. 43 (Joseph of Arimathea); John iii. 1–10, vii. 50, xix. 39 (Nicodemus); 1 Kings xviii (Obadiah); Acts v. 34–5 (Gamaliel). Nicodemus' secret discipleship was a central argument used to justify the outward conformity of persecuted French and Italian Protestants: see Ginzburg, *Il Nicodemismo*, passim; Eire, 'Calvin and Nicodemism'; idem. *War Against the Idols*, ch. vii; Zagorin, *Ways of Lying*, chs iv, v.

religious conduct in which a temporal ruler had the right to command submission.

The tract was immediately brought to the notice of Robert Persons and George Blackwell, who collaborated to draft and distribute in the city and provinces a concise and caustic corrective – an '*antidotum*' to Langdale's alluring arguments. Highly motivated missionaries well versed in the tenets of recusant ideology, they scoffed, were rapidly making his advice ridiculous and redundant – such 'upholstering of mens sinnes weareth out of credite'. Yet in the interim, refutation of the treatise was still an affair of the utmost urgency, for the work contained 'seede of great sedition, with matter of great advauntage to the enemye, and with utter subversion of the Catholike cause, if it should goe forwarde'. This 'daungerous sequell' could not be suffered.[10] The impact of Langdale's piece of case divinity and special pleading was indubitably heightened by the critical context in which it appeared. As one associate of the Jesuits despaired, 'it dothe worke the greater impression especially at this tyme, when such as be frayle would be glad to have such a cushion put under there elbowes, to ease there pressures'. It was likely 'to make greate motion coming together with the storme of persecution' – the impending passage of the stringent 1581 legislation.[11]

Few clerics were willing to commit to paper, much less print, views so obviously at odds with official teaching and propaganda. Yet Langdale was evidently not alone in considering recusancy an overly harsh doctrine that might be waived or mitigated in practice. Discredited as a 'scandalous newter' who had wickedly seduced and destroyed 'many simple soules' by the Jesuit missioners, Dr Robert Pursglove, formerly suffragan bishop of Hull, similarly maintained that churchgoing was tolerable if performed solely for the sake of secular loyalty. He remained 'exceedinge farre out of the right way' until his death, it was said.[12]

Suggestions that a public expression of the limited political character of one's conformity could furnish an excuse for schismatic behaviour seem to have had fairly wide currency in the 1580s and early 1590s.[13] In the same period, Cumberland and Westmorland priests were reputedly advising their flocks that attendance at church was lawful provided no credit was given to Calvinist worship. Father William Hart expounded a gendered version of the doctrine of recusancy in Yorkshire, claiming 'women that had no learning to defend their cause' might yield their presence at Common Prayer.[14] The priest James Bosgrave was called upon by exiled Catholic leaders to justify formally visits he had made to heretical churches, ostensibly in order to acquaint

---

[10] 'Against going to Churche', BL, Add. MS 39830, fos 19r, 14r. See also Pollen, 'Father Persons' Memoirs', 7; idem. 'Memoirs', 180; Southern, *Elizabethan Recusant Prose*, 139.

[11] Edward Chambers, in Pollen, 'Memoirs', 179.

[12] I. G., 'An answere to a comfortable advertisement', ch. iv.; Garnet, *Apology*, 149. See also Aveling, *The Handle and the Axe*, 37–8; *DNB s.v.* Pursglove.

[13] Garnet, *Treatise of Christian Renunciation*, 159–60; Knox, *Letters and Memorials*, 100; idem. *Douay Diaries*, 354–5.

[14] 'The informations of John Warrener c. March 1590': in Pollen, *Unpublished Documents*, 179ff., esp. p. 182; Morris, *Troubles of Our Catholic Forefathers*, iii. 427.

himself with their observances and improve his mastery of the vernacular – to reconcile his notion that conformity was 'lawfull to some one for certen causes' with the universal duty of dissent.[15] Government harassment was likewise taking its toll of obstinate adherents to this principle among the captured clergy themselves. A 'Mr Aufield' consented under torture to resort to church once, with a host of qualifications; some of those held in the Tower with Campion in 1582 were also sorely tempted by the prospect of release if they would but 'salute the churches of the Protestants even from the threshold'; John Paschal, a young gentleman who had accompanied the Jesuits from the Continent, was forced to fulfil his promise to conform in front of an assembled multitude in a London city hall.[16] And 'uncertayne rumour' reached the north that the metropolitan priesthood had agreed with 'uniforme consente' that one of their number could be authorised to 'stand by secretlye to heare' Anthony Tyrrell's recantation of Catholicism from the most public pulpit in the realm, Paul's Cross, in January 1588.[17] Such instances hardly reinforced the drive for obdurate lay religious resistance.

Rather more troublesome to the organisers of the English mission was the Jesuit nephew of Alban Langdale. Following a distinguished career as an ecclesiastical diplomat and a penitentiary in Rome and Loreto, Thomas Langdale, 'leasing upon the soddaine, as it were, his witt and judgement rane out of Italy', reappeared in his native land in 1583 and began systematically to sanction not only occasional conformity, but reception of the reformed eucharist. Posing as a papal legate sent 'to restore to their former liberty the consciences of Catholics' ensnared by fellow Jesuits and seminarists, his persuasive opinions spread rapidly – perhaps even under the licence of the Council of the North and the bishop of Durham. This was seen by insiders as a providential punishment on his irregular and unfortunate uncle. Langdale's subsequent apostasy was an unexpected windfall for the cause of Protestant evangelism.[18]

---

[15] 'The satisfaction of Mr James Bosgrave the godly confessor of Christ, concerning his going to the church of Protestants at his first coming into England', in Allen, *A true report*, 32v–4v, esp. pp. 34r–v.

[16] 'Aufield'(probably Thomas Alfield) is cited in ibid. 'An admonition to the reader' (unpaginated); Pollen, 'Father Persons' Memoirs', 41; Paschal's case is in ibid. 11 and idem. 'Memoirs', 196. On Alfield, see Patrick McGrath, 'Gloucestershire and the Counter-Reformation in the reign of Elizabeth I', *Transactions of the Bristol and Gloucestershire Archaeological Society* lxxxviii (1969), 15–17; and more generally, idem. 'Apostate and naughty priests in England under Elizabeth I', in D. A. Bellenger, *Opening the Scrolls: essays in Catholic history in honour of Godfrey Anstruther*, Bath 1987, 50–83.

[17] I. G., 'An answere to a comfortable advertisement', ch. iv. On this occasion Tyrrell unexpectedly began a speech in the opposite direction, retracting his former confession of conversion and violently denouncing Protestantism. Later that year, on 8 December, he successfully delivered his 'true repentance' at the Cross after defecting once again from the Roman Catholic camp; this was published as *The Recantations as they were severallie pronounced by Wylliam Tedder and Anthony Tyrrell: (sometime two Seminarie Priests of the English Colledge in Rome, and nowe by the great mercie of almightie God converted, unto the profession of the Gospell of Jesus Christ) at Paules Crosse, the day and yeere as is mentioned in their severall Tytles of theyr Recantations*, London 1588. See also *DNB s.v.* Tyrrell; McGrath, 'Apostate and naughty priests', 62–3; M. C. Questier, 'English clerical converts to Protestantism, 1580–1596', *RH* xx (1991), 463–6.

[18] Pollen, 'Memoirs', 181–2, at p. 181; I. G., 'An answere to a comfortable advertisement', ch.

It was the influence of one of their own Counter Reformation recruits, however, which most seriously jeopardised the progress of the campaign for recusancy. Labouring heroically in Lancashire since 1582, Thomas Bell, locally nicknamed the 'bishop of Chester', produced and circulated a series of manuscript tracts in the early 1590s, condoning afflicted Catholics who lapsed into church papistry.[19] Although none are extant, the Jesuit rebuttals of these 'comfortable advertisements' by Garnet and I. G. offer ample evidence of the major elements of his 'defence of schism'.[20]

Bell's pamphlets substantially borrowed and elaborated the arguments developed by Alban Langdale and Robert Pursglove, whom he instanced as previous promoters of his teaching: one of his critics 'marvelled' that he had 'remembred not' the 'apostata' Thomas Langdale as well.[21] He supplemented the list of Old Testament prototypes for conformity with the stories of Shadrach, Meshach and Abednego, the children of Babylon who attended the solemn dedication of Nebuchadnezzar's idol, but refused to reverence it, and of Jehu, who feigned his consent to sacrifices to Baal with the object of furthering his scheme to assassinate idolatrous priests.[22] Bell produced a list of points to counter the proposition that churchgoing was a 'sign distinctive' between religions in England; he likewise expanded the theme of 'just fear', protesting that in the face of Protestant cruelty, conformity was the involuntary act of a constrained will. Equal emphasis was given to the familiar notion that nominal presence at heretical worship was an action located within the scriptural category of *adiaphora*. Forbidden by the positive laws of the Church alone, it could potentially be ecclesiastically dispensed – if not innocently practised without transgression of a Christian's obligation to acquit himself to the edification, rather than offence of his peers. It was in fact 'noe synne *but* in respecte of scandall' and simulation.[23] Bell also boldly underlined the honest and commendable intentions of devout Catholics who yielded to

---

iv; Pollen, 'Father Persons' Memoirs', 101–5, at p. 104. See also Henry Foley (ed.), *Records of the English Province of the Society of Jesus*, 7 vols, London 1877–84, iv. 50, 678–80; Morris, *Troubles of Our Catholic Forefathers*, ii. 21–2; McGrath, 'Apostate and naughty priests', 68.

[19] Haigh, *Reformation and Resistance*, 289. Bell was a Church of England curate converted by reading a Catholic devotional book, who travelled to Douai in 1576 and from there to Rome in 1579, returning to England in 1582. See *DNB* (Supplement) *s.v.* Bell; P. Renold (ed.), *Letters of William Allen and Richard Barret 1572–1598* (CRS lviii, 1967), 232 (Allen to James Tyrie, 1593); Anthony G. Petti (ed.), *The Letters and Despatches of Richard Verstegan c1550–1640* (CRS lii, 1959), 79, 83, 114 (Verstegan to Persons, 15 Oct. 1592; Verstegan to Roger Baynes, 18 Oct. 1592; Verstegan to Persons, 1 Apr. 1593, respectively); P. Renold (ed.), *The Wisbech Stirs 1595–1598* (CRS li, 1958), 205; *APC*, xxiii. 164, 166; Foley, *Records of the English Province*, ii. 349; vi. 16.

[20] By 1593 Bell had apparently written a number of items on the subject: a 'Comfortable Advertisement', an 'Addition', an 'Answer to the syxt objections', a reply to the reproving letter of certain priests, and, perhaps, a 'Defence of Schism'. Bell is discussed by McGrath, 'Apostate and naughty priests', 52–3, and Questier, 'English clerical converts', 468–9, 476 nn. 109, 117. Bell's arguments are reconstructed from Garnet's *Apology* and from I. G.'s 'An answere to a comfortable advertisement'. Cf. Holmes's discussion in *Resistance and Compromise*, 95–8.

[21] I. G., 'An answere to a comfortable advertisement', ch. iv.

[22] Garnet, *Apology*, 17ff., 26ff. (Daniel iii, 2 Kings x).

[23] On 'just fear', Garnet, *Apology*, 41ff.; on 'signs distinctive', I. G., 'An answere to a comfortable advertisement', ch. vii; on things indifferent, ibid. chs iv and vi (my emphasis), and Garnet, *Apology*, 51ff.; on church law, ibid. 46.

comply with the adversary so as to protect their families and preserve their property and capital – the resources of a future regime.[24]

'Mr Advertiser', moreover, used the case of Naaman Syrus as 'a principall grounde of all his procedinges'. It occupied a prominent place in tracts that self-consciously outlined a stance attractively consistent with the doctrine of political non-resistance to an earthly prince. Bell claimed that his interpretation of the text from Kings had an indisputable stamp of imprimatur: his views had previously been approved by no less than Robert Persons and the Trent theologians, a medieval exegete, Nicholas de Lyra, and other distinguished Catholic authorities including Cajetan, Navarrus and Sylvester. In citing Naaman, he significantly invested Elisha's blessing for a royal retainer's deference to his ruler with wider relevance. Bell highlighted the corresponding hierarchical relationships between servants and masters, wives and husbands, parents and children to suggest that conformity might be warrantable for English Catholics generally. Reiterating Langdale's thesis that the Act of Uniformity and later recusancy laws were devised merely to test temporal loyalty and expose enemies of state, he decided that individuals could therefore freely satisfy the queen in this respect. The contention that the underlying intent of such statutes was the extraction of civil allegiance rather than theological consent or spiritual homage verged on a justification of government policy itself. Indeed, I. G. thought it 'verye lyklye that the Lord Treasurer and our comfortour in this poynte were both disciples to one Master'. Bell, he sarcastically observed, spoke 'more favourablye' for the Protestant cause than its own propagandists.[25]

Deliberate disrespect for heretical devotions, contemptuous silence during the intercessions, and absence from sacramental rites diminished the dangers of misleading the weak. So too did a daring declaration made in the presence of the whole congregation, since it 'sett open to the hearers our secrete internall mynd and affection'. Bell had even formalised this 'protestation', the keynote of his conformist creed, for the convenience of his readers: 'Good people I ame come hither not for any lykinge I have of any sacramentes, service, or sermons accustomablye used in this place, or to exhibit any reverence to the same, but only to give a sygne of my allegiance and true loyalty to my prince, This is the onlye cause of my cominge and no other.'[26] Far from scandalising its audience, an open statement of this kind would uplift and enlighten: it was comparable to the meritorious enterprise of zealously declaiming the Catholic faith, or defiantly crying out against heresy at a public preaching cross. It was identical, Bell averred, to the protestation long since advocated and allowed by Gregory Martin – and, by extension, by Cardinal Allen and the entire College of Rheims, at whose behest and under whose auspices the *Treatise of Schisme* had been written.[27]

---

[24] Ibid. 46ff. and 102.

[25] Ibid. 29ff. and 34ff.; I. G., 'An answere to a comfortable advertisement', chs iii, iv, vi.

[26] Ibid. chs i, ii, ix. See also Garnet, *Treatise of Christian Renunciation*, 149–70: 'Whether it be lawfull for Catholickes to go to hereticall churches with a protestation that they come not for liking which they have of the Religion there professed.'

[27] I. G., 'An answere to a comfortable advertisement', ch. ii; Garnet, *Treatise of Christian Renunciation*, 150–1. For the relevant passage in Martin's *Treatise of Schisme*, see sigs F6r–v.

More originally, Bell revived the 'Extravagant', the fifteenth-century Pope Martin V's bull *Ad evitanda*, which had ordained that Christians were not bound to abstain and separate themselves, even at times of divine service, from persons collectively, as opposed to personally excommunicated by ecclesiastical decree. This document 'for the avoydinge of many scandalls and manye perils and for the helpinge of timorous consciences', he argued, justified beyond doubt the behaviour of Elizabethan church papists.[28] Recusancy, his tracts none the less admitted, was the 'more perfecte' path for English Catholics – scriptural exhortations against conformity were not strict commandments but discretionary recommendations for aspiring martyrs.[29]

Aired at another important juncture in official attempts to extirpate recusancy – between the hostile 1591 proclamation and the severe parliamentary measures ratified two years later – such writings were liable to have perniciously pervasive influence.[30] Garnet was acutely aware that Bell's words would free Catholics from the 'yoke of slavery' planned for the 1593 statute. I. G. too feared for the 'many weaklinges' under the charge of his northern brethren who would eagerly follow this 'plausible advise':

some over readye (god knowethe) of themselves with every litle puffe of persecution to fall, and some glad to take any smale occasion or apparancye for sufficient reason, to yeald to the extreamitye of the tyme therby to escape trouble, worldlye dangers and temporall harmes: and fynallye almost soe weryed with sufferinge these cruell and intollerable vexations wherwith the heretykes contynuallye oppresse them.

Bell, he acknowleged, 'may thus easelye perverte the simple and ignorante which lyke unto chafe are in daunger to be blowne out of godes churche': a substantial sector of the populace was clearly teetering on the brink of church papistry.[31]

Obviously, such 'disordered dealings' required instant and fierce reproof – not least because Bell's 'defence of schism' proceeded partly by the divisive and destructive method of revealing internal contradictions within recusancy theory itself.[32] Even more so after the admonishments of local priests failed to reclaim him to orthodoxy, and furthermore, allegedly provoked him through 'excess of revenge' to discredit his opponents by displaying their faults and denouncing their names to the Protestant authorities.[33] I. G. then stepped in to assist his overworked colleagues slaving for 'godes harvest' in distant parts and framed an abusive and uncompromising 'answere' to the principal points paraded by this singularly irascible individual. This was to be presented to Bell

[28] Garnet, *Apology*, 33ff., 159; I. G., 'An answere to a comfortable advertisement', ch. v. I quote from I. G.'s translation of the bull.
[29] Ibid. chs x, xii.
[30] See Hughes and Larkin, *Tudor Royal Proclamations*, iii, no. 738; *SR*, 35 Eliz. c. 1-2.
[31] For Garnet, see Renold, *Wisbech Stirs*, 206; I. G., 'An answere to a comfortable advertisement', preface, ch. ii.
[32] Ibid. esp. ch. xi.
[33] Ibid. ch. ii.

as a personal reprimand, as well as spread abroad for 'the staye of the simple'.[34]

I. G. did not mince words. His manuscript vigorously denounced Bell's flimsy and fallible reasoning and cynically scorned his 'lovelye conceite' and 'childishe evasion'.[35] Not only were Bell and his followers living in a 'folishe paradise' in avowing this wicked new doctrine, but their delusion had been plotted by the devil, the 'father of discorde' himself, in order to drown the faithful in the 'fylthye puddle of schisme'.[36] While the 'comfortour' professed himself to be motivated by a 'tender harte' and 'exceadinge great compassion' for his country's calamities and his flock's miseries, his attempts in reality emanated from singularity and obstinacy, from vain-glory and complacency. This pernicious and passionate 'spirite of contradiction and pryde' had led Bell to stand out saucily against his superiors, disregarding the injunctions of his colleagues and dispensing with the consent and approbation of the Catholic hierarchy on the Continent – all for the 'vayne puffe of popular credite'.[37] He had, I. G. judged, 'overshote himselfe very groslye in this matter of going to churche'. Further defence and execution of such purposes would bring the laity to doubt and disdain their spiritual fathers – and confirm the Protestant prejudice that Catholicism was a religion riding on dissimulation and deceit. If there existed 'any sparckle of the sense of god and humiltye' within him, Bell would abandon his perverse, private opinions and return to the straight and narrow way. If, however, he remained immovable, the time for discreet and friendly remonstration would pass, and he would be pulled down from his pillar and cut off. Indeed, hearsay had it that he had been threatened with nothing less than personal excommunication by the pope, a sentence procured at Cardinal Allen's behest.[38]

Bell's ostentatious return to the Church of England in 1593 must therefore have been a source of considerable relief to leading Catholic priests: arguably, they had in fact engineered it. His apostasy opened an opportunity for Garnet to severely castigate and reject the renegade publicly in print – a strategy that was both unsafe and inexpedient while Bell formally lingered within Counter Reformation missionary ranks. But his renunciation of Rome was two-edged. In some quarters it may well have been an effective antidote to his former teaching; in others the deserter probably dragged his congregations with him into the Calvinists' clutches.[39] The damage, moreover, was done: Bell's

---

[34] Ibid. preface, ch. xiii.

[35] Ibid. chs ii, vi.

[36] Ibid. ch. x, preface, ch. xii respectively.

[37] Ibid. preface, chs i, xiii, x respectively.

[38] Ibid. chs xii, x, xiii, ix respectively. The rumours of his excommunication were recorded over a decade later by Francis Walsingham, a convert to Catholicism, in *A Search made into Matters of Religion*, [St Omer] 1609, 58–9.

[39] Cf Holmes, *Resistance and Compromise*, 95. After his apostasy, Bell was initially sent by the government to Lancashire to help in the 'better searching and apprehending of jesuits and seminaries'. He then went to Cambridge and began a career as a prolific anti-Catholic polemicist. Until his death in 1610, he published a series of scurrilous polemical tracts against popery, including *Thomas Bels Motives*, Cambridge 1593; *The survey of Popery*, London 1596; *The Hunting of the Romish Foxe*, London 1598; *The Anatomie of Popish Tyrannie*, London 1603; *The Downefall of Poperie*, London 1604. See STC 1814–1833, and Questier's discussion in 'English clerical

credible extension of casuistical teaching approached a reasoned vindication of conditional outward conformity. He came close to synthesising an alternative ideology for ordinary Catholics.

Similar doubts as to the moral necessity of recusancy were voiced in the context of the 'Wisbech stirs' of 1595–8. Tempers flared among the priests detained in the isolated East Anglian prison over the question of churchgoing, as well as over domestic scandals. But the 'impious efforts' of clergy who 'dared' to affirm that attendance at heretical services was lawful were not confined to those behind bars: the activities of at least a dozen 'schismatical' priests steadily defecting to Protestantism were causing consternation as far away as Rome.[40] Ignoring the early exertions of Marian priests against attendance at heretical services, and glossing over the continuing rupture within ecclesiastical ranks in 1598, Robert Persons announced that contention about the lawfulness of outward conformity was indisputably past history. Theoretical discrepancies had been eliminated: 'by tyme and by practise, zeale and authority of priests comminge from the Seminaries beyond the seas and by good Catholike men at home, the matter hath byn cleared and the negative parte fully established to the confusion of heresy and edification of all forrayne nations'.[41]

But Persons's partisan version of the origins and success of the sustained assault on church papistry simply reflected the extent to which the issue had become implicated in the interclerical quarrels that culminated in the Archpriest controversy of 1598–1602. Indeed, conformable conduct was a convenient stick with which to beat one's opponents among the secular clergy: in 1602 Persons publicly disgraced William Watson's 'great folly' and 'soule fal' in this respect in a brutally insulting tract. Thomas Lister too, may have been attempting to score a double point when he maintained in his controversial but unprinted 'Treatise of Schism' that divines who denied the Archpriest's jurisdiction should be expelled as 'schismatics'.[42] As the Tridentine offensive against formalists and conservatives merged with one against the Appellants, and defence of the mission contracted to an

---

converts', 471ff. On his activities after conversion, see Strype, *Annals*, IV. 211; *CSP Dom 1591–1594*, 283 (30 Oct. 1592) and ibid. 288 (Nov. 1592).

[40] Renold, *Wisbech Stirs*, 173, 203ff. (letters from Garnet to Aquaviva, 16 Apr., 10 Dec. 1596). See p. 205, where a number are listed, including Edward Gratley, Gilbert Gifford, Anthony Tyrell, William Tedder, Isaac Higgins, Thomas Bancroft, Thomas Langdale, and Rowland Morgan. For Tedder and Tyrell's published recantations, see *The Recantations*. They made no outspoken admissions on this score at the Cross.

[41] Pollen, 'Memoirs', 62, cf 178. This is quoted from the manuscript 'A storie of domesticall difficulties', written at the time of the Archpriest controversy (c.1600) to neutralise the harmful effects of clerical infighting on the laity. Originally intended for publication, it was superseded by Persons's *A Brief Apologie, or Defence of the Catholike Ecclesiastical Hierarchie*, [Antwerp 1601], which censured the Appellants and presented a Jesuit version of the history of the dispute for 'the true information and stay of all good Catholikes'. Cf Garnet, quoted from papers in the Jesuit Archives, Rome, in Caraman, *Henry Garnet*, 108–10.

[42] Robert Persons, *A Manifestation of the Great Folly and bad spirit of certayne in England calling themselves secular priestes*, [Antwerp] 1602, 84r. On Lister, see Gillow, *Bibliographical Dictionary*, ii. 280–3; *DNB s.v.* Lister. Thomas Worthington's 1601 *A Relation of Sixtene Martyrs* also included a declaration 'That the Seminarie Priests agree with the Jesuites'.

exoneration of the Jesuit venture, the question of conformity continued to be a focus for internal rivalries – a potential source of polemical mileage in the strife surrounding the appointment and administration of the notoriously unpopular George Blackwell.

Persons was refuting an impressive new challenge to strict separatist doctrine as late as 1606 – the year in which Paul V repeated the papal interdict against church attendance in negative response to an Appellant petition. *Quaestiones Duae* sought to demolish the authoritative proofs of a fellow Jesuit, Thomas Wright, who had not only revived the concept of 'going with a Protestation' of civil obedience, but introduced the 'new fangle' of frequenting church exclusively at sermon time. By 'such dangerous cankers', lamented outraged colleagues, 'whole counties and shires run headlong without struggle unto the heretics' churches'. More perniciously, disseminating this 'sermonizing doctrine' was tantamount to conceding a round to the Protestant adversary: by it 'the glory of our English Church [is] obscured and defaced, which yet was held in admiration of all other Christian countries for the beauty and perfection thereof'.[43]

As the reverberations of the controversy persisting into the later seventeenth century imply, it is both distorting and improper to view clerical divisions over conformity as a simple manifestation of antagonism between Marian and Counter Reformation clergy. This is to perpetuate the blatant bias of Jesuit and seminarist apologists, who displayed a particular addiction to belittling the role of the 'auncient' priesthood in the rehabilitation of Elizabethan Catholicism.[44] The contemporary ecclesiastical politics of 'schism' were rather more complex and confusing.

Jesuit and Douai/Rheims propagandists denounced the clergy who condoned church papistry as a profound embarrassment to the principles of the English Counter Reformation. They aimed and claimed 'to represse the singularity' of a refractory few. The 'singuler', however, took an alternative view. Thomas Bell boasted that 'all the preestes in England some fewe odd persons excepted' shared his sentiments on the subject; in tolerating lay presence at heretical services, he had the backing of the 'best learned' in the land. Bell's brag was strongly contested by his detractors, but even I. G. had

---

[43] On Paul V, see Rose, *Cases of Conscience*, 242 (he did, however, allow Catholics to enter church buildings for the discharge of 'secular business'); Persons, *Quaestiones Duae*, passim esp. pp. 128–9. On Thomas Wright, the Jesuit, (who is not to be confused with the Carthusian monk who authored *The Disposition or Garnishmente of the Soule* cited in ch. ii, above), see Foley, *Records of the English Province*, iv. 371–4 (Father Robert Jones to Robert Persons in Venice, 2 Oct. 1606, and to Richard Blount in London, 20 Oct. 1606), iv. 284 (a letter from Father Robert North to Robert Persons, 30 Oct. 1606). Wright's opinions were based on those of the well known Spanish casuist, John Azor, whose *Libri Institutionum Moralium* was published after 1607, for which see Rose, *Cases of Conscience*, 85–8.

[44] See for example, Garnet, *Treatise of Christian Renunciation*, 13–14; and John Radford's *Directorie Teaching the Way to the Truth* (written 1599, published 1605), with its lengthy endorsement of recusancy doctrine, which was dedicated to George Blackwell and urged its readers to avoid 'suche as bee and were priests of olde and yet for feare of loosing their livings will teache you (as thee tearme it) to beare a little with the time till a better world come'(p. 496). For the later seventeenth century: Rose, *Cases of Conscience*, 246ff. For pertinent points, see MacCulloch, *Later Reformation*, 147–8, and Haigh, 'The continuity of English Catholicism', 202.

to confess that in 1593 many still exercised 'as muche as he speakethe of & more to[o] and so his assertion might have some shewe to be a comon practyse in the realme'.[45] Scrutiny of the practicalities of the mission's operation suggests his remark was not solely a comment on a disturbing degree of indiscipline within the ranks.

Scholars have long stressed that the priests sent to England after 1574 are better characterised as the emissaries of a pastoral organisation than an evangelical movement.[46] The instructions entrusted to departing Douai seminarists and the first Jesuits sharply defined the priorities and objectives of the enterprise: clerical resources were deliberately to be directed to rallying and resuscitating a pre-existing constituency – to transforming careless 'catholykes in there hart' into conscientious confessants, who first and foremost 'abhorreth all communion and participation with the sectaryes in there servyce and sacraments'.[47] The reconciliation and reformation of church papists was the major focus of missionary energies in the field, as the manuscript pamphlets containing 'papistical reasons' for recusancy that fell into government hands document.[48] Private exhortations against conformity were being distributed in the north by one John Boste; William Hart's preaching to his urban congregation in York in the early 1580s chiefly concentrated on the wickedness of dwelling in 'the tabernacles of our new-faced protestants'.[49] Richard White had summarised Persons's *Brief Discours* for the benefit of his illiterate countrymen and women in a Welsh carol – resorting to popular culture was his response to a sound suspicion that 'John Howlet's' 'counsel has not been followed'.[50] Based on the methods employed by Persons and Campion, their lay disciple and devotee George Gilbert set down detailed guidelines in 1583 as to 'How to proceed with schismatics': they clearly constituted a substantial sector of the populace deemed reclaimable to the Mother Church.[51]

---

[45] Garnet, *Treatise of Christian Renunciation*, 168; I. G., 'An answere to a comfortable advertisement', ch. iv.

[46] Meyer, *England and the Catholic Church*, 62; Rose, *Cases of Conscience*, 74; Haigh, 'The fall of a Church or the rise of a sect?', 184; 'From monopoly to minority', 136; 'The continuity of English Catholicism', 194–5; Dures, *English Catholicism*, 19–20.

[47] Knox, *Letters and Memorials*, 35; Hicks, *Letters and Memorials*, 319ff.

[48] See, for example, *CSP Dom 1547–80*, 644 (Jan.[?] 1580), 'Reasons why a Catholic cannot attend the Protestant Church, and that he cannot be required by law to do so'; ibid. 676 (Sept. 1580), 'Certain Papistical reasons set down for the withdrawing of men to come to the church, sent from the Sherriff of Wiltshire'. Numerous others were probably circulating. In 1593 I. G. referred to 'a little dialogge written by a catholye preeste a yeare agoe': 'An answere to a comfortable advertisement', ch. viii.

[49] 'An Exhortation by John Boste against going to Protestant churches', in Pollen, *Unpublished Documents*, 68–9; J. C. H. Aveling, *Catholic Recusancy in the City of York 1558–1791* (CRS Monograph Series ii), London 1970, 74.

[50] Pollen, *Unpublished Documents*, 93–5.

[51] Hicks, *Letters and Memorials*, 331–40: 'A way to deal with persons of all sorts so as to convert them and bring them back to a better way of life.' See also p. 61. The memoirs of John Gerard and William Weston are full of accounts of 'winning back' schismatics: Gerard, *Autobiography*, 19–21, 25, 37, 39, 79–80, 149, 174; William Weston, *William Weston: the autobiography of an Elizabethan*, trans. Philip Caraman, London 1955, 36–8, 61–2, 148–50.

But successfully grooming lapsed Catholics for Rome's resumption of ecclesiastical and political supremacy called for a subtle and supple approach. The uncompromising strictures of recusancy tracts were more likely to drive church papists into the arms of the heretics than clinch their commitment to the 'Old Religion' – as William Allen, president of Douai College, was only too well aware. Defending the activities of his past pupils in 1577, he dwelt on the 'variety of humours' priests confronted in their flocks, 'so diversely to be delt withall, some to be handled softly, some hardly'. Insistence on the precise keeping of Church law was essential, but pedantry was ill-judged:

> yet how warely soever they walke, except they followe a little the fantasyes of theire favourers and followers or bere more or lesse with there schisme or synne, and be content cunningly to convey the matter so that they may serve the one syde without the offence of the other . . . they shall not possibly gaine the favour and good word of the world.

His particular recommendations to priests thus included advice on: 'howe and where to condiscende without synne to certaine feablenesse growne in manns lyfe and manners these ill tymes, not always to be rigorous, never over scrupulous, so that the church discipline be not *evidently* infringed, nor no acte of schisme or synne *plainly* committed'.[52] They were to strike a balance at their own discretion.

Catering for those who found the conflict between comfort and Catholicism peculiarly acute also called for accurate, if elementary, ecclesiastical training in the resolution of difficult moral cases. Part of a new emphasis on sacramental confession across Catholic Europe, casuistry was a developing theological science that occupied an important place in the curriculum of the English seminaries.[53] Students were supplied with manuals examining specific cases they might commonly encounter in the course of their exertions, guiding their judgement of whether given actions involved mortal or venial sin, and the mitigating circumstances that could make normally forbidden behaviour permissible. These were matters which the laity were ill-qualified and ineligible to decide.[54]

---

[52] Knox, *Letters and Memorials*, 31–2, 34 (letter to Chauncy, prior of the English Carthusians in the Low Countries, 10 Aug. 1577, my emphasis).

[53] See Delumeau, *Catholicism between Luther and Voltaire*, 196; idem. 'Prescription and reality', 148; Edmund Leites, 'Introduction' to idem. *Casuistry and Conscience in Early Modern Europe*, Cambridge–Paris 1988, 1–11, esp. p. 6, and idem. 'Casuistry and Character', in ibid. 119–33, esp. 119–20; Bossy, *Christianity and the West*, 127–8; Rose, *Cases of Conscience*, esp. ch. vi; Clancy, *Papist Pamphleteers*, 17ff.; Zagorin, *Ways of Lying*, ch. viii. The key textbook in the seminaries was Navarrus' *Enchiridion*. Casuistry was nevertheless an area of expertise in which the mission was apparently undermanned. Persons requested that learned Spanish and Italian casuists be sent to help solve the many cases of conscience brought to the Jesuits: Hicks, *Letters and Memorials*, 46 (Persons to Agazarri, Rector of the English College). Allen also warned the clergy to refer cases or questions above their knowledge to their superiors: Knox, *Letters and Memorials*, 34, cf 66. For Jesuit educational policy, see Edward A. Fitzpatrick, (ed.), *St Ignatius and the Ratio Studiorum*, New York 1933, 125, 165–7.

[54] See Holmes, *Elizabethan Casuistry*, 1–9; and idem. *Resistance and Compromise*, ch. viii, for further discussion.

Two booklets compiled for the instruction and use of trainee priests in the late 1570s and early 1580s minutely analysed the implications of the exacting doctrine of recusancy outlined in printed Catholic literature. The casuists in no way denied that nonconformity was the ultimate duty of every Catholic, but they did allow markedly more scope for exception. They reflected an unmistakable element of clerical indulgence towards a large body of individuals understandably hesitant to embrace a stance involving harassment and hardship, pecuniary loss and persecution. And prominent recusancy propagandists including Allen and Persons, Martin and Bristow were at least partially responsible for these rulings.[55] Pre-eminently, priests are urged to use '*practical* considerations to judge the present practice in England'.[56] Ambiguous and marginal cases were to be heard with a sympathetic ear. Grace, for example, fell outside the sphere of activity covered by the rules of ecclesiastical separation. Remaining present could safely be sanctioned because blessings before a meal were not formal, public prayers performed in the name of the Protestant Church. It was even permissible to remove one's hat out of civility and politeness.[57]

More pertinently, the manual framed in 1578–9 gave guarded approval to noblemen and women who accompanied the queen to chapel to render a temporal service such as carrying books or cushions. Naaman's conformity was acknowledged as a valid precedent not merely for Elizabethan courtiers: it was in addition tacitly used to exempt from censure servants and underlings who followed their masters to the parish church.[58]

In the later set of cases, '*Resolutiones quorundam casuum nationis Anglicane*', which probably postdates the 1581 legislation instituting the monthly £20 'mulct', yet more latitude was offered to those tempted to compromise intermittently with the Establishment. Openly assuming that Catholics were obliged to avoid heretical churches and sermons *only* by human law, its writers invoked standard casuistical principles to pronounce papal dispensation for outward conformity a genuine possibility.[59] Conventional, astute and unashamedly pragmatic arguments were advanced in support of a concession, primarily for journeying Catholics forced to join Protestant travelling

---

[55] Idem. *Elizabethan Casuistry*, 6–8. The contributors to the collection of cases compiled in 1578–9 probably included Richard Bristow, Laurence Webbe and William Allen. The decisions in '*Resolutiones quorundam casuum nationis Anglicane*', dated to *c*.1585, are attributed to Allen and Persons. Another possible co-author is Gregory Martin.

[56] Ibid. 49, my emphasis.

[57] Ibid. 38, 48, 69.

[58] On courtiers, ibid. 51. They were better advised to beseech the queen to be excused on account of their consciences, however: ibid. 120–1. On servants, 50, cf 95–6.

[59] These principles were briefly laid down in the preface, ibid. 61–2. Actions contravening divine law could not be made lawful by papal dispensation, except where the conflict of two divine precepts required violation of one of them. Human and canon law could be dispensed on reasonable grounds. Indeed, they ceased to be of effect immediately when they contradicted divine and natural law. Technically, Jesuit casuistry was associated with probabilist and probabiliorist theories, rather than tutorist ones (based on the premise that the safer and stricter rule was always to be followed). Probabilists held that a given action was permissible if any respectable authority had defended it; probabiliorists called for a balanced assessment of all authorities and their arguments. See Rose, *Cases of Conscience*, 72.

companions in singing psalms, reciting prayers or actually attending the odd church service, but also for others similarly pressed by 'importunate requests' and unable to reveal their religious identity without grave risk. The commentators alluded to Naaman Syrus and to Martin V's *Ad evitanda*; they noted that it was unlikely that convinced Catholics would be 'infected' by witnessing Protestant worship, and they stressed the undesirability of alienating weak-willed schismatics who might consider the Church 'too strict, and as a result . . . gradually slip into heresy'. A dispensation was held to be especially urgent for upper-class church papists because conserving their assets and authority was a precondition of the reconversion of England: 'It is important to keep noble and rich families in their former positions of honour and dignity, so that, after the death of the queen, they can stand up for the faith with their full authority and protect it with their strength and power against the audacity of heretics.'[60]

The casuists, however, subsequently rendered these considerations virtually redundant by advising apprentice missionaries that regardless of the outcome of this appeal, Catholics were justified by the over-riding natural law of self-preservation in yielding their presence at church in life- or livelihood-threatening situations – when faced with family and financial ruin. 'Just fear' and dire necessity absolved one from divine punishment for a damnable offence. Individuals who intended to take advantage of this immunity should exercise an aggressive vigilance against the temptations to which they would be exposed. They were to take precautions by preparing their minds through prayer and virtuous acts for a rare encounter with Protestantism – girding themselves 'as one going to fight a duel with the Devil', disregarding the litany, and consulting their spiritual counsellors at the first hint of vacillation.[61] Without a true calling from God, in fact, it was 'generally a sort of temerity to put oneself into open danger of death' and wilfully seek martyrdom.[62] The faithful were in honour bound to differentiate themselves sharply from heretics, but it was absurd to assume that churchgoing automatically negated one's religious identity. To regard recusancy as the sole stamp of Catholic affiliation was seriously to underestimate the extent of continuing sympathy for the 'Old Religion', because church papistry, however much it might be regretted, was endemic:

Many of those who go to heretic churches at present in England, not only among the Catholics but even among the heretics, are Catholic and most Catholic and they do not show themselves to be heretics by going into these churches, but simply do not reveal themselves to be Catholics, as they are not bound to do, except in cases of necessity.[63]

---

60 Holmes, *Elizabethan Casuistry*, 74–6, at pp. 76, 75 respectively, cf 95.
61 Ibid. 76–7. Garnet admitted that the Church could not command its members to risk death or serious inconvenience rather than break canon law. He maintained, however, that recusancy was a divine law and thus could not be dispensed: *Apology*, 46.
62 Holmes, *Elizabethan Casuistry*, 72.
63 Ibid. 95.

The lawfulness of occasional conformity was the unambiguous message priests were to carry home and communicate to pious male heads of households in the seclusion and secrecy of the confessional.

These casuists effectively exonerated and reinstated principled church papists as full and respectable members of the Catholic community. 'Who is properlie called a Schismatike, and so, per consequens, excommunicated?' was the perplexing question they re-addressed. The category defined in reply was decisively narrower than that denoted in recusancy tracts – it excluded conformists '*unless* their hearts are turned against the faith and against the unity of the Catholic Church'.[64] While persistent frequenters of Protestant worship remained utterly beyond the social and spiritual pale, those who seldom and unwillingly complied, and who registered their dissent by the scrupulous segregation from heretics and schismatics in secular affairs on which these manuals continued to insist, were not to be debarred mechanically from the spiritual and sacramental benefits of membership of the Church of Rome. People who *considered* themselves Catholics, abstained from communion, but were not yet firmly resolved to forsake heretical churches and sermons entirely might be admitted safely to mass and confession none the less – although not formal absolution.[65]

Educators were clearly not wrong in anticipating the ticklish topics that would vex those under the charge of the Counter Reformation clergy. In the early 1590s, a case was 'moved to the best about London' by one of Elizabeth's ladies-in-waiting, who hoped to be allowed to attend the Chapel Royal if she wore 'some sygne about her necke, as a peare of beades a crucifyx or the lyke wherby she might be knowne to be a catholyke'. The metropolitan priesthood took a hard line in this instance, but only after six months of deadlocked debate.[66] Other occasions revealed varying degrees of laxity. 'Whether I may not be present at any schismatical service: so that I neither communicate with them in prayer nor in sacraments' was also among the ethically equivocal questions propounded to a learned Jesuit, perhaps Edmund Campion, in 1580. Discovered that year in a gentleman's study, the paper discussing it sharply reinforced the view that recusancy remained compulsory, but conceded that it might be justifiable to attend out of inquisitiveness, merely 'to observe their manners'.[67] Gaoled in the Fleet at Manchester, John Finch was advised that he could eat his paltry prison dinner while a minister read from the Geneva Bible without fault, especially if he protested that he abhorred all false translations of Scripture and detested heretical devotion – 'seeing he came to that place purposly and with intention only to take his meale and repast, and not to heare heresie eyther read or taught'.[68] The author of a short set of cases of conscience surviving from the second half of the reign came to the conclusion that

[64] Ibid. 49, my emphasis.

[65] On mass, ibid. 84ff., cf 20; on confession, 94–5, cf 37. As Holmes has emphasised, these tracts nevertheless outline a social doctrine for Elizabethan Catholics which is marked by a distinct bias towards separation from heretics and schismatics: *Resistance and Compromise*, ch. ix.

[66] I. G., 'An answere to a comfortable advertisement', ch. iv.

[67] Strype, *Annals*, II. ii. 349.

[68] Pollen, *Unpublished Documents*, 82.

periodic church papistry could be given assent, though he made no mistake that regular attendance at Common Prayer was insupportable.[69]

The reasoning behind the authorisation given by official and locally active casuists for occasional conformity strikingly echoed – or was echoed by – the argumentation which characterised the 'erroneous' teaching of Langdale and Bell. In a sense, those allegedly 'deviant' clerics were at fault largely for publicising confidential information about accepted penitential practice – for betraying the private leniency of a religion that projected itself as resolutely and invincibly uncompromising. The exposure of casuistical qualifications of the doctrine of recusancy proved as much of a handicap to Catholic publicists as revelations at the trials of Southwell and Garnet in 1595 and 1606 about the furtively sanctioned use of equivocation and mental reservation by tortured priests. It merely substantiated Protestantism's traditional vilification of popery as an inherently duplicitous and hypocritical system of belief.[70]

Furthermore, although easily eclipsed by the dense jungle of arguments assembled against conformity, printed recusancy propaganda itself contained quibbling concessions to the church papist. Robert Persons's *Brief Discours* cautiously recognised the test case of Naaman Syrus as a legitimate paradigm for aristocratic royal servants and advisors required to discharge some known temporal function or ceremonial office in a church for the queen – to literally 'bear the sword'. This slender exception for the predicament of men at the highest levels of government was also ratified by I. G. and Garnet, and more tentatively by Martin who sanctioned it only for a 'vehement heretike lately converted'.[71] A courtier refusing to show any reverence or honour for the service by kneeling or doffing his hat could scarcely be said to 'attend church' at all, 'seeing he goeth in this case . . . to

---

[69] This Bodleian manuscript is discussed in Holmes, *Resistance and Compromise*, 105–6. At the turn of the century, two prominent Continental casuists, the Spanish Jesuits, Azor and Azpilcueta (Navarrus), set down coherent and authoritative theological justifications for occasional conformity. See Rose, *Cases of Conscience*, 85ff., and on Azor, n. 43 above.

[70] See Johann P. Sommerville, 'The "new art of lying": equivocation, mental reservation, and casuistry', in Leites, *Conscience and Casuistry*, 159–84; Zagorin, *Ways of Lying*, ch. ix passim; Holmes, *Resistance and Compromise*, 12ff.; Rose, *Cases of Conscience*, 89ff. Indeed, these casuistry manuals were used by anti-Catholic propagandists, including Bishop Thomas Bilson, *The True Difference betweene Christian Subjection and Unchristian Rebellion*, Oxford 1585, sig. A4v; Matthew Sutcliffe, *A New Challenge made to N.D.*, annexed with separate title page to *A Briefe Replie to a certaine odious and slanderous libel*, London 1600, 54, 112, 115–16, 117, 121, 94 [*sic*], 132; and Thomas Morton, *An Exact Discoverie of Romish Doctrine in the Case of Conspiracie and Rebellion*, London 1605, 2, 4, 6, 40, 42; see also Zagorin, *Ways of Lying*, 198–200. Casuists allowed Catholics to equivocate regarding their conformity itself, although again, this was publicly denounced: see Garnet, *Apology*, 19, 58. Some manuscript tracts endorsing the practice survive. See, for instance, PRO, SP 12/136/15, 'A briefe advertisement howe to Answere unto the Statute for not coming to Church both in Law and Conscience' (1580); PRO, SP 12/279/90, 'Directions [for Catholics] as to the lawfull manner of answering questions of going to Church' (1601). A large section of the former document was devoted to demonstrating that a Catholic was not legally bound to answer the question as it was improper in common law. See Rose, *Cases of Conscience*, ch. v and pp. 83ff; Holmes, *Resistance and Compromise*, 106.

[71] Persons, *Brief Discours*, 24v, 62r–3v; I. G, 'An answere to a comfortable advertisement', chs iii, iv; Garnet, *Treatise of Christian Renunciation*, 156; idem. *Apology*, 54–5; Martin, *Treatise of Schisme*, sigs F6v–7v.

that material house or buyldinge, which is their Church: nether goeth he to it as to a Church, but as to a house to doe his busines in'.[72] Likewise, because the appointed location of cabinet discussions of foreign policy and civil matters was 'accidental' and irrelevant, it was admissible to attend such meetings in the Chapel Royal, provided the individuals concerned behaved themselves as if they were in a 'common towne house or market place'.[73] Frankly admitting that the 'materiall fact' of going to church was not *in itself* evil, Garnet had to agree that a protestation was 'sometimes profitable' and to acknowledge that 'some manner of going [was] not reprehended'. He balanced his list of instances of 'Unlawfull going' with a collection of occasions when yielding one's presence was in fact defensible: conformity at court, walking through a church, participating in a Catholic mass with a heretic, listening to private preaching or hearing grace, visiting a Protestant church in a foreign city as a 'curiouse beholder', and appearing at service time to accomplish a premeditated act of iconoclasm, disturbance or ridicule.[74] Licensing some varieties of political atheism and secular 'schism', however, had serious theoretical consequences in an Erastian state. They undeniably laid the groundwork for more general application.

The casuistry associated with the clerical leaders of Elizabethan Catholicism thus significantly tempered the vehement public condemnation of schismatics central to their own Counter Reformation polemic. Condoning conformable conduct, securing a measure of official pity for convinced but compromising Catholics, was a pastoral policy and practice actively sponsored by William Allen – a cardinal enjoying the relative ease of exile. Eager to offer succour and relief to the persecuted faithful in England, he interceded on their behalf in 1581 – an intervention directly prompted by the government's new assault on wealthy recusants, the extortionate monthly fine. 'Very charitably according to his accustomed tendernes', panegyrised Garnet, recounting the episode a decade later, he had consulted with theologians at the Sorbonne in Paris and with Francis Toledo in Rome as to the lawfulness of going to heretical churches with the proviso of a Protestation. But his efforts were apparently to no avail – the authorities stood firm on the utter illegality of even qualified conformity.[75] Puritans calling for sharper measures against the papists in 1584 unhappily sensed that exacting outward compliance was 'little good', because it was widely suspected that Allen had undertaken to obtain a papal dispensation on this point.[76] In 1592, a verbal assurance from Pope Clement VIII at last enabled him to 'require and advertyse' the priests of his mission in a personal communication that although they were on no account to advocate or defend 'schism':

---

[72] Persons, *Brief Discours*, 62v–3r.
[73] I. G., 'An answere to a comfortable advertisement', ch. iv.
[74] Garnet, *Apology*, 20, 21, 54–6, 57ff. ('Unlawfull going'); Garnet, *Treatise of Christian Renunciation*, 155–7.
[75] Ibid. 159–60. See also Renold, *Letters of William Allen and Richard Barret*, 31–3; Knox, *Letters and Memorials*, 100.
[76] 'Three Answers to the Archbishop's [Whitgift] Articles, 1584', in Peel, *Seconde Parte of a Register*, i. 175.

I would have you use great compassion and mercyfulnes towards suche of the laytie especially as for meere feare or savinge theire family, wyfe and children from ruyne are so far only fallen as to come sometymes to theire churches or be present at the tyme of their service. For though it be not lawfull to do so muche, nor in yt selfe any waies excusable, yet suche necessity in that kynde of men maketh the offence lesse and more compassionable, yea and more easily by you to be absolved.[77]

Occasional conformists who humbly confessed their infirmity and exhibited sincere remorse should not be treated roughly or rigorously, even if they had lapsed repeatedly and were likely to backslide again. 'Schism' was a transgression of divine law, yet none the less 'no more severity is to be required of the penitent then in any other synnes that be subject to the sacrament of penance, and perhappes [less] all circumstances well and discretly [weighed]'. 'Be assured', Allen wrote, 'that in most cases of this kind *tutior est via misercordiae quam justitae rigoris*', the way of mercy is safer than the rigour of justice.[78]

Allen's dispatch represented a timely and realistic reappraisal of the character of Elizabethan Catholicism: the harsh 1593 statute following closely in its wake made the advantages of church papistry almost irresistible. Benevolently bearing with the frailty of a harassed laity was clearly vital: but local and individual relaxation of ecclesiastical discipline was to be achieved at the expense neither of Catholic resistance – nor of the arresting image of a audaciously recusant community. Anonymous persons might individually and occasionally efface their identity but Catholicism's collective facade and polemical veneer of defiance must in the end emerge untarnished. Explicit reference to the pope's mitigatory sentence and Allen's compassionate directive was therefore singularly unsuitable. It was Thomas Bell's error to rashly appropriate them to persuade his readers of the lawfulness of qualified conformity. Garnet intimated as much in the printed propaganda he prepared to counter the 'comfortour'. In a desperate bid to cover up this disastrous leak of classified information, he ingeniously turned the tables. This 'Italian letter' was conversely the 'certaine ground' upon which his contention that conformity was altogether unpardonable rested: the document was cited 'word for word' as a statement of the 'infallible autority' of 'Peters chaire' against schism. But – redeeming his reputation as an equivocator – Garnet silently omitted all mention of Allen's exhortation to gentleness. It must not 'seeme straunge', he bluffed, 'that herin I go about to publish so private a thing: whan I do nothing else but onely geve a necessary preservative, against diverse venemous tounges, which out of so sweete and pleasant a flower having gathered poison, are every where busie to disperse the same'. Bell's chief crime was certainly his indiscretion.[79]

---

[77] Knox, *Letters and Memorials*, 343–6, at pp. 344, 345 respectively. The letter is also preserved in the Elizabethan State Papers, see *CSP Dom 1591–4*, 291–3 (1592).

[78] Knox, *Letters and Memorials*, 345.

[79] Garnet, *Treatise of Christian Renunciation*, 161–3, at p. 161; Garnet, *Apology*, 11–12; I. G., 'An answere to a comfortable advertisement', preface, ch. xiii. Cf Questier, 'English clerical converts', 476 n. 109.

By the late sixteenth century, the church papist was a clerically acknowledged sector of the Catholic community. As the Elizabethan government unleashed an ever more venomous volley of penal laws, unbending insistence on recusancy was prudently but reluctantly relinquished as impractical idealism – dogmatism that threatened to erode the loyalties of an already disheartened flock. But grudging acceptance of occasional conformity as an adequate mark of commitment to the 'Old Religion' did not signal final resignation to the permanent status of a dissenting minority and oppressed sect. On the contrary, covert accommodation of the church papist was one manifestation of the adaptability of Counter Reformation activists still clinging optimistically to the vision of a restored Church. It was both a temporary necessity and a political strategy to ensure the survival and to preserve the resilience of a healthy and wealthy Catholic body – to maximise its potential for the complete recovery of institutional and social control. As Peter Holmes rightly concludes, in the eyes of these activists, a degree of quiet compromise with the Establishment remained an option for lay Catholics only as long as there was a real prospect of England's eventual return to Rome, a glimmer of hope for a reversal of the Reformation.[80] The motives behind their patience with upper-class conformists were unusually pragmatic. In the words of the casuists, 'Once these men have gone', 'religion in England will be finished, or virtually finished'.[81]

And these were tactics of which prying Protestants themselves had an inkling. There may be an element of truth as well as obsession in Richard Topcliffe's report to the Lord Treasurer around 1590 that priests dispensed certain 'papists' from recusancy 'to the end they may the better, and with the less suspicion, serve the turn of their cause catholic . . . when their day of Jhesus cometh'.[82] The Privy Council was evidently convinced that Catholic missionaries had unlimited secret faculties to absolve people from the sin of conformity: as a matter of high priority it sent a spy to Valladolid College in Spain to investigate this ominous possibility. And were the 'informations' of one John Warrener regarding papal pardons for churchgoing under 'a pretensed Cullor . . . to blind the eyes of the protestants' entirely the unreliable rumours of a professional taleteller?[83]

Why was there such disparity – so fundamental a gap – between published clerical literature emphatically insisting on undeviating nonconformity, and the sympathetic casuistical discussion and relaxed practice closely associated with and advanced undercover by those same priests? This superficial ideological inconsistency is not difficult to account for. If recusancy tracts are recognised as confessional polemic designed to outwit and overcome Protestants, as much as the private devotional manuals of a

---

[80] Holmes, *Resistance and Compromise*, 2, 108, 124; and idem. *Elizabethan Casuistry*, 5, 110. Cf Zagorin, *Ways of Lying*, 140–1.
[81] Holmes, *Elizabethan Casuistry*, 61–2.
[82] Strype, *Annals*, IV. 54.
[83] Pollen, *Unpublished Documents*, 182; *CSP Dom 1595–7*, 59–60 (June 1595). One of the arguments that weighed against the intended clause for compulsory communion in the 1592 Act was the possibility that dispensation might be obtained and Catholics thus made more invisible: see Talbot, *Recusant Records*, 120.

cohesive Catholic 'community', then the reticence of the Counter Reformation hierarchy becomes explicable. Propagandists who made use of a maturing medium to mount an assault on the mendacity and depravity of a heretical Church could hardly disclose the dissimulation and opportunism upon which their own faith had come to rely. Behind the scenes – off the international and English stage – conformity might be countenanced. Not, however, in that forum in which the politics of early modern religion was increasingly being played out – print.

Historians have often presented Catholic ideology and culture in the post-Reformation period in terms of a dichotomy between clergy and laity. More specifically, a sharp line of division has been drawn between missionary priests who adamantly demanded absolute obedience to the precepts of the doctrine of recusancy and separation, and laypeople more disposed to yield the minimum of compliance to the Elizabethan government and outwardly conform – who, nevertheless, gradually submitted to the directives of their ecclesiastical superiors. Caroline Hibbard, for example, suggests that church papistry was the conceivable corollary of a laity left to devise its own *modus vivendi*, free of the domineering interference of the Jesuits and seminarists.[84] However, as Holmes has observed, contemporary Catholic casuistry alone questions the adequacy and accuracy of this model: the clergy were neither blind to the conveniences of concession and compromise, nor unwilling to exercise laxity in the confessional.[85]

It is equally misleading to interpret lay attitudes as direct reflections of the indoctrinating efforts of a clerical elite, to accept unquestioningly the docile deference of people to priests. Indeed, in view of the growing dependence of the missionaries on the financial patronage and physical protection of noble and gentry families, seigneurial interests may well have critically influenced the clerical construction of the working arrangement of occasional conformity. Anthony Browne, Lord Montagu's reprehensible 'schismatic conduct' was imputed to that much maligned cleric, Alban Langdale, by the hagiographer of his saintly wife. But the ostentatious act of contrition he allegedly performed when reproached by Langdale's seminary-trained successor was perhaps partly an edifying fiction, a piece of poetic licence: 'Instantly putting of his hat, and falling on his knees, both with gesture of his whole body, and with his tongue, he most humbly submitted to the censure of the Catholic Church, and piously promised never thence forward to be present at hereticall service, which all the rest of his lyfe he exactly observed.'[86]

Was clerical flexibility the consequence, as much as the cause, of an enterprising and manipulative conformist lay Catholicism? Were priests carried along by a swelling tide of pressure from the parochial communities

---

[84] Hibbard, 'Early Stuart Catholicism', 16–18, 21. See also Bossy, 'The character of Elizabethan Catholicism', 39–59; idem. *The English Catholic Community*, ch. ii; Aveling, *The Handle and the Axe*, 69–70. For discussions directed towards political thought and developments, see Trimble, *The Catholic Laity*, 16–21, 264–6; Pritchard, *Catholic Loyalism*, passim esp. ch. iii.

[85] Holmes, *Resistance and Compromise*, 176ff., 183.

[86] Richard Smith, *The Life of the Most Honourable and Vertuous Lady, The Lady Magdalen Viscountesse Montague*, [St Omer] 1627, sigs B2r–v. See also Manning, *Religion and Society*, 160ff., 221, 231; Dures, *English Catholocism*, 6–7; Scarisbrick, *The Reformation and the English People*, 142.

they served? Did they retrospectively give official endorsement to what was already an established pattern of observance?

So, at least, recusancy propagandists implied. I. G. thought that those of his colleagues who justified churchgoing were pandering to their powerful sponsors: Thomas Bell's downfall had been 'to to [sic] much carnall affection to the temporal estates, of his worldly frendes, whose yealdinge a litle thus dissemblinglye to the state in this poynte might not onlye . . . be his owne more quiete and saftye but also ther temporall comoditye and ease'. Bell, 'by lykelyehoud', had been browbeaten – duped by a rumour-monger, 'some good fellowe desyrous of his comforte', who had brought him news that casuistical concession was widespread in the south, 'for a newe years gifte because he did know him to be delighted with toyes'.[87] To Gregory Martin's mind, conformity was likewise 'foolish pietie', contrived by overawed divines 'to sooth the feareful humour of their carnal frendes'. And when Robert Persons denounced the 'underpropper' Langdale's 'damnable trade' in 1580, he expostulated against such 'as laye handes very greedily on this mans newe devise . . . and doo seeke to set it abroache by all meanes possible, and to drawe other men to the participation of their evill resolution'.[88] 'Pamphlettes and perswasions of such Lay persons as amongst the simple have an undeserved conceite of vertew and learning', Garnet added, were presenting a disconcerting challenge to the hegemony of clerical authority. He set out 'to impose eternall silence unto so froward and impudent brabblers', to smother the 'flattering doctrine' engineered by these 'grave interpreters' – 'our newe Laye schismaticall Devines'.[89] It was 'the half hearted and the schismatics' whom George Birkhead, superior of the Secular Clergy, similarly identified behind manouvering at the highest levels for a temporary withdrawal of Counter Reformation activists and a slackening of the mission's pace.[90] But these were the frustrated and futile outcries of priests incapable of stemming the inexorable flow of control from the spiritual to the secular sphere. Lay church papistry was a force to be reckoned with.

---

[87] I. G., 'An answere to a comfortable advertisement', ch. xii, postscript, ch. iv respectively.
[88] Martin, *Treatise of Schisme*, sig. C6v; 'Against going to Church', BL, Add. MS 39830, fos 19v, 14r.
[89] Garnet, *Treatise of Christian Renunciation*, 18–9, 161–3, 169; *Declaration of the Fathers*, 5–6.
[90] Pollen, 'Father Persons' Memoirs', 147, 155.

4

Church Papists

Heretics they are, and they are our neighbours. By us and amongst us they lead their lives. – Hooker, *Works*, i. 363.

John Bossy has examined the post-Reformation Catholic community as 'a branch of the English nonconforming tradition'. He has characterised its emergence as 'the withdrawal of a separating body from the Church of England', and the experience of its members as involving a progressive severance of those bonds of collective behaviour which cemented late sixteenth- and early seventeenth-century society.[1] Bossy adopts a familiar approach to early modern Catholicism; his book is a sophisticated sociological contribution to the well-established field of 'recusant history'. But a study of the church papist requires an adjusted perspective on evidence that only obliquely and imperfectly registers the phenomenon of non-recusant Catholicism. In this chapter, I wish to offer some conjectural rather than conclusive comments on the consequences of focusing on religious and cultural integration as well as segregation, on co-operation as opposed to separation.

The categories of 'recusant' and 'church papist' are by no means mutually exclusive. The providential tales and stories of exemplary repentance collected, enhanced and recirculated by priests and hagiographers suggest outward conformity was a temptation to which even the most scrupulous succumbed in moments of weakness. Divine wrath and remorse in the form of a raging and unquenchable thirst fell upon one pious West Norfolk gentleman who deluded himself it would be 'rash and regrettable . . . to refuse to purchase immunity from disaster by a single visit to church'. A conscience-stricken blacksmith at Winchester was remanded in 1584 as a madman for the perverse enthusiasm with which he accepted public flogging as a personal penance. Tormented by the sin of once consenting to conform, the priest Richard Griffiths likewise sought to repair the scandal his hypocritical presence had given a Bridewell congregation by recklessly declaring his error in their midst.[2] But it is harder to dismiss as moralising propaganda the compelling case of attempted suicide reported to Francis Walsingham by the bishop of Chester in 1583, of the 'very seditious recusant' of a Manchester

---

[1] Bossy, *The English Catholic Community*, 7, 144, 108 respectively, and passim.
[2] Weston, *Autobiography*, 148ff.; Pollen, 'Father Persons' Memoirs', 141 (a letter from Persons to his superior from Paris, 11 June 1584); Challoner, *Memoirs of Missionary Priests*, 142 (for Griffiths, alias Watson). For similar examples, ibid. 118–19; Morris, *Troubles of Our Catholic Forefathers*, iii. 57; Hicks, *Letters and Memorials*, 59; Weston, *Autobiography*, 178–9. See also W. E. Rhodes (ed.), 'The apostolical life of Ambrose Barlow, O.S.B.', *Chetham Miscellanies. New Series. Vol. II* (Chetham Society, n.s. lxiii, 1909), 10–11.

parish who endeavoured to drown himself after attending Common Prayer.[3] For some individuals, taking advantage of the loopholes evolved by Catholic casuists was psychologically impossible.

If the lists of recusants compiled by ecclesiastical commissioners in York in 1580 or the Exchequer rolls of the 1590s are any indication, however, a large fraction of those indicted in church and civil courts were less fastidious. Faced with the tangible prospect of imprisonment and impoverishment, persisting in overt dissent was a course of action requiring either indomitable courage or fanaticism. Marmaduke Thurkeld gratefully yielded to Protestant persuasions and 'godly motion[s]', and 'willingly entered into recognisance in £100' at Ripon for the full conformity of himself and his family. Eleven days of incarceration in York Castle convinced Ralph Lawson of Brough of the merits of time-serving, and one tussle with the High Commission was enough to permanently deter a Cheshire villager who fervently promised in 1581 to 'frequent the Churche ever duringe his naturall lyffe, God willinge'.[4] The certificates of conformity surviving in Essex archives and the King's Bench records also index the extent to which local pressures and the increasingly stringent legislative measures produced the capitulation of previously intransigent recusants. No less a personage than Bishop John Aylmer attested to the 1587 'reformation' of Jeffery Thorowgood of the parish of Walden, who now came 'very orderly' to weekly service and received the holy sacrament.[5] A brush with the law may well have precipitated a complete abjuration of 'popery': perhaps more often it merely recommended the unmolested existence enjoyed by the church papist.

In a society relying on the efforts of unpaid amateurs for the correction of deviance, 'conformity' could be but a temporary expedient, a brief, even unrepeated, response to the harassment of a singularly zealous magistrate or crusading prelate. Richard Eldershawe, 'a householder professinge phisicke' in the Cheshire community of Andlyn, whose name reappeared on the regional blacklist of 1595 after a short spell of 'schism', was far from unusual in reneging on his pledge of obedience as soon as authority's gaze was averted. An immediate return to intractable recusancy and Catholic activism in rural Staffordshire likewise followed the dramatic surrender which secured Thomas, Lord Paget's release from custody at Windsor in 1580.[6]

Honouring a formal undertaking to comply could sometimes be avoided altogether: the 'dissembling schismatics' of whom Henry Garnet disapproved

[3] *CSP Dom 1581–90*, 131 (28 Nov. 1583).

[4] Hughes, *The Reformation in England*, iii. 427–40 (a transcription of PRO, SP 12/141/28), quotations at pp. 428, 438, 430 respectively; Wark, *Elizabethan Recusancy in Cheshire*, 32. On Exchequer records, Calthorp, *Recusant Roll No. I, 1592–3*, p. xxi and passim; Bowler, *Recusant Roll No. 2 (1593–4)*; Walker, 'Implementation', esp. chs v, ix.

[5] Emmison, *Morals and the Church courts*, 95, cf 90. See also *CSP Dom 1581–90*, 319 (11, 12 Apr. 1586); *CSP Dom 1580–1625 Addenda*, 27 (Dec. 1580); Talbot, *Recusant Records*, 5, 71; J. T. Cliffe, *The Yorkshire Gentry from the Reformation to the Civil War*, London 1969, 181–2; O'Dwyer, 'Catholic Recusants in Essex', 80; Dorothy M. Clarke, 'Conformity certificates among the King's Bench records: a calendar', *RH* xiv (1977), 53–63, which includes transcriptions of some sample certificates.

[6] Talbot, *Recusant Records*, 73, cf 76, 85; *VCH Staffordshire*, iii, ed. M. W. Greenslade, Oxford 1970, 99–100.

included individuals who hollowly agreed to churchgoing or feigned their conformity, split hairs by sending a proxy or offered an assortment of frivolous, if credible, excuses for their absence.[7] Common alibis, ranging from pressing business, labour and lawsuits to old age, illness and babysitting, may more often mask simple slackness than ideological conviction, but one known Cheshire recusant explained his non-appearance in 1594, saying 'he hath not his ordenary usuall seate therein'. At least in the opinion of diocesan officials who compiled a register of nonconforming Catholics in the adjoining county, Anna Standish of Wigan deanery pretended 'some distraction of mind'. Perhaps Edward Dillick of Dedham's pretext that 'he being out of apparel was ashamed to go to Church' was equally specious, a cover for conscientious, clerically approved Catholicism.[8] Yet attendance at Protestant services became a point on which the laity might justifiably equivocate, according to Catholic casuists. Manuscript tracts discussing the evasive and unincriminating answers one might make to the question 'Do you go to church ?' passed from hand to hand. Recusants mindful of the duties of offending the weak and of the duty of open confession of the faith, could nevertheless conceal their failure to obey the statute from inquisitorial churchwardens and magistrates by a range of prevaricating replies. Dodging the consequences of one's religious delinquency and sidestepping its financial penalties in this way was itself a variety of church papistry.[9]

Neither were regular, if infrequent, acts of compliance with the Church of England regarded as inconsistent with committed Catholicism. Monthly appearance at Common Prayer was the personal compromise devised by a Cheshire woman Anne Scarisbrick. The wife and daughters of the eminent Sussex justice and lawyer, Edmund Pelham, confined their outward conformity to thrice annually in 1596; he himself satisfied the law 'but slackly'. For the members of one East Anglian household, toeing the line was a distinctly seasonal obligation – neither Mr George Dinley nor his servants came to church, 'but at Christmass', according to 1595 episcopal recusancy returns.[10] In the same year, a vigilant Lancashire Protestant was warning of gentlemen papists who refrained from church except 'for one Sundaye or two before the Assizes' as an insurance against prosecution, a means whereby they 'shadowe their hypocrasie'. It was also a calculated measure of submission to an admittedly legitimate, if heretical and persecuting regime: the private bargain of Catholics who had reached a

---

[7] Garnet, *Apology*, 58, cf Martin, *Treatise of Schism*, sigs C4r–v.

[8] Wark, *Elizabethan Recusancy in Cheshire*, 122; Talbot, *Recusant Records*, 78; Emmison, *Morals and the Church courts*, 90. For other possible examples, see ibid. 79ff.; Talbot, *Recusant Records*, 71. But note Martin Ingram's cautions on this subject: *Church Courts, Sex and Marriage in England, 1570–1640*, Cambridge 1987, 106.

[9] See, for example PRO, SP 12/136/15, 'A briefe advertisement howe to Answere unto the Statute for not coming to Church both in Law and Conscience' (1580); ibid. 12/279/90, 'Directions [for Catholics] as to the lawfull manner of answering questions of going to Church' (1601).

[10] For Anne Scarisbrick and George Dinley, see Talbot, *Recusant Records*, 84, 111. For Pelham, Strype, *Annals*, IV. 402; cf *DNB s.v.* Pelham. See also Anthony Fletcher, *A County Community in Peace and War: Sussex 1600–1660*, London–New York 1975, 94–5.

tacit understanding with the provincial representatives of central government.[11]

In John Gerard's view, many practised their religion 'precisely' only if and when circumstances permitted. Widespread sympathy for the 'Old Religion' in the north-west made 'conversion' a comparatively easy task – in the short term: 'People of this kind come into the church without difficulty, but they fall away the moment persecution blows up. When the alarm is over, they come back again.'[12] Expectations of toleration under a new king engendered a massive increase in recusancy in Lancashire and Yorkshire in 1603–4. The village hierarchy of Farnworth, Suffolk, was also prompted to enumerate 'all such people as have revolted from the said Chappel and from receiving the holie and blessed Communion since her Majesties death'. Catholicism's 'gains' in this period might realistically be attributed to the movement of cautious and previously undetected schismatics into fully-fledged nonconformity. Indeed, a substantial number of the 'newly seduced' lapsed back into less daring modes of dissent after the Gunpowder Plot of 1605 disillusioned James of his ecumenical ideals.[13] Visitation articles framed for use in a number of dioceses that year disclose ecclesiastical awareness and mistrust of a portion of the populace which oscillated unpredictably between recusancy and church papistry: vicars and churchwardens were to enquire whether the 'popish recusants' of their parishes were offenders of 'long time or only since his majesty's reign' and to monitor carefully the conformable conduct of those recently reclaimed.[14] Progression into dedicated and unyielding recusancy was typically pro-longed and punctuated by episodes of backsliding. Unbending adherence to the rigorous doctrine outlined by clerical propagandists was simply impractical piety.

Further regional studies are likely to confirm J. T. Cliffe's conclusion that most Catholic landowning families in Yorkshire had 'schismatic' branches – to subvert assumptions that an inbred race of recusants, with residences directed by domiciled priests, and diligently fulfilling a quasi-monastic cycle of rituals and devotions, was the chief prop of Elizabethan Catholicism.[15] According to a confidential dispatch on the 'State of Religion' in Northumberland sent to Robert Cecil in 1607, the principal domestic establishments in that county were bristling with 'Church Papists'. And although the Cheshire family of Masseys was among those suspected of being 'vehemently infected with Popery' by a puritan informer of the late 1570s, few of its members were ever accused or convicted of recusancy.[16] A surprising number of the Jesuit novices entering colleges on the Continent after 1597 admitted that their parents,

[11] HMC, *Fourteenth Report, Appendix, Part IV* (Kenyon MSS), London 1894, 585.

[12] Gerard, *Autobiography*, 32–3.

[13] For the Yorkshire figures, see Dickens, 'Extent', passim esp. pp. 30ff.; for Lancashire, Haigh, *Reformation and Resistance*, 277; for Farnworth, Talbot, *Recusant Records*, 147.

[14] See, for example, Cardwell, *Documentary Annals*, ii. 112–13 (1605), and 'Archbishop Bancroft's letter touching recusants, 1604', ii. 97ff.

[15] Cliffe, *The Yorkshire Gentry*, chs viii, ix, passim esp. p. 182; J. C. H. Aveling, 'Catholic households in Yorkshire, 1580–1603', *Northern History* xvi (1980), 85–101.

[16] Talbot, *Recusant Records*, 150–3 (also in HMC, *Salisbury, Part XIX*, London 1965, 3–5); Wark, *Elizabethan Recusancy in Cheshire*, 49–50, 158–9.

siblings and close relatives were conformists, and confessed moreover to having complacently spent their own childhood and youth in 'schism'.[17] In 1579, the casuists at Rheims were already lamenting that intermarriage with schismatics, not to say heretics, 'is nowe a dayes made no matter of conscience, or a Trifle'.[18] The late sixteenth-century English Catholic community was apparently far from incestuously recusant.

Indeed, daunted by the potentially crippling penalties of the statutes of 1581, 1587 and 1593, perhaps an increasing rather than dwindling number of heads of otherwise model dissenting gentry households resorted to occasional conformity to prevent the shattering of their property and the derogation of their status.[19] By the time George Gilbert penned his paper on evangelising methods in 1583, it was already a strikingly conventional stance – a regrettably pragmatic arrangement that often occasioned considerable conflict of conscience:

> These men have no other recourse but a number of feeble excuses, namely that God sees their good intention, that they believe in the Catholic faith and have a hatred for heresy, and they hope that they will be held excused in as much as they cannot live in any other way owing to the strict laws and persecution or to old age which does not fit them to endure hardship or imprisonment. They will say too, that, though they are not acting well, they are awaiting a favourable time when they will make satisfaction for the past; meanwhile they will throw themselves on the mercy of God and will act rightly to this extent that wife, children and servants shall not go to the heretical churches; they will give alms, and will support a priest at their own charges to reconcile them if the need should arise: and in this fashion they flatter and deceive themselves thinking to have their sins condoned by doing good to others.

Ralph Buckland's implacable Jehovah similarly reproved this 'crafty generation' that hoped to make amends by punctiliousness in other religious observances: 'ye fast the Eves and keepe Holy-daies, possibly more then ordinary, in discerning of meates, many of you are more precise then you neede'.[20]

---

[17] On 'schismatic' relatives, Foley, *Records of the English Province*, i. 68, 142–3, 146–8, 166, 183, 295–6; iii. 108, 148–50, 183–4, 186–7, 489; iv. 17–8, 204, 289–92, 403–4, 418, 422–4, 435, 603; Anthony Kenny (ed.), *The Responsa Scholarum of the English College, Rome: part one: 1598-1621* (CRS liv, 1962), 25, 29, 74, 76, 79, 88, 93–4, 111, 116, 121, 134, 154–5, 175–6, 196, 198, 219, 221, 232, 236, 262, 274, 285, 297, 304, 309, 316, 325. McCann and Connolly, *Memorials of Father Augustine Baker*, 16ff., 74ff. On the 'schismatic' backgrounds of aspiring priests, Foley, *Records of the English Province*, i. 68, 146–7, 183, 193; iii. 150, 184, 187; iv. 19, 285, 603, 418, 655; Kenny, *Responsa Scholarum*, 74, 76–7, 94, 116, 154, 172, 188, 196, 198, 232, 275, 316, 325. Even Robert Persons ruefully recalled in his memoirs that he had been but a Catholic 'at heart' until the resignation of his Oxford fellowship in 1573: Pollen, 'Memoirs', 18ff.

[18] Holmes, *Elizabethan Casuistry*, 30.

[19] Bowler, *Recusant Roll No. 2 (1593-4)*, p. xliii; Aveling, 'Some Aspects of Yorkshire Catholic recusant history', 110; Hibbard, 'Early Stuart Catholicism', 17; Cliffe, *The Yorkshire Gentry*, 227.

[20] Hicks, *Letters and Memorials of Father Robert Persons*, 337–8; Buckland, *Embassage from Heaven*,

Church papistry of this ilk was a patriarchal responsibility, a necessary evil to preserve the prosperity, respectability and purity of domestic and seigneurial Catholicism. It was an obligation that devolved by the logic of primogeniture, a principled line of conduct, which in spite of Bossy's scepticism, could be pursued by eldest sons across several generations.[21] Yielding to compromise with Protestantism soon after coming of age and succeeding to an inheritance was deplorably common among those of rank and wealth, according to Robert Wigmore, who left Herefordshire to begin his clerical training abroad in 1610.[22] Gestures of conformism by a series of heirs enabled the Meynells of North Kilvington, Yorkshire, to retain their estates, and their dignity substantially intact into the 1650s.[23] While insisting on the strict recusancy of his spouse and younger offspring, the Sussex gentleman Sir Garret Kempe explicitly instructed his first-born in the hereditary task of outward conformity and 'did very often urge and perswade him to goe to the protestant churches'.[24] J. C. H. Aveling, J. A. Hilton and A. D. Wright have rightly stressed the critical significance of this practice in sustaining the 'Old Faith' as a viable religious option in upper-class families and thus postponing their decline into social and political impotence. It was church papistry that paradoxically ensured the survival of aristocratic recusancy.[25] Presentments for nonconformity in the diocese of Chester in 1595 indirectly suggest it became an equally marked tendency among yeomen and artisans: Owen Wilbram, a smith by trade, is conspicuous by his absence from the Malpas parish lists that included his wife, two daughters and their housemaid. It may be, in fact, that Catholicism among the 'middling sort' predominantly took this form. As a group they were far more prone to be emasculated by the ballooning fines for recusancy than the gentry, who could better afford a luxury tax on their religious heterodoxy.[26]

Does the exceptional prominence of women, particularly married women, in the administrative and legal records of Elizabethan and Jacobean recusancy itself reflect the prevalence of conscientiously Catholic, but 'conformable' *men*? The statistically high incidence of law-abiding males with more obstinately 'popish' spouses received considerable contemporary attention at the regional and parliamentary level, and it has generated much subsequent discussion by

10, 80–1, 78. Cf Hide, *Consolatorie Epistle*, sig. C6v; Wright, *The Disposition or Garnishmente of the Soule*, sig. D1r. On maintaining priests and intending full reconciliation before death, see Weston, *Autobiography*, 36–8; Foley, *Records of the English Province*, i. 142–3.

[21] Bossy, *The English Catholic Community*, 158–9.

[22] Foley, *Records of the English Province*, iv. 423, cf iv. 291.

[23] Aveling, *The Handle and the Axe*, 160–1. Cf Foley, *Records of the English Province*, iv. 18; Kenny, *Responsa Scholarum*, 77 (John Smith admitted both his father and grandfather had been 'schismatics').

[24] Fletcher, *A County Community in Peace and War*, 98. See also Foley, *Records of the English Province*, iii. 183.

[25] See Aveling, *The Handle and the Axe*, 162; idem. *Catholic Recusancy in the City of York*, 67; J. A. Hilton, 'Catholicism in Jacobean Durham (1)', *RH* xiv (1977), 78–85, esp. p. 84; Wright, 'Catholic history, north and south', 148.

[26] Talbot, *Recusant Records*, 68. For this family, see also Wark, *Elizabethan Recusancy in Cheshire*, 170. In addition, see MacCulloch, *Later Reformation*, 150; Hilton, 'Catholicism in Elizabethan Northumberland', 57.

historians.[27] As early as 1578, the Privy Council was receiving communications on the matter from Hampshire; Lancashire authorities registered their concern in 1584, requesting official guidance on the correction of men who 'go to church, but have mass at home for their wives'.[28] In the last decade of the reign, the earl of Huntingdon, president of the Council of the North, and Lord Chief Justice Popham were mounting aggressive campaigns to eradicate female recusancy by imposing burdensome fines on the husbands of offenders – to persuade them to 'work their wives' conformity'. Such schemes, adjudged the Jesuit William Blount in 1600, 'doth touch chiefly schismatics'.[29]

Implementing these measures proved to be legally awkward because under common law a man was not liable for the debts of a *'femme covert'*. The failure of a controversial over-riding clause in the 1593 Act to adequately remedy the situation, however, forced the government to rethink some of its narrowly traditional assumptions about contemporary gender relations, specifically the susceptibility of the 'weaker vessel' to male discipline.[30] Yet, as administrators and legislators slowly realised, the intractability of nonconforming wives was by no means unequivocal evidence of their

---

[27] See Dickens, 'Extent', 39–40; O'Dwyer, 'Catholic Recusants in Essex', ch. iv; Bossy, *The English Catholic Community*, ch. vii, esp. pp. 150–68; Aveling, 'Catholic households', 88; Marie B. Rowlands, 'Recusant women 1560–1640', in Mary Prior (ed.), *Women in English Society 1500–1800*, London–New York 1985, 153ff.; Retha M. Warnicke, *Women of the English Renaissance and Reformation* (Contributions in Women's Studies xxxviii), Westport, Conn. 1983, ch. ix.

[28] For Hampshire, Bossy, *The English Catholic Community*, 154, and *CSP Dom 1547–80*, 687 (14 Nov. 1580); for Lancashire, *CSP Dom 1581–90*, 214 (Nov.? 1584). See also, for Bedford, Calthorp, *Recusant Roll No. I, 1592–3*, p. xxi; for Worcester, Talbot, *Recusant Records*, 129; for Cheshire, Wark, *Elizabethan Recusancy in Cheshire*, 83, 135; for the diocese of York, Ryan, 'Diocesan returns of recusants for England and Wales 1577', 6–9, and Aveling, *Catholic Recusancy in the City of York*, 59, 65–6, 68; for Hereford in 1604, J. H. Matthews (ed.), 'Records relating to Catholicism in the South Wales Marches', in *CRS Miscellanea II* (CRS ii, 1906), 293–6; for Durham, Hilton, 'Catholicism in Elizabethan Durham', 6; Talbot, *Recusant Records*, 69, 76–7, 129; HMC, *Fourteenth Report, Appendix, Part IV* (Kenyon MSS), 584–5. Such concerns persisted into the Civil War period: in Dec. 1641, the mayor of Berwick wrote to a member of the Long Parliament of 'papists' in his town, noting that 'divers persons have lived here divers years, who have repaired to church themselves and their wives and divers of their children and servants recusants': HMC, *Thirteenth Report, Appendix, Part I* (Portland MSS), London 1891, 28–9. (I am grateful to Amanda Whiting for this reference.)

[29] On Huntingdon, see Walker, 'Implementation', 320–30, 387; Bossy, *The English Catholic Community*, 154–5; Morey, *The Catholic Subjects of Elizabeth I*, 152ff. On Popham, Morris, *Troubles of Our Catholic Forefathers*, i. 194ff. Even a superficial survey of the *responsa scholarum* of Blount's colleagues substantiates his surmise: the vast majority of 'schismatic' fathers had 'Catholic' wives. For only a few examples, see Foley, *Records of the English Province*, i. 183. 295–6; iii. 183–4, 186–7; iv. 17–8, 289–92, 423–4, 435, 603; Kenny, *Responsa Scholarum*, 25, 77, 116, 154, 196, 198, 274, 285, 304, 309, 316, 325.

[30] *SR*, 35 Eliz. c. 1. § X; this was reinforced in 7 Jac. c. 6. § X. See Bossy, *The English Catholic Community*, 154–5; Bowler, *Recusant Roll No. 2 (1593–4)*, p. xlvi; Neale, *Elizabeth I and her Parliaments*, ii. 396. MPs' sensitivity on this matter may be an indication of wider opposition to intrusion in private family affairs; it may equally be a comment on the extent of crypto-Catholic influence within Parliament itself. Two lawyers who attempted to take advantage of this loophole and pleaded law on behalf of their Catholic wives in the early 1590s, however, were deprived of their professional practice, fined and disgraced on the pillory at York: see I. G., 'An answere to a comfortable advertisement', ch. i.

resistance to conjugal control. John Goldsmith of Exton, Hampshire, earnestly protested that he was 'not hable to overule his wiefes pevish disposicion in that behaulf': but was this the white lie of a careful conformist who quietly supported the recalcitrance of his spouse – who merely *chose* not to 'lay his commandment unfeignedly' upon her?[31] It is perhaps similarly misleading to regard Sir Ralph Grey's toleration of his lady's patronage of seminary priests and supervision of a strictly Catholic home at Chillingham, Northumberland as proof of his timid deference to a domineering wife.[32] And the regiment of forty-five married women cited for recusancy in the Lancashire town of Wigan in 1595 is hardly conclusive proof of the existence of a disproportionately large plebeian population of A. L. Rowse's henpecked husbands.[33]

A recusant wife consequently called into question the reliability of her professedly Protestant partner. In the experience of Thomas Cooper, bishop of Winchester, no man with an incorrigibly nonconforming spouse was sound himself. What convincing rejoinder could the mayor of York, John Dinley, who found himself in this position in 1577, offer to contradict the charge that 'he is unmete to govern a citie that cannot govern his owne household'? Three years later the city council agreed that men with dissenting dependents were untrustworthy citizens and should be disenfranchised. On the astute advice of Sir Francis Knollys, Lord Burghley was expelling such slippery individuals from county magistracies in 1587: entrusting those who 'pretend to be good subjects, and yet do suffer their wives to be open recusants' with high office was an 'open window' to an explosion of popery.[34] This policy was enshrined in statute law in 1606, when the nonconformity of a married woman became adequate grounds for depriving her husband of civil promotion and appointment.[35]

Church papistry, then, did not invariably signal a weak-kneed surrender of male religious initiative: on the contrary, it was often the qualified conformity of the *paterfamilias* which rendered feasible the very establishment of an internal recusant regime. A husband's concentration on protecting the family's resources and reputation could both enable and necessitate his wife's assumption of a more energetic role in safeguarding its spiritual integrity. Ironically, a woman's inferior public and legal identity afforded her superior

---

[31] *VCH Hampshire and the Isle of Wight*, ii, ed. H. A. Doubleday and William Page, London 1903, 77; Morris, *Troubles of Our Catholic Forefathers*, iii. 268.

[32] Bossy, *The English Catholic Community*, 155.

[33] Talbot, *Recusant Records*, 78 (of the 73 recusants in this parish, only 7 were men, and 21 other women were single, widowed or married to recusants). A. L. Rowse, *The England of Elizabeth: the structure of society*, London 1973 (first publ. 1950), 488, 491, cf Bossy, *The English Catholic Community*, 153.

[34] For the bishop of Winchester, see *CSP Dom 1581–90*, 291 (10 Dec. 1585); Dinley's case is cited in Walker, 'Implementation', 76–7; for the city council decision, see Morris, *Troubles of Our Catholic Forefathers*, iii. 269. On Burghley, see M. A. Tierney, *Dodds' Church History of England*, 5 vols, London 1839–43, iii. 100–1n. Magee, *The English Recusants*, 86f. notes that the 1606 recusancy returns for Hampshire, Wiltshire, Dorset, Somerset, Devon and Cornwall, were annotated with the comment: 'Many women Recusants, and their husbands come to Church, but *permit* their wives to continue Recusants and seduce others' [my emphasis].

[35] *SR*, 3 Jac. c. 5. § VII.

devotional status, fuller membership of the Roman Catholic Church – at least in the eyes of its hierarchy.[36] It would be foolish to ignore the energetic proselytism, autonomy and enterprise of recusant women like Viscountess Montagu or Dorothy Lawson, Margaret Clitherow or Lady Babthorpe. But in the light of the church papist, Bossy's depiction of the post-Reformation Catholic community as a matriarchy requires some qualification. The importance of wives in the history of recusancy does not indisputably demonstrate that they played a pivotal part in the history of early modern English Catholicism. Twentieth-century, no less than early modern commentators have sometimes interpreted nonconformity as a peculiarly female folly, one manifestation of an innate predisposition to religion – 'a certain preciseness of conscience incident to diverse of [that] sexe, without reason or measure oftentimes'.[37] Yet in this context, female recusancy seems just as often a natural division of labour in the management of dissent.

'Schismatics' who diligently reared their children as devout Catholics, kept personal chaplains and 'popish' schoolmasters, sent younger sons for priestly instruction in the Low Countries, and prudently married their daughters into recognised recusant families were hardly men of lukewarm faith.[38] Nor were the poor church papist parents who solicitously installed their boys as servants to captured priests at Wisbech in the late 1590s, hoping they would thereby imbibe the more stalwart Catholicism which circumstances prevented them from practising at home.[39] Fanatical anti-Catholics drew little distinction between temporisers and dissenters: the barbarous maltreatment two fraudulent pursuivants meted out to local papists in North Kilvington, Yorkshire, in 1609, was directed against members of the Meynell family 'conformable . . . to his Ma[jes]ties Lawes', as well as their more stubbornly separatist co-religionists. The lawyer, Ambrose Griffith, 'an halfe Recusant, and a dangerous man' was among the Catholics whose influence most alarmed civil servants in Hereford diocese in 1604: 'though he goeth to the church, yet he runneth the Jesuites' courses most violentlye'.[40] Many of the conforming Cheshire gentlemen whose houses were 'greatlie infected with popery and not loked unto' in 1579 were suspected to be 'cherishers' and 'common interteynors' of Marian and missionary clergy. As inquisitive Protestants

---

[36] Cf Rowlands, 'Recusant women', 153.

[37] These were the words of the Chief Justice of Chester, speaking of Lady Egerton: Wark, *Elizabethan Recusancy in Cheshire*, 34. For other contemporary perceptions, see Hooker, *Works*, i. 75, 152–3; John Dod and Robert Cleaver, *A godly forme of householde government*, London 1612 (first publ. 1598), sig. P3v; and my references to Hill and Dove in ch. ii. For later commentators, Dickens, 'Extent', 39; Keith Thomas, 'Women and the Civil War sects', in Trevor Aston (ed.), *Crisis in Europe 1560–1660: essays from Past and Present*, London 1965, 317–40, esp. p. 321; Bossy, *The English Catholic Community*, 157.

[38] For examples, Hibbard, 'Early Stuart Catholicism', 17; Foley, *Records of the English Province*, ii. 587; iv. 289–92, 423; Wark, *Elizabethan Recusancy in Cheshire*, 49–50; Aveling, *The Handle and the Axe*, 146; Talbot, *Recusant Records*, 75 (George Yate); Warnicke, *Women of the English Renaissance and Reformation*, 171; McCann and Connolly, *Memorials of Father Augustine Baker*, 74; Anthony G. Petti (ed.), *Recusant Documents from the Ellesmere Manuscripts* (CRS lx, 1968), 70.

[39] *CSP Dom 1598–1601*, 319–20 (1599); Weston, *Autobiography*, 152; Kenny, *Responsa Scholarum*, 111.

[40] Morris, *Troubles of Our Catholic Forefathers*, iii. 460 and Talbot, *Recusant Records*, 279–81; Matthews, 'Records relating to Catholicism in the South Wales Marches', 297, 295 respectively.

discovered, 'schismatics' could in fact 'do most mischief' in this respect, 'having dispensacion to entertaine priestes when manie recusantes dare not for feare of penall statutes'.[41] Loath to accept the financial inconveniences and social disadvantages of refusal to attend church, conformists nevertheless voluntarily risked and sometimes even sacrificed their lives to shelter, assist and sustain the clerical agents of sacramental grace and moral advice – no less than a capital crime. Their willingness to do so assuredly added an element of obligation to the casuists' evolution of approval for occasional conformity.[42]

Being two-faced had obvious uses to a religion forced into an underground existence. That notable Catholic matriarch, Elizabeth Vaux, for example, circumspectly recruited conformist tutors after she was required to notify the Privy Council regarding the private education of her son. John Gerard found it convenient to ignore the principles of his own propaganda when he employed a 'schismatic' Norfolk weaver, William Suffield, as his housekeeper and district deputy.[43] 'Papists in heart' had a clear advantage in treacherous efforts to 'overthrowe the course of the Gospell' and 'hazard and indanger the state of the common weale' Bishop Cooper of Winchester feared in 1589 – conformity could effectively camouflage conspiracy. The 'Church-Papist', agreed an early seventeenth-century divine, his namesake, was 'the most dangerous subject the land hath'.[44] And Sir John Petre, who maintained a schismatic Catholic household at Ingatestone, Essex, defended the legality of attendance at Common Prayer 'for fashion sake' and urged his retainers to mimic his example in arrestingly similar terms: 'Do you think there are not that go to the church that bear as good a mind to Godwards as those that refuse, yes, and if occasion serve, will be able to do better service than they which refuse to go to the church [?]'[45] Had plots or the Armada succeeded, the architects of a new Roman Catholic regime may well have included erstwhile church papists.

Neither did conforming Catholics lack leverage or recognition within the Protestant political nation. Acknowledging the case of Naaman Syrus was more than a theoretical milestone. William Byrd, composer at the Chapel Royal, was a church papist until 1585; thereafter he led a double life, casuistically combining stalwart recusancy at home with unqualified conformity at court.[46] The future earl of Northampton, Lord Henry Howard, was singularly scrupulous in availing himself of Elisha's licence:

---

[41] Wark, *Elizabethan Recusancy in Cheshire*, 49–50; Scarisbrick, *The Reformation and the English People*,155, quoting from PRO, SP 12/168/35 (Feb. 1584).

[42] For the case of a 'schismatic' Yorkshireman, denounced by his turncoat schoolmaster, and subsequently hanged, see Morris, *Troubles of Our Catholic Forefathers*, i. 244.

[43] Gerard, *Autobiography*, 174, 248 (Elizabeth Vaux); 55, 172 (Suffield).

[44] Thomas Cooper, *An Admonition to the People of England*, London 1589, 29; Thomas Cooper, *The Cry and Revenge of Blood*, London 1620, 26. Cf Cooper, *Certaine Sermons*, 192–3 [sic], and Richard Topcliffe, in Strype, *Annals*, IV. 54.

[45] Foley, *Records of the English Province*, ii. 587–9, at p. 589, from 'A declaration of certain Papists', by George Eliot, Petre's apostatising servant; see also O'Dwyer, 'Catholic Recusants in Essex', 81.

[46] Edmund H. Fellowes, *William Byrd*, London 1936, ch. iii; A. C. Edwards (ed.), *English History from Essex Sources 1550–1750* (Essex Record Office xvii, 1952), 13 (Byrd's citation for recusancy in the courts of the archdeacon of Essex in 1605).

[He] would come and continue at prayers when the Queene came, but otherwise would not endure them, seeming to performe the duty of a subject in attending on his prince at the one tyme, and at the other using his conscience. He would runne out of the Queenes chamber in hir sicknes when the chaplein went to prayer. Their prayer, for him, [was] like a conjuracion for a spirit.[47]

For Philip Howard, earl of Arundel, however, dissembling his religion and accompanying Elizabeth to church increasingly reeked of Machiavellianism, a political atheism to which he eventually found himself unable to stoop – by November 1584 he was walking feverishly in Westminster Abbey's aisles during sermons and inventing excuses for absence from service.[48] Banking on papal permission for her conduct, James I's consort, Anne of Denmark, yielded to the importunities of her husband's bishops and regularly frequented prayers and preaching, although she consistently refused to receive the Calvinist communion.[49]

At the local and county level there were apparently many Catholics who failed to see any conflict between theological adherence to the Church of Rome and the exercise of political responsibility for the preservation of civil law and order. As studies in Lancashire, Cheshire and Sussex have shown, even a generation after the purges of the mid-1560s, church papistry persisted within the commission of the peace and town corporations, parliament and the highest posts of rural governance. It also enabled Catholics of the calibre of the Elizabethan jurist Edmund Plowden to rise to the heights of the legal profession.[50] Occasional conformity secured Sir Nicholas Throgmorton's presidency of the principality of Wales and ensured that Lord William Howard of Naworth, Cumberland, remained a trusted royal servant in the civilisation of the Border counties until his death; in order to qualify for public office in the 1580s, Sir Randolph Brereton modestly compromised his nonconformity by appearing at sermons 'at the assises tyme with the Justices' of Cheshire.[51] But if the north-country justice Thomas Walmsley, who endeavoured to switch the attention of district authorities from popish

---

[47] John Bruce (ed.), *The Diary of John Manningham, of the Middle Temple, and of Bradbourne, Kent, Barrister at Law 1602–3* (CS, o.s. xcix, 1868), 170–1.

[48] Pollen, *Unpublished Documents*, 307–9 (a letter of Robert Southwell to Father General Claude Aquaviva, 25 Jul. 1586). In 1586, Elizabeth's ministers specifically pressed the case of Naaman as a precedent, but Howard's resolution was 'not to swerve a hairs breadth from his duty as a Catholic'. See also, J. H. Pollen and W. MacMahon (eds), *The Ven. Philip Howard Earl of Arundel 1557–1595: English martyrs vol. II* (CRS xxi, 1919), 99ff. (letter of earl of Arundel to the queen, 11–14 Apr. 1585); *DNB s.v.* Howard.

[49] Albert J. Loomie, 'King James I's Catholic Consort', *Huntington Library Quarterly* xxxiv (1971), 303–16, esp. pp. 305, 308, 310; Morris, *Troubles of Our Catholic Forefathers*, i. 197–8. For further comments on court crypto-Catholicism, see Aveling, *The Handle and the Axe*, ch. v.

[50] On Lancashire, Haigh, *Reformation and Resistance*, 284–5; on Cheshire, Wark, *Elizabethan Recusancy in Cheshire*, 49–50; on Sussex, Manning, *Religion and Society*, pp. xv, xvi, 81, 241ff.; and on Northumberland, Talbot, *Recusant Records*, 150–3, and HMC, *Salisbury, Part XIX*, 3–5. On Plowden, Geoffrey de C. Parmiter, *Elizabethan Popish Recusancy in the Inns of Court* (*BIHR* Special Supplement xi, 1976), passim esp. pp. 6–7.

[51] Foley, *Records of the English Province*, iv. 289; *VCH Cumberland*, ii, ed. James Wilson, London 1905, 88–9 and *DNB s.v.* William Howard; Wark, *Elizabethan Recusancy in Cheshire*, 49.

recusancy to puritan indiscipline, is at all indicative, crypto-Catholicism was a complicating factor in the drive against recusancy, an offence which the statutes progressively placed within the jurisdiction of secular officials.[52] Within the microcosm of the village, 'schismatic' constables, bailiffs and, not uncommonly, churchwardens could be correspondingly unco-operative in the achievement of legislative objectives. The parish clerk of Swyne, Yorkshire, was neglecting his ecclesiastical duties in 1567, when he was presented as 'a defender and mainteyner of the Romish religion and saieth it will never from his harte'; his counterpart at Holy Trinity, Hull, used all his ingenuity to hinder the Protestant revolution, including setting 'forwarde the clocke, that ther can be no conveniente tyme for the worde to be preached'.[53]

For gentlemen anxious to demonstrate their loyalty to the crown and their conservative dedication to upholding the traditional class structure, on the other hand, participation in the weekly worship of a Church whose supreme governor was also the head of State was almost unavoidable. Refusing to be present at services whose very seating arrangements visibly embodied and reinforced the social hierarchy was, as Bossy observes, a grave dereliction of one's duty to bolster parochial discipline and stability. It offered an evil example to those of 'mean calling', as well as anarchic sectaries and separatists: some Yorkshiremen of wealth and estimation were making 'earnest promises . . . in that behalf' to the Council of the North in 1573.[54] Periodic appearance at Common Prayer was a pointed gesture of submission. The movement into full recusancy of the Suffolk landowner, Sir Thomas Cornwallis, in 1584 was accompanied by the new guarantee of entering into a Bond of Association, and when John Jenison of Durham attended church in 1609 he vowed he did so not as 'a reformed Protestant but . . . only in obedience to the Kings laws'.[55]

In announcing his intention to tolerate conforming papists in his opening speech to the parliament of 1604, James I was implicitly acknowledging the political potency of church papistry. Misunderstood and rejected by the papacy, his 1606 Oath of Allegiance was at least partly designed to resolve precisely the predicament from which conformity already rescued Catholics – the problem of fidelity to a monarch possessing God-given secular authority, and yet championing an accursed and diabolical faith. As a proclamation issued four years later to dispel some of the controversy surrounding it insisted, the Oath was 'only devised as an act of great favour and clemency towards so many of our subjects, who though blinded with the superstition of popery, yet carried a dutiful heart towards our obedience'. No less than his subjects, James was contributing to the sharpening of the boundaries between

---

[52] Haigh, *Reformation and Resistance*, 284–5. According to George Gilbert, it was not uncommon for office-holding conformists to publicly harass recusants but secretly favour them: Hicks, *Letters and Memorials*, 337. Cf the York mayor John Dinley, cited in Walker, 'Implementation', 78.

[53] Purvis, *Tudor Parish Documents*, 191, 227–9, cf Talbot, *Recusant Records*, 77. See also R. C. Richardson, *Puritanism in North-west England: a regional study of the diocese of Chester to 1642*, Manchester 1972, 164.

[54] Bossy, *The English Catholic Community*, 124; Morris, *Troubles of Our Catholic Forefathers*, iii. 234.

[55] On Cornwallis, see Morey, *The Catholic Subjects of Elizabeth I*, 159. Jenison is quoted in Hilton, 'Catholicism in Jacobean Durham', 84.

'religion' and 'politics', to their differentiation as separate spheres of theory and activity.[56]

How, indeed, did individuals reach a temporal truce with neighbours who were allegedly their spiritual enemies? Surviving and thriving in communities comprised largely of Protestants called for a decided measure of accommodation and collaboration – not least because the Church of England remained the administrative agent for parish rates and an important source of personal income and prestige for tithe farmers, and those who enjoyed the patronage rights of ecclesiastical property. In 1604, for instance, puritan petitioners were complaining about 'popish' gentlemen in Staffordshire who still held sway as impropriators and lay rectors of livings and benefices.[57] There were similarly sound reasons for continuing to utilise its 'social services': the taint of illegitimacy blighted infants whose baptisms were not officially registered, and serious legal difficulties over the settlement of estates could follow clandestine marriages contracted by missioners. Bribing the parson to fiddle the books and double ceremonies were not uncommon, but 'unseasonable coming in' at the end of official services for the administration of the sacraments was equally 'well knowen' to a group of grumbling Lancashire preachers and 'faithfull Professors' in 1590.[58] Desire to be interred in consecrated ground also compelled many to acquiesce in Protestant burial rites or conduct their own nocturnal funerals in the churchyard.[59] While the growing insularity of the Catholic community is unquestionable, living in frosty isolation from people who were in principle the agents of heresy and the devil, but in practice friends, acquaintances and relatives, was largely an impracticable polemical ideal.

There were more ways of expressing disapproval of the Reformation and distinguishing oneself from Protestants than the illegal, anti-social act of self-definition prescribed by clerical zealots. As Ralph Houlbrooke's research on ecclesiastical court records in the Tudor dioceses of Norwich and Winchester has revealed, dissent was by no means incompatible with maintaining 'a toehold within the institutional structure of the national church'.[60]

One appealing alternative to insolent refusal to attend weekly services was deliberate abstention from holy communion. A sacramental rite in which ecclesiastical injunctions and canons required the laity to participate only

---

[56] Tanner, *Constitutional Documents of the Reign of James I*, 28; Cardwell, *Documentary Annals*, ii. 147ff., esp. p. 153. Cf James's reply to the earl of Northumberland, in October 1603, quoted in D. H. Willson, *King James VI and I*, London 1956, 18–19. For the Oath, *SR*, 3 Jac. I. c. 4, § IX. See also John J. LaRocca, ' "Who can't pray with me, can't love me": toleration and the early Jacobean recusancy policy', *Journal of British Studies*, xxiii (1984), 22–36.

[57] Peel, 'A Puritan survey of the Church in Staffordshire', 345, 351. Catholic casuists themselves agreed that Catholics were 'bound to observe the custom' of paying tithes and church rates: Holmes, *Elizabethan Casuistry*, 58, cf 105; and Strype, *Annals*, II. ii. 349–50. For examples, see MacCulloch, *Suffolk and the Tudors*, 185, 210.

[58] Raines, 'A description of the state . . . of Lancaster', 4, 1 respectively. See also Garnet, *Apology*, 61–2; Bossy, *The English Catholic Community*, 134ff.

[59] Raines, 'A description of the state . . . of Lancaster', 6. For examples, see Bossy, *The English Catholic Community*, 140–1; Morey, *The Catholic Subjects of Elizabeth I*, 154; Aveling, *The Handle and the Axe*, 144. Penalties for this offence are described in *SR*, 3&4 Jac. c. 5. § X.

[60] Houlbrooke, *Church Courts and the People*, 249, 257.

three times each year, it may have been a relatively rare event in many parishes. Although non-communicating was not a civil offence in the Elizabethan period, as an ecclesiastical transgression it was in theory ultimately subject to the highest censure of the Church, excommunication. But this spiritual disincentive was arguably less significant than any financial deterrent since it could always be alleged that heretical discipline was in any case invalid, a power unjustly usurped from the pope. It was an empty threat, moreover, for to expel Catholics from the Church of England simply played into their hands.

Charged in 1590 with failing to communicate for twelve years, John Widley of Wistaston, Cheshire, for example, showed no signs of graduating to that higher degree of conscientious objection enjoined by the Counter Reformation; a contentiously Catholic Chester shoemaker, who declared that 'the Word of God is not in England' and was 'accostomed to goe downe to the castle amongst the recusantes to serve them with shoes upon the Sondaie morninges', notwithstanding chose to confine his own nonconformity to boycotting the Easter eucharist in 1594.[61] When Mrs Marie Whitfield, 'a long recusante' of Bolton in the diocese of Carlisle, eventually submitted to her vicar's persuasions to attend church she flatly refused to partake of communion. In 1582, John Burse of Barking, Essex, presented by churchwardens for his breaches in this respect since 1559, just as defiantly declared 'he wolde not receyve so long as he lyved'.[62] The more timid concealed their motives by pleading embarrassment and fear of arrest as debtors, as did William Shakespeare's father in Stratford-upon-Avon in 1592. Others contrived to be at variance with a neighbour or unable to reconcile a dispute with an adversary, and thus officially unfit to participate. Placing one's self temporarily 'out of charity' was an equally striking and disturbing symbol of ritual separation from the social and sacral community.[63] This brand of church papistry was widespread in the 1560s and 1570s, but those who felt that mere churchgoing might be stomached, but not Calvin's Supper, may have been just as common at the end of Elizabeth's reign.

As a method of reconciling rebuttal of the Reformation with the letter of statute law, non-communicating was effective not least because it was often

---

[61] Wark, *Elizabethan Recusancy in Cheshire*, 25–6, 124. Numerous other examples might be cited: see Hughes, *The Reformation in England*, iii. 440; Emmison, *Morals and the Church courts*, 99–110.
[62] Talbot, *Recusant Records*, 66; O'Dwyer, 'Catholic Recusants in Essex', 56. Cf *VCH Oxfordshire*, ii, ed. William Page, London 1907, 44 (William Lenthall of Wilcote, had similarly 'reformed himself thereof, but for the receiving of the Communion he is not yet satisfied in his conscience' in 1593).
[63] Collinson, *Birthpangs*, 58, and idem. 'The Church: religion and its manifestations', in John F. Andrews (ed.), *William Shakespeare: his world, his work, his influence*, 3 vols, New York 1985, i. 38–9. For examples of individuals claiming to be 'out of charity', see Purvis, *Tudor Parish Documents*, 46; Wark, *Elizabethan Recusancy in Cheshire*, 7, 122ff.; Emmison, *Morals and the Church courts*, 108ff. Ministers were not permitted to admit a 'malicious person out of charity' to communion; for two examples of this requirement in visitation articles, see Cardwell, *Documentary Annals*, i. 357 (Matthew Parker's articles for Canterbury, 1569); i. 402 (Edmund Grindal for the same region, 1576). For a penetrating analysis of this phenomenon in early modern Germany, see David Sabean, in *Power and the Blood: popular culture and village discourse in early modern Germany*, Cambridge 1984, 37–60.

indistinguishable from innocuous residual folk practices and the behaviour of religious radicals at the other extreme. Even in London, the medieval habit of making an annual Easter communion survived into the late Tudor and early Stuart period.[64] Nor did reluctance to receive always signal Romanist rejection of Protestant eucharistic theory. Donald Spaeth's study of Restoration Wiltshire suggests that superstitious dread of the divine judgements the liturgy warned would be visited on unworthy communicants gave rise to more widespread shirking of the sacrament. Thus failure to share in the consecrated bread and wine frequently expressed vigorous endorsement of, rather than indifference to or dissent from the Established Church – it unexpectedly indexes the vitality of parochial Anglicanism after 1660.[65] More than half a century earlier, non-communicating may similarly attest as much to that osmotic process by which the Book of Common Prayer instilled a Protestant consciousness in contemporary minds, as to the scruples of the categorically Catholic.[66] And the ecclesiastical authorities in Essex who summoned twenty-seven Inworth villagers for their absence from the Easter communion in 1592 evidently suspected they were dealing with Familists rather than papists, because they interrogated the delinquents with 'frivolous questions' concerning 'what should become of their bodies when they were in the grave and whether all the world should be saved'.[67] Were these individuals staging some kind of mass Anabaptist demonstration or a popular protest against Protestantism in general? Or was their entirely typical laxity simply the target of a new and more systematic drive to improve standards of pious observance? The confusion cautions against any attempt to anatomise religious positions in early modern society on the basis of forms of worship and communal conduct alone.

Non-communicating nevertheless progressively acquired public, Protestant recognition as a 'popish' pestilence that demanded eradication or containment as urgently as recusancy itself. Presentment of adult parishioners who contravened the relevant rubrics was a standard article of enquiry at visitations after 1559, but in numerous dioceses and peculiars episcopal initiatives in this sphere became increasingly linked with their preoccupation with popery. Indeed, Elizabeth's bishops were particularly active, if unsuccessful, in promoting bills in the House of Lords to unite communion with church attendance as the accepted legal meaning of 'conformity', and they continued to strike at this class of church papists through the High Commission.[68] As early as 1577, Bishop Aylmer was discussing with

[64] J. P. Boulton, 'The limits of formal religion: the administration of holy communion in late Elizabethan and early Stuart London', *The London Journal* x (1984), 135–54, esp. p. 138; Ingram, *Church Courts, Sex and Marriage*, 106.

[65] Donald A. Spaeth, 'Common prayer? Popular observance of the Anglican liturgy in Restoration Wiltshire', in S. J. Wright (ed.), *Parish, Church and People: local studies in lay religion 1350–1750*, London 1988, 125–51, esp. pp. 131–9.

[66] Collinson, 'The Elizabethan Church and the new religion', 169.

[67] Emmison, *Morals and the Church courts*, 101.

[68] For episcopal measures against non-communicating, see Kennedy, *Elizabethan Episcopal Administration*, ii. 51 (Chichester 1577); ii. 59 (Worcester 1577); ii. 94 (York 1578); ii. 108 (London 1580); ii. 120 (Chester 1581); ii. 130 (Middleton 1582); iii. 140, 148 (St David's 1583); iii. 164 (Coventry and Lichfield 1584); iii. 183, 219 (Chichester 1585, 1586); iii. 248 (Salisbury

Walsingham the imposition of fines 'for contemptuose refusinge of receavinge
the communion', and the Privy Council's nation-wide investigations in 1586
were revealing 'manie papistes in diverse counties which come to church but
receve not', hence evading arraignment.[69] Censuses in northern jurisdictions
in fact suggested that a substantial rise, rather than a steady decline in such
culprits had coincided with the growth of recusancy in the following decades;
for Suffolk bureaucrats attempting to detect and quantify 'popery' in 1595
they were unequivocally twin aspects of the task. And while the parish of
Prescot was considered one of 'most infected' in Lancashire shortly after the
queen's death, the character of its Catholicism was hardly exceptional –
official figures revealed a clear local bias towards non-communicating. All but
six of the ninety-two offenders at Kirkby Malzeard, catalogued in a
government survey of Yorkshire a year later, also contented themselves with
this mode of resistance.[70] These insights were formally endorsed in 1604, when
the newly framed Canons instructed vicars and curates to discriminate
between 'Popish recusants' and those 'popishly given' – between the 'absolute
recusants' and 'half recusants' who inhabited their parishes.[71] Royal outrage
after the sinister events of 1605 allowed parliament to push through a bill that
negated the principles of James's avowed policy of indulgence. Instituting an
annual fee of £20 to punish conformed recusants who jibbed at communicating, it lashed out directly at 'divers persons Popishly affected [who] doe
nevertheless, the better to cover and hide their false Hearts, and with the
more safety. . .to execute theire mischievous Desseignes, repaire sometimes
to Church to escape the Penaltie of the Lawes'.[72] The 1606 statute proved to

1589); iii. 260 (York); iii. 289, 291 (Shoreham); iii. 320 (Nottingham 1599); iii. 348 (London
1601). Cardwell, *Documentary Annals*, i. 371 (York 1571); i. 412 (Canterbury 1576); ii. 33
(Salisbury 1588); ii. 108, 112 (a general form to be used in several dioceses, 1605). For
Lancashire, see Haigh, *Reformation and Resistance*, 260, and for Winchester and Norwich dioceses,
Houlbrooke, *Church Courts and the People*, 247. On the parliamentary activities of the bishops and
their use of the High Commission, see Walker, 'Implementation', esp. pp. 67ff., 80ff., 124–6.
[69] Ryan, 'Diocesan Returns of Recusants for England and Wales 1577', 1ff.; Wark, *Elizabethan
Recusancy in Cheshire*, 64. Civil officials such as the earl of Huntingdon used it as a check of loyalty:
Morris, *Troubles of Our Catholic Forefathers*, iii. 73–4.
[70] For Prescot, which enumerated 207 recusants and 244 non-communicants (a pattern in
keeping with the ratio of 2400 to 3683 calculated for the entire region under his jurisdiction by
Bishop Richard Vaughan), see Talbot, *Recusant Records*, 146. For Kirkby Malzeard, see Dickens,
'Extent', 35. For Chester, see Purvis, *Tudor Parish Documents*, 79, 80–1; for Suffolk, Talbot,
Recusant Records, 108ff. On Yorkshire, Dickens, 'The first stages of Romanist recusancy', 168–82,
and 'Extent', 30ff.; on the city of York, Morris, *Troubles of Our Catholic Forefathers*, iii. 281ff.; on
Ely and London in 1603, Magee, *The English Recusants*, 84; on Bristol, Walker, 'Implementation',
410; on Hampshire, Paul, 'Hampshire recusants', 77–81; on Wiltshire, Ingram, *Church Courts,
Sex and Marriage*, 108. Particularly telling are the Lancashire returns of 1613: Haigh, *Reformation
and Resistance*, 277. Although John Bossy's efforts to estimate the size of the early seventeenth-
century 'Catholic community' are equally problematic, his conclusions reinforce rather than
contradict contemporary assessments: nearly half the statistical weight of a body Bossy
qualitatively describes in terms of recusancy is in fact 'church papist': *The English Catholic
Community*, 182–94, esp. p. 192.
[71] For the 1604 canons, Edward Cardwell (ed.), *Synodalia: a collection of articles of religion, canons, and
proceedings of convocations in the province of Canterbury from the year 1547 to the year 1717*, 2 vols, Oxford
1842, i. 309.
[72] *SR*, 3 Jac. I. c. 4. § I.

be chiefly a paper victory, but it marked a realisation that outward conformity was no solution to the old, almost obsolete, struggle to accomplish religious uniformity. It embodied a redefinition of 'recusant' to embrace the non-communicating church papist. Repudiation of the Protestant eucharist seems less a 'first sign' of recusancy than a definitive conscientious stance itself.[73]

It may be just as distorting and artificial, however, to regard refusal to communicate as the 'most meaningful line of division' between 'Catholic' and 'Protestant' in this period.[74] There was probably a body of yet more fully conforming Catholics who earned the reputation and stigma 'papist' among their peers or were supposed to be 'favourers of the Roman Church and Religion' by local magistrates. The 'popish' parishioners who troubled puritan ministers with 'notorious disorders' at Easter eucharists in Lancashire in 1590, for instance, afford a glimpse of an equally vigorous strain of non-recusant Catholicism – occasional communicating. Many, it was said, intruded themselves to receive the sacrament 'who before have not been present at divine service, nor at any part of the prayers before the communion' and behaved 'tumultuously' during the actual administration, so as to be dismissed quickly from this disagreeable annual test of their 'conformity'.[75] Not all the 'lewd Company' which voluntarily assembled for mass at Agden, Cheshire, in Passion Week 1582, had apparently fully internalised the clerical doctrine of recusancy: the celebrant felt bound to conclude the ceremony with 'certen speaches of exhortacion . . . perswading them to forsake the service and the Churche and to come home and cleave unto the Masse and the auncyent catholike Churche'. Only a handful of the twenty-nine individuals arrested for attending proscribed rites in a Lancashire district two decades later did not readily agree to 'conform themselves' to Protestantism.[76] Some of those who 'mainteyne[d] their errors openly in talke', according to ecclesiastical visitors in Cheshire in 1578, were neither recusants nor non-communicants; a case in point is the Suffolk man presented in 1595 solely because he 'scorneth the marriage of ministers terming their wives and children villainouslie'.[77] William Flamstedd of Preston Capes, Northamptonshire, was 'vehemently suspected of Papistrie' and coherently defended prayers to the saints, Mary and the dead, as well as his belief in the Real Presence, but saw no major contradiction in coming to Protestant service every Sunday.[78]

Such regularly attending church papists were often anything but fence-sitters. In a sense, a church was the most appropriate forum in which to dramatise one's ridicule and repudiation of the Reformation, to enact a form

---

[73] Bossy, *The English Catholic Community*, 123.

[74] Rose, *Cases of Conscience*, 6; Hibbard, 'Early Stuart Catholicism', 17n. Cf Manning, *Religion and Society*, 256–7.

[75] Raines, 'A description of the state . . . of Lancaster', 8. See also Richardson, *Puritanism in North-west England*, 172.

[76] Wark, *Elizabethan Recusancy in Cheshire*, 42–4. He ejected two who openly confessed 'they had byn at church'. For Lancashire, Haigh, *Reformation and Resistance*, 277, 292–3, and see idem. 'The continuity of English Catholicism', 184.

[77] Wark, *Elizabethan Recusancy in Cheshire*, 17; Talbot, *Recusant Records*, 109.

[78] Peel, *Seconde Parte of a Register*, i. 295.

of ritual iconoclasm against the 'newe no gospell', and to combat Calvinism with the very culture regarded as most inimical to its popular advance. In the 1560s and 1570s, Sir Richard Shireburn impudently blocked his ears with wool against the execrable tones of heretical devotion; Sir Thomas Cornwallis sat contemptuously perusing a Lady Psalter while others were on their knees at prayer in Suffolk; Sir Nicholas Gerard loudly chanted Latin psalms as soon as the minister at Etwall, Derbyshire commenced the reformed service.[79] Many persisted in offering their bare presence with no intention of following the liturgy, or sitting soberly and attentively in their pews – engaging instead in devotional reading, concentrating on their rosaries, or deliberately disrupting and interrupting proceedings by scuffling or chattering. 'Parsons Howlets hypocrites', complained John Field in 1581, came to church:

> without all reverence, either nodding or sleeping in the time of the exercise, or else walking and jangling, or carried away with idle and unprofitable imaginations, or else occupied in some popish paltry book either printed at home or brought from beyonde the seas, or else they are watching for some advantage, agaynst the painfull and godly minister, evermore lying in waite, to stir up strife, and to disquiet the Church.[80]

Nor was making a public 'protestation' combining a profession of political loyalty with a statement of one's Catholic objections to the Protestant liturgy necessarily the soft option of the pusillanimous. One of its chief Jesuit opponents inadvertently admitted as much in objecting that, far from relieving the distresses of those who practised it, a declaration along these lines actually exacerbated them since it placed the 'protesters' in peril of prosecution for a scurrilous attack on the Book of Common Prayer. I. G. was stretching a polemical point, but he was probably correct in suggesting that such statements would provoke rather than mollify a 'hott spirited minister' or justice of the peace.[81]

The whole gamut of such 'unconformable' and unruly behaviour was still offending puritan interests in Lancashire during the last decade of the century, especially the 'scornefull laffinge Countenance' of those who withdrew themselves to the 'farthest partes' of the building, arrived late or departed early to avoid that central proselytising mechanism of a religion of the Word, the sermon.[82] Kneeling at the communion table in 1569, Mrs Kath Lacy of Sherburn, in Yorkshire's East Riding, proceeded to remove the sacrament from her mouth and to disdainfully 'treade the same breade under her fote'.

---

[79] For Shireburn, Bossy, *The English Catholic Community*, 122; for Cornwallis, Morey, *The Catholic Subjects of Elizabeth I*, 159; for Gerard, *VCH Derbyshire*, ii, ed. William Page, London 1907, 24. Admittedly Gerard, crippled by gout, was forced to attend by his brother, who was anxious to avoid detection by local authorities. For similar cases see Morris, *Troubles of Our Catholic Forefathers*, iii. 217; Manning, *Religion and Society*, 46; Parmiter, *Elizabethan Popish Recusancy*, 10.

[80] Field, *A Caveat for Parsons Howlet*, sigs D8r–v. See also Frere and Douglas, *Puritan Manifestoes*, 29, 115, for the same complaint in the Admonitions of 1572; Gifford, *Dialogue between a Papist and a Protestant*, 2r–v.

[81] I. G., 'An answere to a comfortable advertisement', ch. i.

[82] Raines, 'A description of the state . . . of Lancaster', 3–4. On sermons, see also Wark, *Elizabethan Recusancy in Cheshire*, 50, 80; Haigh, 'Puritan evangelism', 47.

Ecclesiastical officers in Essex arraigned John Willemcom 'for a railer', because he would 'gooe throwe the church in despite of the parish, in at one dore and out at the other in the services'. Thomas Wintringham declined the eucharist at Skeffling on Christmas Day 1595, and 'did mocke and flowte at them that did'.[83] The presence of such Catholics was a mixed blessing; as disgruntled Protestants admitted, it 'dothe more hurte, then theire absence did'.[84]

Yet church papists held no monopoly on irreverent and unseemly conduct in church. The 'disturbers and mislikers' of divine service that late sixteenth-century bishops were expecting to discover and discipline in regions as diverse as York, Chichester and Middlesex, were not merely conforming Catholics appeasing their consciences by obstructing and prophaning heretical worship. No more were the heterogeneous congregations Archbishop Abbot was confronting when he issued visitation articles for the province of Canterbury in 1616.[85] Efforts to celebrate Common Prayer in a suitably holy atmosphere were also frustrated by puritans, whose irregular attendance and studiously disrespectful manners betokened their outcry against a half-finished reformation – and by the instinctive impiety and impropriety of that multitude of 'cold statute protestants' it had manifestly failed to convince and convert. When Henry Wakefield of Bulphan in prodigiously Protestant Essex 'openly rebuked the parson for preaching false doctrine' on the last Sunday in Advent 1591, was he objecting to Protestant innovation or 'Romish' recidivism? Was the villager of not so distant Earls Colne presented for 'contemptuous behaviour in church and for swearing by St Anne and St Lucy' in 1587, consciously Catholic or just residually so?[86] Conformity renders almost invisible an indeterminate number of silent sympathisers of the Old Faith, whose Catholicism was above all an attitude not an act. Perhaps few men and women who, like the Finchingfield tailor George Binkes, 'desyreth and wolde be called by the name of a papyste', signalled that sentiment and affirmed their identity by bluntly refusing to go to church.[87]

The implications of extricating early modern English Catholicism from the polemical definitions of its clerical propagandists, of rejecting a narrow perspective which overemphasises specific acts of nonconformity are, I would suggest, far-reaching.

There is perhaps an inevitable class bias in a history of Catholicism that is a history of recusancy. In a culture imbued with hierarchical assumptions, official interest and anxiety logically centred on that social elite whose overt defiance of the law was deemed to offer so dangerous a precedent to their

[83] For Kath Lacy and Thomas Wintringham, see Purvis, *Tudor Parish Documents*, 68, 59 respectively. For John Willemcom, O'Dwyer, 'Catholic Recusants in Essex', 54.

[84] Raines, 'A description of the state . . . of Lancaster', 3.

[85] Kennedy, *Elizabethan Episcopal Administration*, ii. 126 (Middlesex 1582); iii. 218–19 (Chichester 1586); iii. 261 (York 1589). Cf ibid. iii. 290 (Shoreham 1589) and iii. 230 (Hertford 1586); Purvis, *Tudor Parish Documents*, 5, 15; Cardwell, *Documentary Annals*, i. 409; Dickens, 'The first stages of Romanist recusancy', 166. For Abbot, Cardwell, *Documentary Annals*, ii. 176ff.

[86] Emmison, *Morals and the Church courts*, 127, 118 respectively, cf 119–20; Purvis, *Tudor Parish Documents*, 86, 137; Wark, *Elizabethan Recusancy in Cheshire*, 25–6.

[87] O'Dwyer, 'Catholic Recusants in Essex', 46–8; also in Emmison, *Morals and the Church courts*, 46.

subordinates. Christopher Haigh has insisted that a 'maldistribution' and 'misdirection' of clerical resources contributed to the contraction of recusant Catholicism into wealthy households and its polarisation into a seigneurially structured minority. While the increasing domestication of the mission may have been as much a natural product of persecution as a deliberate strategy, circumstances certainly weighed against the durability of plebeian recusancy.[88] But is the gentry and aristocratic dominance which distinguishes Bossy's 'Catholic community' and Trimble's 'Catholic laity' partly an optical illusion?[89] If inaccessibility to the priestly agents of sacramental grace and ideological instruction forced poorer Catholics – outside the select sphere of a manor house or beyond missionary circuits – into complete or qualified conformity, their commitment to the 'Old Religion' can scarcely be considered inferior because it did not take shape as a provocative gesture.

The humble 'hungry souls' thirsting for reconciliation and eager 'to shake off the yoke of bondage, heresy' in outlying Hampshire around 1590 are likely to have been conformists. So too perhaps, were a substantial proportion of the 'mean papists' 'whose malice be hot and barbarous' worrying Richard Topcliffe that same year.[90] Rural villagers who perpetuated 'popish' habits on the north and west fringes of England constituted a reservoir of far from resolute recusants that was in constant danger of depletion by conformist retrogression. This was evidently the impression of the parliamentarians who initiated and promoted a 1601 bill that would have injected new life into the disused shilling fine imposed by the Act of Uniformity for absence from Common Prayer – a rusty, but still the sole mechanism for dealing with impecunious and intermittent offenders. The 'papists' who had been 'so earnest' against it, insisted a petitioner to the House of Lords, knew all too well that strict enforcement of this penalty would draw many of 'the common sort' into church on Sundays – and into 'schism'.[91] There is, therefore, at least an even chance that the labourer of Moulsham, Essex who announced 'I am a Papist and I will pray for the Pope' in the aftermath of the 1588 Armada was technically a 'schismatic'.[92] John Gerard's notion that there were few 'Catholics' among the ordinary people of East Anglia possibly just betrays an inflexible Counter Reformation outlook.[93]

---

[88] Haigh, 'From monopoly to minority', passim esp. pp. 133ff.; idem. 'The continuity of English Catholicism', 201ff.; and 'Revisionism', 403ff. Haigh is endorsed by Guy, *Tudor England*, 300–1, but contested by McGrath, 'English Catholicism: a reconsideration', 420ff., and Wright, 'Catholic history, north and south', 120–34. On the class bias of the Jesuit mission, see the instructions given to Persons and Campion in 1580 in Hicks, *Letters and Memorials*, 320. And see Bossy, *The English Catholic Community*, esp. chs vii, xi.

[89] Ibid. esp. ch. vii; idem. 'The character of Elizabethan Catholicism', 39–59 passim; and 'The English Catholic community 1603–1625', 91–105; Trimble, *The Catholic Laity in Elizabethan England*, passim. See also, Norman, *Roman Catholicism in England*, 31; Aveling, *The Handle and the Axe*, 162–3; Fletcher, *A County Community in Peace and War*, 94ff.

[90] Challoner, *Memoirs of Missionary Priests*, 595; Strype, *Annals*, IV. 55.

[91] 'To the most Reverend Archbishops, and right reverend Lord Bishops of both provinces', dated Dec. 1601, printed for refutation in *A Briefe Censure upon the Puritane Pamphlet: Entituled, (Humble Motyves . . .)*, [English secret press] 1603, 25, 35. See also Neale, *Elizabeth I and her Parliaments*, ii. 396–406; Walker, 'Implementation', ch. x.

[92] Emmison, *Disorder*, 56.

[93] Gerard, *Autobiography*, 33. For further comments on lower class Catholicism, see Haigh, 'The

The sizeable artisan contingent that is a marked feature of urban Catholicism in York and Ripon presumably included many who likewise failed to fulfil strictly the clerical criteria for membership of the Church of Rome.[94] And the people in the congregation that crowded to hear a Jesuit preacher in London's Blackfriars in 1623 and perished when the makeshift chapel collapsed were by no means exclusively from genteel backgrounds. How many of the less privileged victims of the 'fatall vesper' unceremoniously buried in a mass grave had unblemished recusant records?[95]

Independent lower class recusancy may have been comparatively rare. Church papists, however, were not necessarily tied to the apron strings of the gentry and nobility. Largely free of the feudal and territorial ties exercising such a stranglehold on the inhabitants of the countryside, poor city dwellers might easily have opted for covert, as opposed to the conspicuous Catholicism pressed upon employees on many isolated gentry estates. The extent to which the paternalistic influence of nonconformist landlords created insular pockets of uncompromising recusancy among their tenants and peasant dependants itself seems sometimes open to question. A Protestant witness testified in 1586 that the servants of Lord Paget of Staffordshire were merely 'ill affected in religion' – occasional conformists and non-communicants – as were most residents of the 'popish' town of Battle, Sussex, a haven for missionary priests and a place of pilgrimage in the heart of Montagu country, in 1596.[96] Popular conformist Catholicism was peculiarly vulnerable to the attrition of time and gradual comprehension within the Church of England. Yet it cannot be summarily dismissed as amorphous and insignificant, even in the Jacobean and Caroline period.

The accepted geography of 'Catholicism' may be suffering from a similar ellipsis. Although the distribution of recusancy was unmistakably concentrated in upland regions, the 'darker corners of the land', Yorkshire, Lancashire and the Welsh Borders, conceivably loyalty to the 'Old Faith' in the south and Midlands was by contrast classically conformist in nature.[97] Did individuals surrounded by 'fierce Protestants' and 'unable to live in peace' abandon their faith altogether? More probably they simply adopted the less spectacular stance of the church papist instead.[98] The 'Catholicism' that has appeared a 'paper tiger' in Peter Clark's Kent, an exaggerated phobia of the

continuity of English Catholicism', 205–7; and 'From monopoly to minority', 143; Scarisbrick, *The Reformation and the English People*, 156–9; Dures, *English Catholicism*, 8, 58–9; Barry Reay, 'Popular religion', in idem. (ed.), *Popular Culture in Seventeenth Century England*, London 1988, 109–11.

[94] Aveling, *Catholic Recusancy in the City of York*, 44, 51, 65, 68–9, 73, 85, 98, 136–47; Dickens, 'Extent', 42. See also Scarisbrick's comments in *The Reformation and the English People*, 156–9.

[95] For one version of the tragedy, which includes a list of the victims, see W. C., *The Fatall Vesper*, London 1623, passim esp. sigs F1r, G1rf.

[96] *VCH Staffordshire*, iii. 99–100; Strype, *Annals*, IV. 402. See also, Talbot, *Recusant Records*, 108 regarding Sir Thomas Cornwallis's servants; Aveling, *The Handle and the Axe*, 45 on Sir Thomas Percy; Foley, *Records of the English Province*, ii. 587–9, on Sir John Petre's wider household.

[97] Bossy, *The English Catholic Community*, ch. v and p. 403. See also Dures, *English Catholicism*, 60–1; Haigh, 'From monopoly to minority', 133ff.; Patrick McGrath, *Papists and Puritans Under Elizabeth I*, London 1967, 402.

[98] Gerard, *Autobiography*, 33.

godly in William Hunt's Essex, and something of chimera or scarecrow in J. A. Hilton's Cumbria is one measured chiefly in terms of ritual refusal to go to church.[99] As Patrick McGrath has emphasised, the absence of formal recusancy does not mean the absence of committed Catholicism. 'Popery' was more impalpable and prevalent than that.[100]

Is separated Catholicism, then, a premature vision in late sixteenth- and early seventeenth-century England? The hypothesis demands detailed investigation at the parochial level. Both persuasive and predictable, however, is Alan Davidson's study of pre-Civil War Oxfordshire, which concludes that Catholicism and recusancy are neither synonymous nor coterminous until after 1688.[101] In the immediate post-Reformation period at least, English Catholicism sits uneasily in the mould of a fully segregated and seigneurial sect. The 'Catholic community' which emerges in skeletal outline when the dictates and preoccupations of governments, hierarchies and apologists are contextualised is, perhaps, radically different.[102] In spite of its intellectual tradition of comprehensive separatism, Elizabethan and Jacobean Catholicism appears a religious culture of dissent marked in practice by a decisive degree of co-operation and compromise. Indeed, parallelling church papistry with its theorised Protestant counterpart, the principled semi-separatism advocated and observed by Henry Jacob and his adherents after 1616, seems more appropriate than any forced comparison with the full-blown sectarianism initiated by the ideas of Browne and Barrow, Penry and Greenwood in the late sixteenth century. No less eye-catching is the resemblance partially conformist Catholicism bears to the secessionist and 'voluntary' tendencies within mainstream puritanism itself. Just as the godly were able to engage in additional and alternative pious practices while remaining within the embrace of the ecclesiastical establishment, so too could the Church of England cosily accommodate the equally eccentric religiosity of church papists.[103] In some

[99] Clark, *English Provincial Society*, 152, 179; William Hunt, *The Puritan Moment: the coming of revolution in an English county*, Cambridge, Mass.–London 1983, 148; Hilton, 'The Cumbrian Catholics', esp. pp. 40, 58. Cf Dickens's disclaimer in 'Extent', 43 and Wark's careful study of Elizabethan recusancy in Cheshire, which explicitly limits itself to scrutinising the handful who openly rebuffed statute Protestantism and adopted a public position by refraining from weekly worship: *Elizabethan Recusancy in Cheshire*, pp. vii, 130.

[100] McGrath, 'Elizabethan Catholicism: a reconsideration', 418. See also Newman, 'Roman Catholics in pre-Civil War England', 148–9.

[101] Alan Davidson, 'Roman Catholicism in Oxfordshire, 1580–1660', unpubl. PhD thesis, Bristol 1970, 18, 22, cited in Hibbard, 'Early Stuart Catholicism', 17n.

[102] Cf Bossy, *The English Catholic Community*, esp. pp. 7, 391, 398–401. For pertinent comments, see Haigh, 'The fall of a Church and the rise of a sect?', 184–5; idem. 'The continuity of English Catholicism', 206–7; and *Reformation and Resistance*, 275; Dures, *English Catholicism*, 39; Hibbard, 'Early Stuart Catholicism', 17.

[103] See Murray Tolmie, *The Triumph of the Saints: the separate Churches of London 1616–1649*, Cambridge 1977, 3ff., 28–34; Patrick Collinson, 'The English conventicle', in W. J. Sheils and D. Wood (eds), *Voluntary Religion* (SCH xxiii, 1986), 223–59; idem. *Birthpangs*, 145ff.; *The Religion of Protestants*, ch. vi, esp. pp. 274ff.; and 'Cohabitation of the faithful with the unfaithful', passim; Christopher Hill, 'Occasional conformity and the Grindalian tradition', in *The Collected Essays of Christopher Hill, Volume Two: religion and politics in seventeenth century England*, Brighton 1986, 301–20. For the argument that the Church of England in this period was an elastic institution, see Collinson, *The Religion of Protestants*, passim esp. p. 282; cf Bossy, *The English Catholic Community*, 397.

respects, Tudor and early Stuart Catholicism might also be better characterised as semi-separating.

Church papistry, in certain guises, was not a posture of apathy, but one of moral dilemma – a scrupulous as well as pragmatic answer to the problem of proscription. Nor was it the outward face of a Catholicism which was 'a complex of social practices rather than a religion of internal conviction', a piety consisting less in doctrinal affirmation than 'a set of ingrained observances'. Far from a brief and embarrassing episode in the 'posthumous history' of medieval or pre-Reformation Christendom – an episode swiftly obliterated by the recusant era triumphantly launched by a Tridentine crusade – conformity was an enduring phase in the evolution of early modern Catholicism. Articulate Catholicism within the Church of England was a lasting feature of a complex contemporary religious scene, rather than a bewildered biconfessionalism that disappeared with Dickens's decades of 'survivalism' in the 1570s.[104]

The 'church papist penumbra' has been a crucial weapon in Christopher Haigh's assault on the Dickens/Bossy thesis that there was a profound and organic discontinuity between the 'survivalism' of the early Elizabethan period and the 'seminarism' subsequently exported from Europe.[105] It has been the key link in his just claim that separated English Catholicism was no novel creation of Continental missionaries, but a logical extension of its immemorial and Marian heritage: the recusant community which emerged into view a generation after the reign began neither wholly displaced nor was sharply distinct from the confused and unco-ordinated collection of conservatives that was its predecessor. Yet Haigh appropriates the church papist largely to inform a debate about the origins of *recusant* Catholicism; to rekindle an historiographical controversy about the speed of the Reformation and the speed of the transfiguration of a Church into a sect.[106] Conformity was not always a transient or protracted stage in an uncomfortable inner struggle towards recusancy; it was as often the final outcome of that struggle itself. Can conforming Catholics be regarded as marginal and peripheral to a 'hard core' of 'absolute recusants'? In the perception of one Protestant petitioner to the queen, it was conversely the latter who made up the minority: three in four 'papists', he estimated in 1601, were 'Papists of state' who obeyed the law for 'fashion'. Only a quarter were so 'altogether possessed of the dreggs of poperie' that they enshrined it in a detectable offence.[107]

---

[104] Idem. 'The character of Elizabethan Catholicism', 41, 39; and *The English Catholic Community*, 4; Dickens, 'The first stages of Romanist recusancy', passim. Cf Haigh, 'The continuity of English Catholicism', 206, 207n., 208; idem. *Reformation and Resistance*, 277; Dures, *English Catholicism*, 6, 26.

[105] Bossy, *The English Catholic Community*, passim esp. introduction; idem. 'The English Catholic community 1603–1625', 101; Dickens, 'The first stages of Romanist recusancy', esp. pp.180–1; idem. *The English Reformation*, 1964 edn, 311–12.

[106] Haigh, 'The continuity of English Catholicism', 207–8; idem. *Reformation and Resistance*, 277; and 'From monopoly to minority', 132. Cf Dures, *English Catholicism*, 87; Williams, *The Tudor Regime*, 275.

[107] The taxonomical and statistical assessment was Thomas Digges's in his petition to Elizabeth 'for assotiation in religion' (1601) printed for refutation in *A Briefe Censure upon the*

The conventional chronicle and chronology of Catholicism locates the 'heyday' of church papists prior to 1580, charts their rapid decline after the turn of the century, and declares them 'a virtually extinct race in 1641'.[108] Yet, in 1621 Sir Edward Giles was prompting a parliamentary committee to 'consider of some law against Church Papists'.[109] And when John Earle published his popular anthology of 'characters', *Microcosmography*, in 1628, the conforming Catholic remained a remarkably familiar figure, a constituent feature of early seventeenth-century English society. In Earle's forthright and witty portraiture of his age:

A Church-Papist Is one that parts his Religion betwixt his conscience and his purse, and comes to Church not to serve God, but the King. The face of the Law makes him weare the maske of the Gospell, which he uses not as a meanes to save his soule, but charges. He loves Popery well, but is loth to lose by it, and though he be something scar'd with the Buls of Rome, yet they are farre off, and he is strucke with more terrour at the Apparitor. Once a moneth he presents himselfe at the Church, to keepe off the Church-warden, and brings in his body to save his bayle. He kneels with the Congregation, but prayes by himselfe, and askes God forgivenesse for comming thither. If he be forced to stay out a Sermon, he puls his hat over his eyes, and frownes out the houre, and when hee comes home, thinkes to make amends for this fault by abusing the Preacher. His maine policy is to shift off the Communion, for which he is never unfurnish't of a quarrell, and will be sure to be out of Charity at Easter; and indeed he lies not, for hee has a quarrell to the Sacrament. He would make a bad Martyr, and a good traveller, for his conscience is so large, he could never wander out of it, and in Constantinople would be circumcis'd with a reservation. His wife is more zealous, and therefore more costly, and he bates her in tyres, what she stands him in Religion.[110]

To the forces behind the controversial Canons of 1640, 'the suppressing of the growth of Popery' required attack on two major fronts: ecclesiastical officials were to inform themselves in an 'especial manner' of 'all recusants above the age of twelve years, both of such as come not at all to church, as also of those who, coming sometimes, thither, do yet refuse to receive the holy eucharist with us'. The Long Parliament majority, led by John Pym, was likewise unshaken in its resolve to take steps 'for the preventing of

Puritane Pamphlet: Entituled, (Humble Motyves . . .), 11, 15. (*Humble Motives*, attributed to William Bradshaw, was published in 1601.) In 1617 the Spanish ambassador, Don Diego Samiento de Acuña (later Count Gondomar) estimated that there were 300,000 recusants and double that number, 600,000 Catholics attending Protestant worship: Gordon Albion, *Charles I and the Court of Rome*, London 1935, 13n.

[108] Bossy, *The English Catholic Community*, 124, 158, 187, and 'The English Catholic community 1603–25', 103. See also Pollen, *The English Catholics*, 97; Dickens, *The English Reformation*, 1964 edn, 312; and Guy, *Tudor England*, 301.

[109] Cited in Magee, *The English Recusants*, 113.

[110] John Earle, *Earle's Microcosmography*, ed. Alfred S. West, Cambridge 1897 (first publ. 1628), 47–8. This character can also be found in BL, MS Harley 1221, no 4, fo. 65v.

feigned conformity'.[111] Nor was the tract which 'discovered' and publicly unmasked 'Church Papists' or 'Popish Protestants' on the very eve of the Civil War in April 1642 purely the product of anti-Catholic delirium: P. R. Newman's comparison of Durham recusancy records and Protestation returns furnishes more concrete evidence that non-recusant Catholicism was still flourishing some eighty years after Elizabeth's 'Reformation'.[112] 'Formerly we had abundance of them that went under the name of Protestants, and were commonly called by the name of Church-Papists', wrote Richard Baxter, from his parish in Kidderminster, Worcestershire in 1659; far from having faded from view, furthermore, there was 'great reason to think that there are more such now'. The terminology was not yet obsolete in 1682; it had simply been secularised – according to Narcissus Luttrell, indefatigable chronicler of late Stuart state affairs, members of the politically conscious nation could expect to be classified under no other headings than 'whig and tory, church papist, tantivee, fanatick, &c'.[113]

Church papists thus demand a more prominent place in the history of post-Reformation Catholicism than they have hitherto been accorded. However, just as recusancy is only part of that story, so too 'Catholicism' is a single chapter in the tale of the church papist. Many individuals who ambiguously straddled the boundaries between official and unofficial religion, who practised, in Christopher Haigh's evocative phrase, an 'ambidextrous religious life', are inappropriately described in terms of articulate adherence or even silent commitment to the Church of Rome.[114] Wedged within the framework of an ostensibly reformed church, 'church papists' equally deserve the consideration of students of English Protestantism. Diarmaid MacCulloch has suggestively spoken of conformity as containing a constant danger of 'haemorrhage' towards the ecclesiastical establishment, but such fringe-dwellers are surely worthy of further speculation.[115]

Did they perhaps provide a popular, parochial basis for seventeenth-century 'Arminianism', the anti-Calvinist reaction within the official Church? Crypto-Catholics with more conciliatory opinions of the status quo who gradually assimilated Protestant habits and attitudes and became comfortably entrenched within the Church of England may well have constituted a reservoir of potential sympathisers for the anti-predestinarian

---

[111] Cardwell, *Synodalia*, i. 393; Conrad Russell, *The Causes of the English Civil War: the Ford Lectures delivered in the University of Oxford 1987–1988*, Oxford 1990, 77.

[112] *The Discription, Causes and Discovery, or Symptomes of a Church Papist*, London 1642 (Thomason Tracts E143 [10]). (I am indebted to Amanda Whiting for drawing this pamphlet to my attention.) Newman, 'Roman Catholics in pre-Civil War England', 148–9. During parliamentary elections in Lincolnshire in 1640, voters were advised to 'Choose no Ship sheriff, nor Court atheist, No fen drainer, nor church papist': David Underdown, *Rebel, Riot and Rebellion: popular politics and culture in England 1603–1660*, paperback edn, Oxford 1987, 133.

[113] Richard Baxter, *A Key for Catholicks*, London 1659, 337; Narcissus Luttrell, *A Brief Historical Relation of State Affairs from September 1678 to April 1714*, 6 vols, Oxford 1857, i. 198–9.

[114] Haigh, 'The Church of England, the Catholics and the people', 200 and passim. See also McGrath, 'Elizabethan Catholicism: a reconsideration', 419; Collinson, 'The Elizabethan Church and the new religion', 174–5.

[115] MacCulloch, *Later Reformation*, 150.

ideas emerging in the 1590s, and for the Laudian revival of ceremonialism and ritualism in the 1630s. It is at least feasible that sidling into an ideologically antagonistic institution and colonising it, they imperceptibly formed the bedrock of what historians are rightly still so wary of calling 'Anglicanism'.[116] The presence of church papists consequently casts a shadow of doubt on Nicholas Tyacke's influential version of pre-Civil War religious history. If lay conformist Catholicism fostered the long term backlash against Calvinism, can 'Arminianism' be viewed as an over-whelmingly clerical phenomenon, an intellectual movement whose origins lay primarily in academic circles? A divisive strain of non-puritan Protestantism persisting inside the English Church does perhaps little to bolster the thesis that Arminians were an innovating clique who sabotaged an existing ecclesiastical consensus and imposed a doctrinal revolution on an edifice steeped in Calvinist theology and practice.[117]

---

[116] Indeed, in denouncing Arminianism as popery in thin disguise, hostile contemporaries were almost literally branding it as a variety of church papistry. On the possibility of continuities between church papistry and anti-Calvinism and 'anglo-Catholicism', see Patrick McGrath's passing comment in *Papists and Puritans*, 31n. Christopher Haigh also offers some interesting speculations on this point at the popular level in 'The Church of England, the Catholics and the people', 218–19, and we look forward to further illumination of the subject in his forthcoming book. Maltby, 'Approaches to the Study of Religious Conformity', however, argues for a body of 'conformist' opinion in late Elizabethan and early Stuart England that was at once and as much anti-Laudian as anti-puritan: passim esp. pp. 13–14. Such a nexus is both tenuous and difficult to establish with any exactitude. But in late Elizabethan Bury St Edmunds religious conservatives and crypto-Catholics (including Sir Thomas Cornwallis and Sir Thomas Kitson) were using their parish patronage not only to appoint Marian clergy, but to install a new generation of anti-Puritan ministers: MacCulloch, *Suffolk and the Tudors*, 210–11. David Crankshaw of Robinson College, Cambridge, is discovering similar practices on a wider scale. For a later period, see John R. Guy, 'The Anglican patronage of Monmouthshire recusants in the seventeenth and eighteenth centuries', *RH* xiv (1981), 452–4. And Nicholas Tyacke has wondered if the small group of church papists in Parliament in the 1620s were a possible source of support for Arminianism – individuals who hoped that less aggressive Protestants might be induced to further schemes for religious toleration of Catholics. His sole but striking example is Sir Thomas Riddell, MP for Newcastle-upon-Tyne in 1621, 1625 and 1628–9, a conformist whose wife and eldest son were indicted as recusants in 1625; it is significant that his unsuccessful candidature in 1624 was sponsored by the Arminian Bishop Neile against local Calvinists: *Anti-Calvinists: the rise of Arminianism c.1590–1640*, paperback edn, Oxford 1990, 147.

[117] The debate on Arminianism is complex and crowded, but see on the one hand Tyacke, *Anti-Calvinists*, passim, esp. the foreword written for the paperback edn, and idem. 'Puritanism, Arminianism and counter revolution', in Conrad Russell (ed.), *The Origins of the English Civil War*, London 1973, 119–43; Peter Lake, 'Calvinism and the English Church 1570–1635', *P&P* cxiv (1987), 32–76, and idem. *Anglicans and Puritans?*, 228–9, 245–9; Russell, *The Causes of the English Civil War*, ch. iv, esp. pp. 84, 91–3, 102–5, 107–11. On the other, Peter White, 'The rise of Arminianism reconsidered', *P&P* ci (1983), 34–54; idem. *Predestination, Policy and Polemic: conflict and consensus in the English Church from the Reformation to the Civil War*, Cambridge 1992; Kevin Sharpe, 'Archbishop Laud', *History Today* xxxiii (1983), 26–30, and idem. 'Archbishop Laud and the University of Oxford', in H. Lloyd-Jones *et al* (eds), *History and Imagination*, London 1981, 146–64; G. W. Bernard, 'The Church of England c.1529–c.1642', *History* lxxv (1990), 183–206. For exchanges, see Nicholas Tyacke and Peter White, 'Debate: the rise of Arminianism reconsidered', and 'Rejoinder', *P&P* cxv (1987), 201–29; also the communications generated by Kevin Sharpe's review of Tyacke's *Anti-Calvinists*, 'How far did the Reformation go?', *Times Literary Supplement* (14 Aug. 1987), 884, published in the issues for 21, 28 Aug. and 4, 11, 18 Sept. For critical surveys of these debates,

And the nickname embraces innumerable Elizabethans and Jacobeans who can only with difficulty – or arrogance – be forced into 'the strait-jackets of "Catholic" and "Protestant" labels'.[118] Conformists shade obscurely into a body of 'mere conformists', whose disinterest in Reformation logomachy – perhaps in 'religion' itself – challenges us to reassess our lingering presupposition that early modern society was fractured by the confessional dichotomies implied by contemporary polemic.

see Richard Cust and Ann Hughes, 'Introduction: after revisionism', in idem. (eds), *Conflict in Early Stuart England: studies in religion and politics 1603–42*, London–New York 1989, 6–7, 23–6; Anne Hughes, *The Causes of the English Civil War*, London 1991, 98–101, 107–13. On proto-Arminianism, see MacCulloch, *Later Reformation*, 80–1, 94–7, 99–100.

[118] Palliser, 'Popular reactions', 55–6.

5

Statute Protestants

It was never merry England since we were impressed to come to the Church. – Browne, the lighterman at Ramsgate, 20 October 1581 – Arthur Hussey (ed.), 'Visitations of the Archdeacon of Canterbury', *Archaeologia Cantiana* xxvi (1904), 32.

Words be often as they be taken, and as the minds of them be that speake them. – Hide, *Consolatorie Epistle*, sig. D3r.

According to George Gifford, preacher and minister of Maldon, Essex, in 1582 the population of East Anglia was infested with 'utter enimies unto the Gospel'. The congregations of the Established Church in this very seedbed of the English Reformation were not chiefly comprised of impeccable Protestants, but swelled by scores of individuals as 'zealously addicted unto popery' as the incorrigibly Catholic 'church papist' who inhabits his discourse. The county, on the contrary, was one of the 'desolate places' abounding in iniquity, and in seeking to spread the light of Scripture and build God's bastion there, Gifford was fighting a losing battle against Satan and his crew.[1]

Gifford's *Dialogue between a Papist and a Protestant* was a contribution to a genre of licensed ecclesiastical libel, anti-Catholic polemic. Gathering in momentum and profusion as the century progressed, such literature symptomises a heightened contemporary sensitivity to the magnitude and immediacy of the Catholic menace – a sensitivity that can seem with hindsight a perplexing and pathological form of collective neurosis.[2]

[1] Gifford, *Dialogue between a Papist and a Protestant*, sigs J3v, J3r respectively.
[2] See Milward, *Religious Controversies of the Elizabethan Age*, for a survey of some anti-Catholic propaganda, literature that has been remarkably neglected until very recently. For the Henrician, Edwardine and early Elizabethan period, see John N. King, *English Reformation Literature: the Tudor origins of the Protestant tradition*, Princeton 1982, 252–70, 283, 311, 351–5, 371–406. For the later Elizabethan and Stuart period, Christopher Hill, *Antichrist in Seventeenth Century England*, London 1971, 14ff.; Carol Z. Wiener, 'The beleaguered isle: a study of Elizabethan and early Jacobean anti-Catholicism', *P&P* li (1971), 27–62; Robin Clifton, 'Fear of popery', in Conrad Russell (ed.), *The Origins of the English Civil War*, London 1973, 145–50, and idem. 'The popular fear of Catholics during the English Revolution', in Paul Slack (ed.), *Rebellion, Popular Protest and the Social Order in Early Modern England*, Cambridge 1984, 141–5; Peter Lake, 'The significance of the Elizabethan identification of the pope as Antichrist', *JEH* xxxi (1980), 161–;78; idem. *Moderate Puritans and Elizabethan Church*, Cambridge 1982, esp. chs iv, vi; 'William Bradshaw, 'Antichrist and the community of the godly', *JEH* xxxvi (1985), 570–89; and 'Anti-popery: the structure of a prejudice', in Cust and Hughes, *Conflict in Early Stuart England*, 72–106, esp. pp. 74ff. Anthony Milton's forthcoming book, *Catholic and Reformed: the Roman and Protestant Churches in English Protestant thought 1600–1640*, a major study of anti-Catholic polemic, will undoubtedly revive interest in this rich, but under-exploited source. (I am grateful to the author for allowing me to read his manuscript prior to publication.) 'Popular' anti-Catholicism disseminated at the level of

Yet these tracts embodied no hysterical reaction to the Counter Reformation's modest endeavour to reclaim 'schismatics', no inflated estimate of the potential impact of an undermanned missionary machine. 'Popery's' prevalence was not to be explained by the superhuman efforts of a handful of Jesuits and seminary priests possessed of inexhaustible evangelical genius, but by the deplorable abuses in the Church of England's own ministry. Instead of crushing the 'coccatrise egges' of an 'viperous generation', the 'swarme' of depraved Marian timeservers surviving within its ranks simply hatched forth 'browdes of this evill kind . . . in great plentie'. Until such 'unlearned Idols' and priests of Jeroboam were replaced by a brigade of godly preachers, Gifford remonstrated, it was inevitable that many would 'stumble and loth the Gospel'.[3]

Underlying much anti-Catholic polemic was therefore a practical, pastoral concern about the Reformation's poor psychological progress and precarious hold at the parochial level. Peter Lake has highlighted the skill with which moderate Cambridge puritan divines exploited the spectre of 'popery' as a source of 'ideological leverage' in their domestic disputes with the ecclesiastical hierarchy.[4] This bugbear was similarly invoked by a plethora of petitions pleading against the silencing of non-subscribing clergymen and lamenting the inadequate provisions for a teaching and preaching pastorate in the 1580s. Such 'boulstring and bearing' of unable and unworthy ministers, such 'defacing and discrediting' of the energetic and conscientious, they announced with one accord, did nothing but harden the obstinate in their 'Romish' errors and nurse and nourish superstition. In consequence, 'Papists' and 'Atheists' were proliferating at an alarming rate: there were good grounds for fearing that they 'do dailie multiplie and increase'.[5] When Francis Bunny entreated local magistrates to procure the planting of additional preachers in the north in 1595, he maintained that this was the only way to disperse the 'popish swarmes' seething in Northumberland. For unfamiliarity with God's word was the soil in which Catholicism best germinated and took root: it made a

---

cheap print has also received relatively little attention in the English context, but see Tessa Watt, *Cheap Print and Popular Piety 1550–1640*, Cambridge 1991, 88, 150–9, 178–9, and cf R. W. Scribner, *For the Sake of Simple Folk: popular propaganda for the German Reformation*, Cambridge 1981.
[3] Gifford, *Dialogue between a Papist and a Protestant*, sigs J4r–v, cf pp. 34rff., 42r.
[4] Lake, *Moderate Puritans*, chs iv, vi, esp. pp. 67ff., 93; idem. 'William Bradshaw', 570–1; 'Significance', esp. pp. 170ff.; and 'Anti-popery', 79ff., esp. p. 83. Some historians have distinguished sharply between puritan 'devotional' writing and 'polemic', and privileged the former as a 'truer' manifestation of the puritan spirit. See, for instance, William Haller, *The Rise of Puritanism: or the way to the New Jerusalem as set forth in pulpit and press from Thomas Cartwright to John Lilburne and John Milton 1570–1643*, New York 1957 (first publ. 1938), passim esp. p. 24; M. M. Knappen, *Tudor Puritanism: a chapter in the history of idealism*, Gloucester, Mass. 1963, ch. xx, esp. pp. 379–80. But the production of anti-Catholic – and, indeed, anti-establishment – polemic was not a separate exercise: it sprang from precisely the same pietistic impulse. For further comments, see Lake, *Moderate Puritans*, 2ff., 284, and passim; Dewey D. Wallace, 'George Gifford, puritan propaganda and popular religion in Elizabethan England', *The Sixteenth Century Journal* ix (1978), 27–50, esp. pp. 28, 49n.; *The Work of William Perkins*, ed. and intro. I. Breward, Appleford, Berks 1970, 24; Peter Clark, 'Josias Nicholls and religious radicalism, 1553–1639', *JEH* xxviii (1977), 141.
[5] Peel, *Seconde Parte of a Register*, ii. 80; i. 225 respectively. Cf i. 76, 174, 185, 191, 216, 226, 253, 256–7, 264, 285; ii. 13, 37, 188, 190–1.

'ready entrance' for Jesuit and seminary-trained missionaries, the false prophets and 'leaping locusts' who could successfully seduce spiritually unschooled 'silly soules'.[6] Josias Nichols, vicar of Eastwell in Kent, asserted much the same in his impassioned apology for the scruples and strategies of those suppressed and slandered as 'Puritanes', *The Plea of the Innocent*. Writing in the run-up to the renewed agitation for further reform that preceded the Hampton Court Conference in 1604, he claimed to have found 'skarse' 'tenne in the hundred' with any knowledge of Calvinist, not to say Christian doctrine in parishes where sermons were still seldom preached.[7]

George Gifford's evocation of the resilient figure of the 'church papist' was a political tactic too: a ploy intended to prompt the queen and Privy Council to remedy the disciplinary flaws he believed continued to impair the Church of England's effectiveness as a proselytising agency. His character was a propagandist construct, the personification of a Church conceived to be 'but halfly reformed'. It encapsulated the subtle, but subversive assertion that the structural and ceremonial legacies of 'popery' inherent in the Elizabethan settlement were the root cause of the conservatism and ignorance of the masses. Gifford's discovery and denunciation of the 'church papist' refracted and projected the ambitions and anxieties about the institutionalisation and internalisation of the Reformation at the centre of his puritan outlook.[8]

Yet his lively moralising *Dialogue* was also part of a pedagogic literature 'applied to the capacitie of the unlearned' and designed to 'serve the turne of the simple'; it was rudely fashioned 'after the manner of ploughmen and carters' rather than framed as 'a disputation betweene deepe Divines'.[9] By providing a comprehensive confutation of doctrinal errors, it sought to remove the stumbling blocks hindering the popularisation and propagation of Protestantism. Fostering a vituperative and apocalyptic anti-Catholicism, arousing cathartic hostility to a habitual system of belief, remained a critical task some twenty years after the religious revolution of 1559 – decades after the legislative landmarks of Henrician and Edwardine Erastianism. It was both the godly's greatest disappointment and gravest embarrassment that a generation after the Reformation's restoration – notwithstanding so much 'painful' preaching – 'popery' had yet to be effectively stifled. Of its undiminished virility and stamina, William Fulke asked despondently in 1580, 'who living in Englande can be ignoraunt?'[10] Even a quarter of a century later, George Abbot, subsequently archbishop of Canterbury, was giving expression to his desire to dispel the 'foggy mists' of Catholicism in a

---

[6] Francis Bunny, *A Short Answer to the Reasons, which commonly the Popish Recusants in these North parts alleadge, why they will not come to our Churches* (bound with *Truth and Falshood*), sigs Aa4r and Aa5v. Cf *Truth and Falshood*, 148v–60vff.

[7] Josias Nichols, *The Plea of the Innocent*, London 1602, 184ff., 212ff., at p. 214.

[8] Gifford, *Dialogue between a Papist and a Protestant*, dedication, sigs J2r–J4v. For other examples, see Field, *A Caveat for Parsons Howlet*, dedication, sigs A2r–3r; William Fulke, *A Retentive to Stay Good Christians*, London 1580, 46; Wiburn, *Checke or reproofe*, 129v.

[9] Gifford, *Dialogue between a Papist and a Puritan*, title and sig. J2v; and his *A Briefe discourse of certaine points of the religion . . . which may be termed the Countrie Divinitie*, London 1598 (first publ. 1581), sig. A2r. Cf Wiburn, *Checke or reproofe*, 6v, 124v; Fulke, *Briefe Confutation*, 1r; Bunny, *Truth and Falshood*, sig. A4r; and idem. *Short Answer*, sig. Aa5r.

[10] Fulke, *Retentive*, 126.

systematic 'unmasking' of 'reasons of refusall', composed 'to the ende that such among our Popish Countrey men as are ordained to salvation, may be plucked out of the fire'.[11] Such propaganda addressed itself to convincing the self-consciously 'Catholic in mind', but perhaps more particularly, to those whose 'popery' was unacknowledged, half forgotten but incompletely abandoned. 'Although they bee not rancke Papists', observed Gifford, 'yet have [they] in them still a smacke and savour of Popish principles' – yet were they 'crammed . . . full of Popish drosse'. John Baxter's corresponding complaint about the 'linsie woolsie religion' of too many of his contemporaries ran: 'Their ave maria sticks close betwixt their teeth, though their Pater Noster was forgot many yeeres agoe.'[12] These assaults on the residual rural Catholicism persisting within the Church of England were an essential aspect of a wider campaign against the pelagian piety of the poor, 'popular' religion – the irreligion 'which is among the common sort of Christians, which may be termed the Countrie Divinitie'.[13]

Gifford thus numbered among those he disdainfully labelled 'church papist' a large multitude whose 'Catholicism' was less a set of defined dogmas capable of being summarised in a catechism, than an intuitive method of thinking and living, a deeply ingrained mentality. Such individuals betrayed their adherence to the Romish AntiChrist not so much in a positive, voiced endorsement of its untenable theology, as in their reactionary resistance to the saving message of the Gospel and its advocates. Vague nostalgia for a golden age, a medieval 'mery world when there was lesse preaching, and when all things were so cheape, that they might have xx. egs for a penny', was but a degenerate strain of 'popery' festering on within Protestant society.[14] The puritan activist John Field also caricatured those who disconsolately repined the passing of the pre-Reformation period, with all its 'good felowship' and 'good chere': 'They whil whisper from place to place, and from one to another and uppon their ale-bench, what dayes are these, what wickednesse is in the world, See the lives of these Gospellers, was there ever such covetousnes.' 'Since there was so much talke of the scripture, since every cobler and Tinker durst meddle with it, and a byble must stand in every window', since Protestantism had put the people on a pedestal, they moped, things had taken a distinct turn for the worse. This, commented Field, was simply the 'common speech of papists'.[15]

And while these 'papists' had imbibed elementary lessons in abusing the pope and slating an idolatrous creed, like the ebullient 'Atheos' of Gifford's tract they displayed an astonishingly superficial understanding of fundamental Calvinist tenets. They manifestly failed, furthermore, to exhibit the arresting spirit of God's word in their ordinary lives. The bare conformity of covert

11 Abbot, *Reasons . . . Unmasked*, sig. Ff2r.

12 George Gifford, *Foure Sermons upon the seven chiefe vertues or principall effectes of faith*, London 1582 (first publ. 1581), sig. C3v; idem. *Countrie Divinitie*, 61, cf 34, 42; J[ohn] B[axter], *A Toile for Two-Legged Foxes*, London 1600, 112. Cf William Harrison, *Deaths advantage little regarded*, 'A Postscript to Papists', sig. N1v.

13 Gifford, *Countrie Divinitie*, title page.

14 Idem. *Dialogue between a Papist and a Protestant*, 2r.

15 Field, *A Caveat for Parsons Howlet*, sigs D8v–E1r.

Catholics sheltering within the law, then, was tacitly equated with the minimal commitment of 'statute protestants'. These were men and women who supposed it sufficient to comply with the ecclesiastical regulations concerning church attendance, to present an honest demeanour, live and labour uprightly to the view of the world – and, above all, to 'meane well' and try hard, naively trusting that 'God will beare with me in the rest'.[16] 'Is it not enough for plaine countrie men, plow men, taylours, and such other, for to have their ten commaundements, the Lords prayer, and the beliefe?', contended Atheos: 'shall we say God regardeth not his prayer, because he doth not understand what he prayeth?'. To his companion Zelotes, such shallow knowledge and uncomprehending utterance of the liturgical formularies appointed for public worship was like physical presence in the parish church, no more than a 'token'. It was a pretence of the Protestant faith – a pretence of faith itself.[17] 'The common sort of people thinke indeed, that all Religion consisteth in the outward service of God, though their hearts bee farre from him', deplored Arthur Dent, the vicar of South Shoebury on the Essex coast, in his *Plaine Mans Path-way to heaven*, first published in 1601. Too many persuaded themselves that they might complacently 'practise it at their leasure'.[18] 'Some imagine', echoed the King's Preacher in Lancashire, William Harrison, reprimanding his congregation at Huyton in 1614, 'that if they be no Recusants, if they be no prophane contemners of the Word and Sacraments: but repayre to the Church every Sabboth day, & heare divine Service & Sermons orderly, as by Law they are enjoyned, they are good Christians, & sure to bee saved.'[19]

But this was not 'religion' in the eyes and to the minds of the godly. Laurence Chaderton exhorted his audience at Paul's Cross in October 1578 to throw off these 'clokes of hypocrisie, and wordes of lyes', for it is not 'the outwarde shewe of Christianitie, in countenannace, worde, and woorke, that avayleth any thing, but only a newe creature in Christ'. Anatomising the abuses and cataloguing the faults of the English nation and its people, the semi-professional writer Phillip Stubbes summed up: 'If Religion consist in wordes onely, then are thei verie religious, but otherwise, plaine irreligious.'[20] In fine, it was not verbal formalities or external gestures that characterised true profession of the Gospel, but 'the inward humilitie of a syncere heart' –

---

[16] Gifford, *Countrie Divinitie*, 9, cf 17–18, 116–17. See also John Dod and Robert Cleaver, *A Plaine and Familiar Exposition of the Ten Commandments*, London 1612 (first publ. 1604), 12, 301; Perkins, *Work of William Perkins*, 407; idem. *A Discourse of Conscience wherein is set downe the nature, properties, and differences therof: as also the way to get and keepe good conscience* (1596), reprinted in *William Perkins 1558–1602: English puritanist*, ed. Thomas F. Merrill, Nieuwkoop 1966, 43.

[17] Gifford, *Countrie Divinitie*, 46, 116, 56 respectively. For Atheos's 'anti-Catholicism' and antagonism towards the pope, see 34ff., 61, 66.

[18] Dent, *Plaine Mans Path-way*, 126, 124 respectively.

[19] William Harrison, *The Difference of Hearers*, London 1614, 20. Cf George Gifford's sermon on the same text: *A sermon on the parable of the sower taken out of the 13. of Matthew*, London 1582, sig. A7r; Dent, *Plaine Mans Path-way*, 25; and Nicholas Breton, *A Merrie Dialogue betwixt the taker and Mistaker*, London 1603, 12–13.

[20] Laurence Chaderton, *An Excellent and godly sermon*, London 1580. sig. E8r and passim; Phillip Stubbes, *Phillip Stubbes' Anatomy of Abuses in England in Shakspere's Youth A.D. 1583*, 2 vols, ed. F. J. Furnivall, London 1877–9 (first publ. 1583), i. 130.

the inner transformative effects wrought on the soul by the Holy Spirit through Scripture.[21]

These were postures and positions perpetuating the pre-Reformation patterns of piety that Protestant zealots traditionally branded as empty spectacle and outrageous sham. Catholicism, went the cliché, exalted observance above insight. It was a counterfeit, skin-deep concept of Christianity measured by mindless muttering of prescribed prayers, mechanical fulfilment of priestly imposed penances, and robotic performance of ritual. According to William Perkins, it constituted no more than 'a carnall service' of God, 'standing of innumerable bodily rites and ceremonies'. The philosophy of the reprobate majority, in Dent's view, thus resembled the outlook of 'Papists, which thinke, if they heare Masse in the morning, they may doe what they list, all the day after'.[22] The infidelity of individuals whose unholy conversation and conduct throughout the week made a mockery of their obedient, if impassive appearance at church on Sunday merely mirrored the 'Old Religion's' innate duplicity and dissipation. It parodied the epitome of that falsity and faithlessness, church papistry. Gifford had no doubt that a vast component of this nominally Protestant population had in fact cheerfully temporised under Queen Mary's restored Romanist regime in the mid-1550s. They were sometime 'mass gospellers', who had been content to keep their consciences carefully hidden and compromise and communicate with corrupt Catholicism. 'Looke whatsoever any Prince doth set forth, that they will professe.'[23] Their exterior decorum belied an interior godlessness.

Seen through a puritan lens, practising the lukewarm religion of 'cold statute protestants' was equivalent to practising no religion at all. Such worldlings were scarcely superior to 'bruite beastes', Indians or infidels who had never been enlightened by the Word. They behaved as if the Scriptures were but 'fables'; they esteemed the Gospel no more than an item of mundane materiality – an 'eg shell' or 'dish clout'; they loved their Maker as negligibly as 'an old shoe'.[24] They were, in Jeremy Corderoy's entirely typical terms, 'atheists', such as 'wil not in words deny God, but by their deeds'. This was not the 'Open Atheisme' of those vocally cynical about the existence of a deity, but what William Perkins called 'Coloured Atheisme' – an infinitely more insidious strain of contemporary scepticism.[25] 'No Sect now in England' was

---

[21] Perkins, *Whole treatise*, 79, cf 51ff., 62.

[22] Idem. *A Reformed Catholicke*, London 1597, 339; Dent, *Plaine Mans Path-way*, 125. Cf Gifford, *Dialogue between a Papist and a Protestant*, 28r–v, 43rff., 50r; Harrison, *Deaths advantage little regarded*, 'A Postscript to Papists', sig. N1r. The stereotyped denunciations of Catholicism's inherent duplicity, hypocrisy, superficiality and carnality which are common to most anti-Catholic propaganda are discussed by Lake, 'Anti-popery', 75ff.; Wiener, 'Beleaguered isle', 37ff.; Clifton, 'Fear of popery', 146ff., and 'Popular fear', 142ff.

[23] Gifford, *Countrie Divinitie*, 34, cf 64–5. The phrase 'mass gospellers' was used by the Marian martyr John Bradford in the tract he wrote against Protestant church papistry, *The Hurte of Heringe Masse* which was published posthumously around 1561, again in 1580, and reprinted in *Writings of John Bradford*, 320.

[24] Gifford, *Countrie Divinitie*, 119; Dent, *Plaine Mans Path-way*, 128, 122, 134; Gifford, *Countrie Divinitie*, 22 respectively.

[25] Jeremy Corderoy, *A Warning for Worldlings*, London 1608, sig. A4v and dedication passim; Perkins, *Reformed Catholike*, 335. Cf Fulke, *Retentive*, 170 [*sic*]; B[axter], *Toile for Two-Legged Foxes*,

'so scattered' asserted the metropolitan pamphleteer Thomas Nashe in 1593. In these last days, Arthur Dent's fictional godly villager, Philagathus affirmed, it was nothing less than epidemic: 'This age indeed aboundeth with many hollow hearted hypocrites, dissemblers and timeservers, which howsoever they make a face, and beare a countenance as though they loved the Gospell, yet their heart is not with it. Their heart is with Atheism: their hart is with Popery. They have a Pope in their belly: they bee Church-papists.'[26] The spiritual and moral tepidity of individuals satisfied with undemonstrative attendance at the obligatory rites of the Established Church was not just an unacceptable substitute for the ethically and intellectually demanding religiosity expounded by clerical elites – it was its very antithesis.

It was a commonplace among Elizabethan preachers that by far the greater number had 'escaped out of the gulfe of superstition' only to be 'plunged into prophaneness': they had fallen from Romish credulity and error into impiety and neutrality.[27] In what must have been a pulpit-thumping sermon at Paul's Cross in January 1581, the Oxford divine James Bisse rehearsed the theme and raised it to new heights of rhetorical hyperbole:

> But alas for pitie, alas for shame, are not many that beare the name of Protestantes, and Gospellers, inferiour too them? We use our libertie as a cloake of loosenesse, wee turne the grace of God into wantonnesse, and the glorious Gospell of Jesus Christ into lewdnesse. Are not wee come from the excesse, to the defect? from blinde zeale, to wilfull ungodlinesse? from ignoraunce in darknesse, to wickednesse in knoweledge? from many Gods, to noe God? from papisme, to Athisme? from superstition, to irreligion?

As George Gifford saw the situation a year later, 'the most in number . . . having Poperie taken from them, and not taught throughly and sufficiently in the Gospell, doe stand as men indifferent; so that they may quietly enjoy the world, they care not what religion come: they are like naked men, fit and ready for any coate almost that may be put upon them'.[28]

Gifford and his Protestant colleagues clearly shared with the agents of the Counter Reformation uneasy apprehensions about the birth of a secularised

---

116; Dent, *Plaine Mans Path-way*, 122, 124, 129; Dod and Cleaver, *Plaine and Familiar Exposition*, 92; Nichols, *Plea of the Innocent*, 212–14; Hooker, *Works*, i. 432. See also Collinson, *The Religion of Protestants*, 200ff.; Haigh, 'The Church of England, the Catholics and the people', passim esp. pp. 205ff.; Wrightson, *English Society*, 204–5; Hunter, 'The problem of "atheism" '; Wootton, 'Unbelief in early modern Europe'.

[26] Thomas Nashe, *Christes Teares Over Jerusalem* (1593), repr. in *The Workes of Thomas Nashe*, 4 vols, ed. Ronald B. McKerrow, Oxford 1966, ii. 121–2, cf 117; Dent, *Plaine Mans Path-way*, 125, cf 128.

[27] Richard Greenham, *The Workes of the Reverent and Faithful Servant of Jesus Christ M. Richard Greenham, Minister and Preacher of the Word of God*, London 1599 (first publ. 1598), 5, 61.

[28] James Bisse, *Two Sermons preached, the one at Paules Crosse the eight of Januarie 1580*, London 1581, sigs D5v–6r; Gifford, *Countrie Divinitie*, sigs A2v–3r. For similar statements, see Gifford, *Dialogue between a Papist and a Protestant*, 38v–9r; Dod and Cleaver, *Plaine and Familiar Exposition*, 76; Wiburn, *Checke or reproofe*, 122v; Thomas Cartwright, 'A generall confession of sinnes to be made at the exercise of fasting', appended to *A very godly and learned treatise of the exercise of fastyng* (1580), in Albert Peel and Leland H. Carlson (eds), *Cartwrightiana* (Elizabethan Nonconformist Texts i, 1951), 144; the bishop of Carlisle, in *CSP Dom 1598–1601*, 362.

society; they backed their rivals' diagnosis of the disturbing long-term consequences of religious upheaval. Alienated by the sectarian squabbles and interminable theological wrangling of the sixteenth century, the bulk of the population seemed to have progressed from the 'Old Religion' to a post-Catholic torpor – into passive conformity and ideological confusion. In 1569, Stephen Bateman's *Christall glasse of Christian reformation* embodied in an emblem his impression that parishes everywhere contained a company of '*Nullifidians*, such as are of no religion, not regarding any doctrine so they may bee quiet to live after their owne willes and mindes'. But when a group of like-minded ministers met in 1604, the category of 'indifferent or plaine neuters' within their 'country congregations' seemed of no less serious proportions.[29] These were those 'luke-warm Laodiceans whom God cannot digest', remarked Henry Peacham in 1638, 'and whom I have knowne both Protestant & Papist alike to have discarded'. Indeed, it was the parallel opinion of Augustine Baker, a Benedictine missionary of Welsh extraction, that thousands of people, 'unawares to themselves', had become: 'neutrals in religion, viz. neither indeed true Catholicks, for perfect knowledg, beleif and practice, nor yet meer Protestants or otherwise hereticks in their beleif, though schismaticall, by their externall accommodation of themselves to the schismaticall service of the English Church'.[30]

But were these commentators witnessing the emergence of an epoch in which religion was shrinking into a peripheral feature of activity and consciousness? Robert Whiting's recent study of the south-west endorses contemporary convictions that the Reformation, far from ushering in Jean Delumeau's era of 'Christianisation' or Christina Larner's 'age of faith', rather initiated the descent from a relatively high level of devotion into conformism, inertia and apathy.[31] Yet his conclusion remains a largely untestable hypothesis: distanced by four centuries, we cannot prize open the mentalities of most men and women, and inspect their souls.

It is equally probable that in articulating growing concerns about conformity and mere conformity, clerical counterparts of irreconcilable doctrinal standpoints were unwittingly disclosing a mutual shift in perception. As William Fulke recognised, the visibility of such groups was partly a function of the rigorous standards and lofty expectations of a progressive and

---

[29] Stephen Bateman, *A christall glasse of Christian reformation*, London 1569, sig. G4r (see frontispiece); HMC, *Lord Montagu of Beaulieu*, i. 39.

[30] Henry Peacham, *The Truth of our Times*, London 1638, 157; McCann and Connolly, *Memorials of Father Augustine Baker*, 16–17. See also George Gilbert's 'A way to deal with persons of all sorts so as to convert them and bring them back to a better way of life' (1583), in Hicks, *Letters and Memorials*, 339–40 ('The method to be adopted with lukewarm Catholics'), and above, ch. ii.

[31] See Whiting, *The Blind Devotion of the People*, passim esp. pp. 171, 186–7, 268. For the debate about secularisation, on the one hand, see Delumeau, *Catholicism between Luther and Voltaire*, passim esp. pp. 159–61, and pt ii, chs iv and v; idem. 'Prescription and reality', 154ff.; Larner, 'The age of faith', 113–26 passim; Margaret Spufford, *Contrasting Communities: English villagers in the sixteenth and seventeenth centuries*, Cambridge 1974, ch. xiii. On the other, Thomas, *Religion and the Decline of Magic*, 189ff., esp. pp. 205–6; Clark, *English Provincial Society*, 156ff. For a broader survey of the issue, see Alan Gilbert, *The Making of Post-Christian Britain: a history of the secularization of modern society*, London–New York 1980, 26ff.; and for succinct comments, Collinson, *The Religion of Protestants*, 198–9.

vocal minority: 'The number of Atheists that are in England are not *made*, but *discerned* by the preaching of the Gospel.'[32] In a culture predisposed to comprehend itself dyadically, in oppositional and binary terms, 'atheist' and 'papist' were polarised stereotypes available for the expression and repression of disquiet about 'aberrant' mental and behavioural tendencies – for the reinforcement and restatement of theoretical norms. They were categories of deviance to which individuals who even marginally departed from prescribed ideals might be assimilated and thereby reproved.[33] It was Francis Bacon who observed that 'all that impugn a received religion, or superstition, are, by the adverse part, branded with the name of atheists'.[34] The identification of papists – and church papists – in early modern society was a correspondingly subjective process: less revealing, perhaps, of the phenomenon itself, than of the shape of the ideological prism through which the classifier viewed it. The use of such words illuminates more lucidly the attitudes of their utterers than the characteristics of the stigmatised. Religious insult and imputation in early modern England intrinsically involved self-definition.

For the propagandists of a resurgent Rome, 'schismatics' represented a threat to the integrity and recusant identity of Tridentine Catholicism. For puritans, 'church papist' was but one synonym for ungodly, a convenient shorthand for all that negated their vision of what it was to be religious – properly 'Protestant'. Indeed, in Gifford's *Countrie Divinitie*, the hallmark of Atheos' 'popery' is his antipathy towards 'trim pulpit men', 'busy controllers', those 'curious and precise fellows' whom he regards as unduly self-righteous and hypocritically holy. Gifford's church papist is above all an anti-puritan – 'if', as his imaginary adversary Zelotes counters, 'ye take the name Puritane for one which hath more care to obey God, then the common sort, and therefore laboureth to keepe himselfe pure and unspotted of the world'.[35] To shrink from and sneer at the optional, ostentatious piety of the 'hotter sort of Protestants' – conduct that could earn one an unsavoury reputation for singularity – was, in effect, to condemn and confess oneself a 'papist'. John Dod and Robert Cleaver accordingly denounced the 'dastardlinesse' of individuals who manifested even the slightest reluctance to keep the Sabbath assiduously or fall in line with the sermon-gadding fad – in short, to serve Calvin's fastidious God – 'lest they should be counted too precise',

---

[32] Fulke, *Retentive*, 109, my emphasis. James I similarly told parliament in Feb. 1621, 'I thinke there are more [recusants] discovered But not that there are more indeede then heretofore': Wallace Notestein *et al*, *Commons Debates 1621*, 7 vols, New Haven–London 1935, iv. 74.

[33] See Clark, 'Inversion, misrule and the meaning of witchcraft', passim; Burke, *Popular Culture in Early Modern Europe*, 185–91. For a valuable theoretical discussion of the sociology of deviance, and its application to the problem of seventeenth century New England witchcraft, see Kai T. Erikson, *Wayward Puritans: a study in the sociology of deviance*, New York 1966, esp. ch. i. Michael Hunter examines 'atheism' in these terms: 'The problem of "atheism" ', esp. pp. 147ff., 153–4. Lake's 'Anti-popery', passim esp. pp. 73, 80, is an important recent discussion of 'popery' using this conceptual framework; Patrick Collinson draws upon these concepts to illuminate puritanism in *The Puritan Character: polemics and polarities in early seventeenth-century English culture*, Los Angeles 1989, 21–3.

[34] Francis Bacon, 'Of atheism', in *Essays*, ed. and intro. Michael J. Hawkins, London 1972, 50.

[35] Gifford, *Countrie Divinitie*, 123. For Atheos's vigorous 'anti-puritanism', see 3–4, 6–7, 13, 15, 26–7, 29, 95, 101, 103, 105, 123.

jeered and laughed at as 'Puritanes'.[36] This was the cowardice of cold Christians and vestigially Catholic conformists.

It was, by extension, conventional wisdom among the 'godly' that the popish and profane multitude had both invented and monopolised current usage of that supremely emotive perjorative, 'puritan'. 'I know no puritans', declared a character in John Udall's dialogue *Diotrephes*, 'but Sathan taught the Papistes, so to name the ministers of the Gospell.' As an anonymous answerer to Whitgift's articles likewise protested in 1584, if any man aired the issue of reforming Church abuses, he was harassed by the bishops, who bustled together with 'the counterfaite papist and bribing Atheist' and 'by one devise or other dubbe him a puritan'.[37] In 1621 too, Timothy Rogers, preacher at Steeple Bumpstead in Essex, deduced that it was 'loose and dissolute liver[s]' and 'Papists' who 'crie out against us, that we are hereticks, schismatickes, Puritanes & what not'. And defending the unfashionable habits of sincere 'Professors of the Gospell' at the turn of the century, Josias Nichols agreed that the 'greater sort of the people beeing olde barrels which coulde holde no newe wine, addicted partlie to Poperie & partlie to licentiousnesse, having many of them no other God, but their bellie, woulde deride and scoffe at them, and called them holye brethren and holye sisterne'.[38] The parochial master-minds behind this protracted backbiting campaign were persons its victims would have imputed 'papists' or 'church papists' in reprisal. 'Gods wrath', predicted one such sufferer in 1586, 'can not but be marvailouslie kindled against those that slaunder, nickname, and mocke his Sainctes.'[39]

Patrick Collinson and Peter Lake have argued that the identification of the distinctive attributes of the reprobate was in fact a vital element in the raising of 'godly consciousness'. Non-separating puritans whose theological and ecclesiological principles constrained them to participate with the unregenerate masses in public prayers and official rites experienced with particular pressure the problem of validating their status as true believers, the invisible company of the chosen concealed within an unreformed Church and a corrupt and malicious world. Avoiding contact with the 'popishly' inclined, forbearing the acquaintance and conversation of contemptibly 'cold statute protestants', separating from the shameless sinners amongst one's neighbours, were at least in theory, critical to the self-vindication and affirmation of the elect.[40] As the puritan patriarch of Dry Drayton in Cambridgeshire, Richard Greenham implied, it was 'a very speciall signe and

---

[36] Dod and Cleaver, *Plaine and Familiar Exposition*, 50, 8 respectively. See also Lake, *Moderate Puritans*, 13; Hunt, *The Puritan Moment*, 145.

[37] [John Udall], *The state of the Church of Englande*, [London 1588], sig. B4r; *Seconde Parte of a Register*, i. 181. The charge that 'papists' had invented the word in fact had some historical substance: see Leland J. Trinterud (ed.), *Elizabethan Puritanism*, New York 1971, 7–9.

[38] Timothy Rogers, *The Roman-Catharist*, London 1621, 40, 7 respectively, cf pp. 37–41; Nichols, *Plea of the Innocent*, 6. For further examples, see Hill, 'The definition of a Puritan', 16; Perkins, *Work of William Perkins*, 34; Dod and Cleaver, *Plaine and Familiar Exposition*, 92.

[39] 'A Copie of Mr. Fullers booke to the Queene' (1586), in Peel, *Seconde Parte of a Register*, ii. 55.

[40] Collinson, *The Religion of Protestants*, 268ff.; idem. 'The English conventicle', 252ff.; 'The godly: aspects of popular Protestantism', in *Godly People: essays on English Protestantism and Puritanism*, London 1983, 1–18; and *Birthpangs*, 145ff; Lake, *Moderate Puritans*, 126ff.; idem. 'William Bradshaw', 579ff.

marke of the true childe of God' to flee and forsake the society of evil and wicked worldlings and to make haste instead to the secular assemblies of the self-selected saints. Dod and Cleaver also confuted the 'blind charity' of those who affably made allowances for their idolatrous enemies: benignly to tolerate 'papists' and 'carnal protestants' amounted to a form of adultery with AntiChrist. To refrain from this austere and unfriendly code of practice, according to Josias Nichols in 1602, was to show 'a verie cold love unto the Ghospell'.[41]

If, then, we seek those who marked themselves out to their peers as 'church papists', our attention must turn to the individuals against whom puritans directed this social doctrine of shunning. It must converge on those 'fraternally' admonished for their impiety and immorality, and on those accused and convicted during the local crusades in civil and ecclesiastical courts against 'sin', against the sub-culture of the ungodly – sabbath-breaking and sexual misdemeanours, alehouse-haunting and 'idle' recreations. It must alight on the urban and rural parishioners at the receiving end of those periodic and increasingly permanent programmes for moral 'improvement' that historians have come to refer to under the rubrics of the 'reform of popular culture' and the 'reformation of manners'.[42] No less consideration is required of churchgoers ejected from the eucharist on the grounds of insufficient catechetical knowledge or 'notorious' offences by puritan ministers determined to reserve the sacraments for privileged factions of the faithful – determined to offer this gift of grace only to communicants who had 'purged themselves of the suspicion of popery which their former life and conversation hath caused to be conceived'.[43] We can catch a glimpse of those regarded as contemptibly 'conformist', for instance, in an incident in East Hanningfield, Essex, in the 1580s, when the rector William Seridge repelled no less than nineteen members of his congregation from one celebration of holy communion on account of their disorderly behaviour and ignorance.

---

[41] Greenham, *Workes*, 178–81, at p. 178; Dod and Cleaver, *Plaine and Familiar Exposition*, 82, cf 203; Nichols, *Plea of the Innocent*, 217 [*sic*].

[42] As studied, for example, by Keith Wrightson and David Levine, *Poverty and Piety in an English Village: Terling 1525–1700*, New York 1979, 111ff., 157ff.; Patrick Collinson, 'Cranbrook and the Fletchers: popular and unpopular religion in the Kentish Weald', in *Godly People*, 399–428, esp. p. 407; Clark, *English Provincial Society*, 149, 156–7; Martin Ingram, 'Religion, communities and moral discipline in late sixteenth and early seventeenth century England: case studies', in Kaspar von Greyerz (ed.), *Religion and Society in Early Modern Europe 1500–1800*, London 1984, 177–93; and more comprehensively in his *Church Courts, Sex and Marriage*. Cf Margaret Spufford, 'Puritanism and social control?', in Anthony Fletcher and John Stevenson (eds), *Order and Disorder in Early Modern England*, Cambridge 1985, 41–57. These developments are more broadly sketched in Burke, *Popular Culture in Early Modern Europe*, esp. ch. viii.

[43] The phrase was Thomas Cartwright's, disputing the point with Whitgift at the time of the Admonition controversy in the 1570s: Whitgift, *Works*, i. 382–6; iii. 101–4, at p. 104. Cf Frere and Douglas, *Puritan Manifestoes*, 13–14, 121, 135; Lake, *Anglicans and Puritans?*, 34–5; Hooker, *Works*, ii. 93, 96. Rejection for these reasons was orthodox practice enjoined by the Injunctions of 1559, the rubrics of the Book of Common Prayer, and numerous Elizabethan visitation articles, although it was perhaps poorly enforced except by puritan vicars. See for example, Hughes and Larkin, *Tudor Royal Proclamations*, ii. 123; Clay, *Liturgical Services*, 180, 190; for representative exhortations in visitation articles, see Cardwell, *Documentary Annals*, i. 402; Kennedy, *Elizabethan Episcopal Administration*, iii. 163.

Such attempts to sift the Protestant wheat from the 'popish' chaff, to convert village churches into the meeting-houses of exclusive gathered sects, give some solidity to the shadowy and insubstantial identity of the Elizabethan church papist.[44]

Inversely, we need to scrutinise those who openly expressed and actively manifested their indignation against interfering and officious assaults on the comfortable values of 'good neighbourhood' carried out by 'busy controllers'; their resentment of 'prattling' preachers who 'meddled' with arcane matters like predestination and fulminated furiously against 'popery'; and their distaste for the introspective, yet exhibitionist religiosity observed inside the ghetto of the 'godly'. Equally to the fore in future research should be Christopher Haigh's 'parish Anglicans' and Judith Maltby's 'Prayer Book Protestants' – the lay people who struggled to compel reluctant ministers to supply the restricted ceremonial and ritual prescribed in 1559, and whose initiatives for liturgical conformity represented an enthusiastic defence of the 'imperfect' Established Church.[45] For it was 'Papistes & other people not well affected to religion and godlines' who were prone to 'pick quarrels' over the surplice and superstitious solemnities, 'to find holes in the Ministers coates', and devise means of molesting them through the authorities. Or so it seemed to the beleaguered godly. 'They which wolde have service sayde accordinge to the booke of common prayer are papists and atheists', was the telling retort of the nonconforming clergyman at Flixton, Suffolk, around 1590.[46]

But perhaps most particularly we must focus on those who vented their anger and animosity at the level of language – on the inhabitants of communities all over late Tudor and early Stuart England who traduced their vicars, churchwardens and fellow parishioners as 'no Protestants but pratlingstants', 'trim mates', 'saints and scripture men', 'pickthankly knaves', 'precise fooles', and above all 'puritans'. From the vantage point of their opponents, these were 'papists' – more literally 'church papists'.

Indeed, nicknames, derogatory epithets like 'papist' and 'puritan', are indices not so much of popery and puritanism, as of anti-popery and anti-puritanism. As Patrick Collinson has observed, it was in 'the context of confrontation' that such stigmas acquired meaning, substance and historical importance. 'There is little point in constructing elaborate statements defining what, in ontological terms, Puritanism' – or for that matter Popery – 'was and

---

[44] Cited in Collinson, *The Elizabethan Puritan Movement*, 349 and Emmison, *Morals and the Church courts*, 105. For other typical examples, see ibid. 103–6, 109–10.

[45] For some of these themes, see Haigh, 'Puritan evangelism', passim; idem. 'The Church of England, the Catholics and the people', esp. pp. 205ff.; Maltby, 'Approaches to the Study of Religious Conformity', esp. pp. 43–50; Richardson, *Puritanism in North-west England*, 161ff.; Margaret Spufford, 'Can we count the "godly" and the "conformable" in the seventeenth century?', *JEH* xxxvi (1985), 428–38. On lay pressure for liturgical conformity, see W. J. Sheils, *The Puritans in the Diocese of Peterborough 1558–1610* (Northamptonshire Record Society xxx, 1979), 43; Purvis, *Tudor Parish Documents*, 158; *VCH Essex*, ii, ed. William Page and J. Horace Round, London 1907, 42ff.. For only a handful of examples of opposition to preaching, evangelising and 'preciseness' in morals, see Emmison, *Morals and the Church courts*, 66, 116–17; Purvis, *Tudor Parish Documents*, 77, 137.

[46] Nichols, *Plea of the Innocent*, 7; Maltby, 'Approaches to the Study of Religious Conformity', 48. Cf Raines, 'A description of the . . . state of Lancaster', 12.

what it was not, when it was not a thing definable in itself but only one half of a stressful relationship.'[47] Labelling and counter labelling arise out of a dialectic and dynamic which is of personal and parochial, rather than general or global significance. The semantic 'sense' of these words is both relative to and of fleeting relevance in the linguistic and cultural circumstances in which they are employed. 'Dost thou call me a papist? If I be a papist, thou be a puritan.' Such was the swift and scathing riposte of Edwin Sandys, archbishop of York to his dean, Matthew Hutton, in an ecclesiastical controversy in Durham in 1578.[48] The estrangement and tension their polemical interplay reflected and aggravated seems of far more consequence than the dubious theological or ideological accuracy of their reciprocal accusations. Equally revealing is the witty word-play executed in the title and the text of Timothy Rogers's 1621 tract, *The Roman-Catharist: Or, The Papist is a Puritane*. This was no sophistical stroke intended to tar both right and left of the religious centre with the same 'schismatic' brush, but instead a brilliant parry by the 'precise' against their 'popish' persecutors – a triumphant turning of the tables. Yet, pressed into service by another author on another occasion, it might have been.[49]

It is with a similar sensitivity to the subjectivity of such intense situations that we must approach the collisions and conflicts perceived and played out in these confrontational terms within contemporary communities. The polarities implied by puritan ministers and unsympathetic parishioners who hurled humiliating appellations at each other in the late Elizabethan period can hardly be given complete credence outside the contexts that engendered them. The organised resistance George Gifford and his partisans encountered when they attempted to establish Calvinist discipline in Maldon in the 1580s, for example, was attributed to 'a multitude of papists, heretics, and other enemies to God and her Royal Majesty'.[50] But their antagonists probably had little time or tolerance for the Bishop of Rome and his Church and minimal affinity with the adherents of radical heterodox sects. The same is true of those who manouvered against John Elliston in Preston Capes, Northamptonshire, in 1584–5, following his endeavours to institute adult catechising and to publicly reprove 'superstition and wicked conversation'. After parish elites reacted by 'molesting' the vicar in the archidiaconal court for blatantly ignoring the rubrics of the Book of Common Prayer, he defensively branded them as 'blasphemers of Gods name, profaners of the Saboath' and 'vehemently suspected of popery, whereof they have shewed manifest tokens'.[51] In Hatfield Peverell, Essex, there was likewise 'great hurle burle in the church' when Thomas Carew's pastoral practice – particularly his custom of examining and debarring intended communicants – affronted a sizeable sector of his flock. To Carew's dismay, the bishop of London, John Aylmer, sided with his 'popish'

---

[47] Collinson, *Birthpangs*, 143. See also his 'A Comment: concerning the name Puritan', 486–8; his review article 'Fundamental objections', *Times Literary Supplement* (17–23 Feb. 1989), 156; and his *The Puritan Character*, esp. p. 19. Cf Lake, *Moderate Puritans*, 10ff.

[48] Quoted in Peter Lake, 'Matthew Hutton – a Puritan bishop?', *History* lxiv (1979), 189.

[49] Rogers, *The Roman-Catharist*, cf Nichols, *Plea of the Innocent*, 1.

[50] Emmison, *Disorder*, 52ff.; Hunt, *The Puritan Moment*, 153; Haigh, 'The Church of England, the Catholics and the people', 214; Edwards, *English History from Essex Sources*, 8.

[51] Peel, *Seconde Parte of a Register*, i. 291–6, at p. 291.

adversaries, dismissing those who appealed against his suspension for nonconformity with 'reprochefull names' like 'precitians', 'puritans', 'fooles' and 'knaves'.[52]

Barnstaple in Devon was also 'devided and distracted into sundrie opinions and strange conceits' in 1585, when its curate, John Farmer clashed with the town's puritan preacher, Eusebius Paget, who had contrived to thwart lay requests for additional celebrations of the eucharist – requests that seemed to savour of 'Romish' sacramentalism. Bewildered and aggrieved at being indiscriminately 'counted papists and raisers of discord', Farmer and his supporters exacted revenge by producing what was no doubt an equally unreliable list of Paget's unorthodox and seditious teachings.[53]

The politics of religious identity was no less a politics of language and labelling in Kingston-upon-Thames, Surrey, where John Udall and the godly crossed swords with 'certaine of the parishe' a year later. If any refused to join with 'he and his faction', alleged the anti-puritans, 'they will not cease to slander him in moste spitefull and ungodly manner, reporteinge him ether to be a papiste, an Atheiste, of the familie of love, or one that hath no religion, or raise some evill slander againste him'. The ill-used, however, retaliated by adopting the same strategy, presenting to diocesan authorities an extended indictment of Udall's innovatory practices and insubordinate conduct.[54] Verbal brawls were growing into and out of ideological brawls in Stanford le Hope, Essex, in 1591 too. The invective of rivalling clerics of 'popish' and 'puritan' leanings who defamed each other from the pulpit as 'dumb dog' and 'prating jack', infected and split the congregation itself. Its members 'multiplied words, one against another', violent speeches that escalated into little short of armed battle in the churchyard.[55]

Of particular pertinence is Joseph Minge's 'just defence' and 'true answer' to the 'slanderous libel' that he had 'brought Ashford from being the quietest towne of Kent to be at deadly hatred and bitter division'. This was, he protested in 1584, solely because of his zeal against 'popery' and its remnants – his labours 'to teach, to admonish, to exhort, and upon occasion given to reprehend temporising papists, which to save all whole will come to Church, but so place themselves and so order the matter that thei will neither see nor heare the mynister, nor pray with the congregation'.[56]

In another district where that 'constreyned union of Papists & of Protestants' within the Church of England was in danger of snapping altogether, Lancashire, William Harrison rounded on those who railed against God's orators, resisted their evangelising efforts, and incessantly bothered and beseiged the godly. They were no more than malicious mobs, 'inhumane bands' of 'Popish Recusants, Church Papists, prophane Atheists, and carnall Protestants which swarmed together like Hornets in those parts'.[57] Events in late Tudor Rye were equally symptomatic of the sophistication with

---

[52] Ibid. ii. 28ff., at pp. 30, 32.
[53] Ibid. i. 286–91, at pp. 290, 291.
[54] Ibid. ii. 39ff., at pp. 41, 44.
[55] Emmison, *Disorder*, 189ff., at p. 190. See also Hunt, *The Puritan Moment*, 147.
[56] Peel, *Seconde Parte of a Register*, i. 238–9.
[57] Harrison, *Brief Discourse*, 5.

which religious terminology was utilised as a tool and a weapon in local quarrels and even secular disputes. Friction between the town's progressive puritan faction and its rather less progressive vicar, Roger Smyth, took the form of a campaign by key members of the corporation to discredit and discharge the unfortunate cleric on the grounds of crypto-Catholicism. But their case for his 'popish' propensities, which rested on the discovery of a crucifix in a letter to his father-in-law in London, was flimsy and flawed, for Smyth had only the remotest recusant or non-recusant Catholic connections.[58]

Religious nicknaming, reflected Josias Nichols in 1602, had its origins in the turmoil of the mid-sixteenth century. It was the teaching and preaching of the Gospel that had stirred up and destabilised early modern society, and it was the rash and widespread resort to 'reproachful termes' that gave sharpest witness to the revolutionary effects of Protestant proselytism.[59] The author of a homily composed at the outset of Edward VI's reign in 1547 had also grumbled that 'words of Contention . . . be now almost in every mans mouth'. Routinely reissued after 1559, its insistence that Reformation strife and dissension was endemic was apparently no less appropriate generations later.[60] Language, apparently, was not merely contributing to the survival of antagonisms but consolidating them. Does the advent of the epithet 'church papist' in the 1580s, then, signal an environment in which religious rifts were widening and intensifying? And were these wars of words triggering what Patrick Collinson has suggestively described as Elizabethan and early Stuart 'street wars of religion'?[61] While such interchanges may ultimately tell us relatively little about religious realities, they at least reveal the looseness and laxity with which labels like 'papist' and 'puritan' were often applied.

To the Jesuit Robert Southwell's chagrin, 'papist' was 'a vantage for everie one, that either oweth them monie, or offereth them injurie, that they can neyther claime their right, nor right theyr wronges'. It was an equally sore point with Josias Nichols that the best method of making an honest man ignominious was 'to entitle him, whom thou wouldest disgrace with the name of a Puritane' – 'a shrewde devise' as a petitioner to the Privy Council acknowledged in 1580. 'We charge the prelatical clergy with Popery to make them odious though we know they are guilty of no such thing': such was one of the jurist John Selden's off-the-cuff remarks preserved in *Table-Talk*.[62] None were impartial reporters, yet beneath their confessional prejudices they were commenting on the adaptability and elasticity of the vocabulary of religious abuse.

---

[58] Graham Mayhew, *Tudor Rye* (Falmer Centre for Continuing Education Occasional Papers xxvii, 1987), 79, 134; HMC, *Thirteenth Report, Appendix, Part IV* (Rye and Hereford Corporations MSS), London 1892, 120–2.

[59] Nichols, *Plea of the Innocent*, 6.

[60] 'A Sermon against contention and brawling', *Certaine Sermons or Homilies*, 90.

[61] Collinson, *Birthpangs*, 127–55. See also Clancy, 'Papist – Protestant – Puritan', 248; and Underdown, *Rebel, Riot and Rebellion*, 142, where he comments on the use of 'cavalier' and 'roundhead' during the Civil War.

[62] Southwell, *Epistle of Comfort*, 77; Nichols, *Plea of the Innocent*, 35 [sic]; *A parte of a register, contayninge sundrie memorable matters*, Middelburg [1593?], 130; John Selden, *Table-Talk: Being the Discourses of John Selden Esq*, London 1689, 43.

'Papist', therefore, was as protean and pliable a term as historians have come to consider the name 'puritan'. It was one whose connotations varied according to the biases and beliefs of those who availed themselves of it. Indeed, the deviating definitions of 'popery' developing as the Tudor period gave way to the Stuart age index divergent tendencies and separating strands within Calvinism itself. As Conrad Russell has recently remarked, we need to differentiate between men and women who displayed a merely cordial and conventional dislike of Catholicism and those who demonstrated a virulent and vicious hatred of it – between individuals who interpreted 'popery' in a limited, even legalistic sense as involving actual complicity and communion with Rome, and those for whom it was a far more fluid and frightening phenomenon.[63] The Arminian and proto-Arminian elements inside the early seventeenth-century Church were apt to make cautious and careful use of the word 'papist' by comparison with clergy and lay people who bandied it about brashly and exploited it as a blanket term of blame – and whom anti-Calvinists on the rise were redefining as 'puritans'. The 'popery' existing in the eyes of these Protestant beholders was increasingly less an external menace flowing from the English Counter Reformation and Catholic powers abroad, than an internal, domestic disease that had infected – or re-infected – the ecclesiastical establishment, a cancer eating the core of Church and state. It was an adjustment in anxieties parallel to that implict in the shifting focus of apocalyptic typology which Christopher Hill first traced twenty years ago: the radicalisation and politicisation of the identification of AntiChrist as it transferred from pope to prelates to the prince himself.[64]

The meaning of 'church papist' in this period, moreover, was as mutable as that of its root word: as a concept, church papistry was as plastic as 'popery' itself. It too came to be employed by particular sections of society less literally and more liberally – in a manner indicative of accumulating disquiet about the changing character of the Church of England and the modifying theological temper of its hierarchy. Its suitability for designating and denigrating self-conscious conformist Catholicism and the residually 'romish' religion of the poor was gradually overtaken by its serviceability as a synonym for the 'backsliding' bent of the Laudian and pre-Laudian Church. As a notion and a nickname, 'church papist' registers a partial alteration in puritan preoccupations, from unease about 'cloaked papists' to unease about a new 'cloaked papistry', from dissatisfaction with a lukewarm laity to outrage about a lukewarm institution.

Just such a shift is evident, for example, in the case of Robert Abbot, vicar of Cranbrook, Kent, between 1616 and 1643, who acquired a reputation for nurturing a pope in his belly. When Arthur Dent used this arresting analogy in 1601, he was alluding to the base and blind appetites underlying popular religion, the 'carnal' Protestantism of the people. Those who applied it to Abbot, however, were making disapproving reference to his unreserved respect for the Established Church in a diocese

---

[63] Russell, *The Causes of the English Civil War*, 75–82.
[64] Hill, *Antichrist*.

by then under the governance of William Laud – a Church Abbot revered as his 'deare mother'.[65]

This kind of criticism was implicit in the fiery sermon Sampson Price, preacher to the city of Oxford, delivered at Paul's Cross in October 1613, on those caustic verses from Revelation iii. 15–16: 'I know thy workes, that thou art neither cold nor hot, I would thou wert cold or hot. So then because thou art lukewarme, and neither cold nor hot, I wil spew thee out of my mouth.' In choosing 'so thundering a Text', Price intended to rock his metropolitan audience from its merely complacent Christianity, to rouse England from the spiritual slumber and 'drowsinesse' that would, he prophesied, prove its downfall.[66] He took this cue to voice his contempt and his condemnation of the hypocritical piety of 'Protestants in shew, and Papists in deed': such conforming Catholics were the very 'Gangrens of this Land'. Their conduct called in turn for castigation of the secular priests who, seemingly by common knowledge and in public view, casuistically condoned it, and of a pope who diabolically dispensed 'his followers to worship God, with their lippes, and dissemble their religion'.[67] Christ's blistering caveat to the Church of Laodicea likewise afforded Price an opportunity to denounce the 'blas-phemous Atheist[s]' and 'doubtfull Neuter[s]' of his age – those doctrinally confused contemporaries who, 'like Mermayds', were 'halfe Flesh halfe Fish'. These were the sins, he menaced, which 'moveth the Highest to great wrath' and which would precipitate a divinely initiated disaster.[68] Yet Price's sermon did more than rehearse familiar Elizabethan themes. It was also the occasion for reproof of interest groups that aimed to advance the 'Machiavillian policie' of toleration and scandalously sought to 'reconcile the Protestant and Papist and have both live together' – reproof, perhaps, of an emerging party of churchmen inclined to take a more moderate line and to steer a middle course between Rome and Geneva.[69]

When Thomas Sutton, lecturer at St Mary Overy, Southwark, preached on the same politically sensitive passage at the same London location eighteen months later, there was, however, rather less ambiguity. Not only did Sutton launch into a scathing attack on those 'scabs, and ulcers of Church and State . . . our Church Papist, who will serve both God and Rimmon, and our nullifidian Protestant, that can serve both God and Mammon', but he proceeded to present a damning diagnosis of 'the maladie that maketh the visage of our Church so wan'. Another strand of church papistry, of quasi-Catholicism, he insisted, cried to heaven for quicker vengeance:

> yee mediators that would gladly conclude a marriage between the Church of God & a Romish synagogue, and patch a religion . . . of good and evill; you that would make an attonement betweene the religion of Protestant & Papist *sacra prophanis*, that would have our gold & their drosse to be stamped

[65] Collinson, 'Cranbrook and the Fletchers', 427–8. I am grateful to Professor Collinson for reminding me of this reference.
[66] Sampson Price, *Londons Warning by Laodicea's Luke-Warmnesse*, London 1613, 4, 7.
[67] Ibid. 26, 54, 22–3.
[68] Ibid. 14, 23, 40, 38.
[69] Ibid. 24.

together, our golden head to stand upon their feet of clay, and Gods eternall truth to be yoaked with foolish and false traditions.[70]

In exposing it, Sutton hoped 'to stop the stentorious mouths, and to pare the Satyricall and bloudy pencils of some men, who in all their learning can finde none that either disquiets or endangers the Church but the strict Precision, who cannot swallow downe some of our Church Ceremonies'. He strove to curb the anti-puritan polemic and policies of controversialists and high ranking clergy who professed to have purged and swept the Church of all her 'imposthumes', and yet ignored and indulged, if not encouraged, the insidious progess of a movement to recatholicise a predominantly Calvinist institution. Unless zealous action was taken to keep this 'Romish fire from our English tinder', 'wee [may] feare that one day wee shall feele Gods hand upon us and see destruction looking in at our gates, and desolation looking in at our windowes, and finde nothing but emptinesse in our Churches, see nothing but Romish spiders weaving their cobwebs in our Pulpit' – 'Italian cobwebs [that] would strangle our English soules'. If Protestantism continued to be thus diluted and debased, nothing more could be expected than that ultimate providential judgement, the removal of God's candlestick, the Gospel.[71]

By 1622 it was not merely tactless but treacherous to allude to this chilling apocalyptic text. Indeed, it proved little short of professional suicide for Richard Sheldon, the Jesuit whose convincing conversion from Catholicism a decade earlier had allowed him to rise rapidly to the rank of royal chaplain. Sheldon received a severe reprimand for the sermon 'Laying open the Beast, and his Marks' which he delivered at the Cross on 1 September of that year: he never fully regained the King's patronage and favour. In the context of the negotiations for the Spanish match, a bold and belligerent line against 'Babylon' had become a profound political embarrassment, a disastrous diplomatic gaffe. Sheldon's unrestrained invective against AntiChrist could only clash with the apparently pro-Catholic policies and priorities of the Crown. Not least controversial was his complaint that papists in consequence were gaining confidence and upgrading the degree of their conscientious objection – 'the covert chaffe of Communion-Recusants, doe now shew it selfe to be Church-Recusants'.[72]

Perhaps even more impertinent and imprudent, however, was the extent to which Sheldon turned his aggressive anti-popery inwards, deliberately directing it against the crypto-Catholic fifth column he perceived to be taking over the Church of England from within. He had the temerity to attack 'our Luke-warm Laodiceanizers', such as 'secretly mutter and mussitate, Rome and the Reformed churches agree in the substance of Religion, that there is no fundamental difference betwixt them and us'. Adopting an insupportable ecumenical stance, these 'neutralizers' and 'Godlesse Adiaphorisers' dared to dogmatise on Catholicism's status as a true church and the possibility of salvation inside her. They dared to 'dreame of Christian union, and brotherly

---

[70] Thomas Sutton, *Englands First and Second Summons*, London 1616, 223–4, 242, 216 respectively.
[71] Ibid. 232–5.
[72] Richard Sheldon, *A Sermon Preached at Paules Crosse*, London 1625, 49. For biographical details, see *DNB s.v.* Sheldon.

consociation' between 'Sion and Babylon . . . Egypt, and Hierusalem . . . Christ, and Antichrist . . . light, and darknesse . . . God, and Beliall'.[73] Rome's utter ruin was inevitable, Sheldon assured his auditors, but they should shun the novelties and subtleties of those who sought thereby to inject a creeping popish poison into English Protestantism.[74] The Laodicean analogy, then, had become a liability: the implicit charge of church papistry carried connotations that were outrageous and offensive to the ears of an ecclesiastical establishment in which anti-Calvinism was ever more ascendant.

'Church Papist, what meane ye by that?', George Gifford's character had innocently enquired in 1582. By the second decade of the seventeenth century the term rang of more than non-recusant Catholicism. It had acquired a distinctly and dangerously anti-Arminian edge.

To approach 'church papists' as if it were possible to engage in an arithmetical exercise in confessional number-crunching is thus to misunderstand the question at issue, to misjudge profoundly the problem posed. For, residing in large part in the minds and discourses of critical contemporaries, 'church papists' (no less than those nicknamed 'puritans') defy statistical analysis. To investigate them is instead to explore the clerical construction of a category of 'unchristian' attitudes and acts, of deviant Catholicism and disappointingly passive profession of the reformed Gospel; it is to explore how priests and pastors struggled to establish what constituted 'religious' consciousness and conduct, to replace the limp lukewarmness of conventional piety with a 'hotter sort' of Protestantism and Popery. It involves tracing the transmutations of an ideological anxiety at the level of the intellectual elite, and scrutinising the multiple ways in which ordinary individuals confronted the task of preserving and proving their Catholic identity. Conformity presented a crucial challenge to the Counter Reformation hierarchy. How could Catholicism's integrity and impeccability as the 'true religion' be upheld if a programme of casuistical concession was openly known to be in operation; how could compromise be allowed if an abolished Church was to be prevented from dwindling into a subjugated sect? Negotiating these contradictions, satisfactorily reconciling the disparity between recusancy theory and 'schismatic' practice, could be accomplished only by sacrificing the respectability of the church papist.

And just as they were pawns in the ecclesiastical politics of the post-Reformation period, so too have they been made puppets in the politics of confessional historiography. Forced out of the picture by the pretentiously pious, discarded in favour of those conspicuous, strident minorities which grabbed the religious limelight, church papists challenge dominant historical models none the less.

Yet, since their presence is perceived chiefly through a haze of contemporary hostility and prejudice, is it in fact anything more than an hallucination, a figment of certain imaginations? In 1605, with a surprising degree of detachment from the circumstances in which he spoke, the statesman Robert Cecil observed: 'whosoever shall behold the papistes with puritane spectacles,

---

[73] Sheldon, *A Sermon Preached at Paules Crosse*, 49, 30 [*sic*], 52.
[74] Ibid. 49.

or the puritan with papistical, shal see no other certeynte, than the multiplication of false images'.[75] This cluster of overlapping illusions, this muddle of apprehensions and misapprehensions, may be deceptive and transitory, but it still has much to divulge about the cultural and religious climate of early modern England.

[75] Strype, *Annals*, IV. 545.

Bibliography

Full bibliographical references to secondary sources will be found at their first citation in the footnotes.

Manuscript Sources

British Library, London:
> MS Additional 39830: 'Against going to Churche' (1580), Tresham Papers, vol. iii, Historical and Theological Collections 1455–1605
> MS Cotton Julius F. VI, fos 167r–9r: 'A copye of the devise for alteratione of religione at the First yeare of Q. Elizabethe' (1558)
> MS Harley 1221: Miscellaneous Tracts and Papers

Public Record Office, Chancery Lane, London:
> State Papers Domestic:
> 121/136/15: 'A briefe advertisement howe to Answere unto the Statute for not coming to Church both in Law and Conscience' (1580)
> 12/144/19: 'A discourse delivered to Mr. Sheldon to persuade him to conform. Arguments to prove it lawful for a Roman Catholic to attend the Protestant service' (1580)
> 12/279/90: 'Directions [for Catholics] as to the lawfull manner of answering questions of going to Church' (1601)

St Mary's College, Oscott, Sutton Coldfield:
> MS E. 5. 16: I. G., 'An answere to a comfortable advertisement, with it addition written of late to afflicted catholykes concerning goinge to churche with protestantes' (c. 1593)

Primary Printed Sources

Abbot, George, *The Reasons which Doctour Hill hath brought, for the upholding of Papistry, which is falselie termed the Catholike Religion; Unmasked, and shewed to be very weake, and upon examination most insufficient for that purpose*, Oxford 1604 (*STC* 37)

Acts of the Privy Council of England, 32 vols, ed. John Roche Dasent, London 1890–1907

Ainsworth, Henry, *Counterpoyson. Considerations touching the points in difference between the godly Ministers & people of the Church of England, and the seduced brethren of the Separation*, [Amsterdam?] 1608 (*STC* 234)

Allen, William, *An Apologie and True Declaration of the institution and endeavours of the two English Colleges, the one in Rome, the other now resident in Rhemes: against certaine sinister informations given up against the same*, Henault [Rheims] 1581   (*STC* 369, *A&R* 6, *ERL* 67)

—— *A true report of the late apprehension and imprisonment of John Nicols Minister, at Roan, and his confession and answers made in the time of his durance there. Whereunto is added the satisfaction of certaine, that of feare or frailtie have lately fallen in England*, Rheims 1583   (*STC* 18537, *A&R* 12, *ERL* 63)

—— *A True, Sincere, and Modest Defence of English Catholics*, ed. R. M. Kingdon, Ithaca, NY 1965 (first publ. 1584)

An answer to a certain godly mannes lettres, desiring his frendes judgement, whether it be laufull for a christian man to be present at the popishe Masse and other supersticious churche service, [Strassburg] 1557   (*STC* 658)

Babington, Gervase, *A Very Fruitful Exposition of the Commandements by way of Questions and Answers for greater plainnesse: Togither with an application of every one to the soule and conscience of man, profitable for all, and especially for them that (being not otherwise furnished) are yet desirous both to see themselves, and to deliver to others some larger speech of every point that is but briefly named in the shorter Catechismes*, London 1596 (first publ. 1583)   (*STC* 1098)

Bacon, Francis, *Essays*, ed. and intro. Michael J. Hawkins, London 1972

Bateman, Stephen, *A christall glasse of Christian reformation, wherein the godly maye beholde the coloured abuses used in this our present tyme*, London 1569   (*STC* 1581)

Bateson, Mary (ed.), 'A collection of original letters from the bishops to the Privy Council 1564 (with returns of J.P.s and others within their respective dioceses, classified according to their religious convictions)', *Camden Miscellany IX* (Camden Society, n.s. liii, 1895)

B[axter], J[ohn], *A Toile for Two-Legged Foxes: Wherein their noisome properties; their hunting and unkenelling, with the duties of the principall hunters and guardians of the spirituall vineyard is livelie discovered, for the comfort of all her Highnes trustie and true-hearted subjects, and their encouragement against all Popish practices*, London 1600   (*STC* 1596)

Baxter, Richard, *A Key for Catholicks, To open the Jugling of the Jesuits, and satisfie all that are but truly willing to understand, whether the Cause of the Roman or Reformed Churches be of God; and to leave the Reader utterly unexcusable that after this will be a Papist*, London 1659

Bedel, William, *An Examination of Certaine Motives to Recusansie*, Cambridge 1628   (*STC* 1786)

Bell, Thomas, *The Anatomie of Popish Tyrannie: Wherein is conteyned a plaine declaration and Christian censure of all the principall parts, of the Libels, Letters, Edictes, Pamphlets, and Bookes, lately published by the Secular priests and English hispanized Jesuites, with their Jesuited Arch-priest; both pleasant and profitable, to all well affected readers*, London 1603   (*STC* 1814)

—— *The Downefall of Poperie: Proposed by way of a new challenge to all English Jesuits and Jesuited or Italianized papists: daring them all jointly, and every one of them severally, to make answere thereunto if they can, or have any truth on their side; knowing for a truth that otherwise all the world will crie with open mouths, Fie upon them, and their patched hotch-potch religion*, London 1604   (*STC* 1818)

—— *The Hunting of the Romish Foxe. Presented to the popes holines, with the kisse of his disholy foote, as an odoriferous & redolent posie fit for his gravitie, so often as he walketh right stately, in his goodly Pallace Bel-vidêre*, London 1598 (*STC* 1823)

—— *The survey of Popery Wherein the reader may cleerely behold, not onely the originall and daily increments of Papistrie, with an evident Confutation of the same; but also a succinct and profitable enarration of the state of Gods Church from Adam untill Christs ascension*, London 1596 (*STC* 1829)

—— *Thomas Bels Motives: concerning Romish Faith and Religion*, Cambridge 1593 (*STC* 1830)

Bilson, Thomas, *The True Difference betweene Christian Subjection and Unchristian Rebellion: Wherein the princes lawfull power to commaund for trueth, and indeprivable right to beare the sword are defended against the Popes censures and the Jesuites sophismes uttered in their Apologie and Defence of English Catholikes*, Oxford 1585 (*STC* 3071)

Bisse, James, *Two Sermons preached, the one at Paules Crosse the eight of Januarie 1580. The other, at Christes Churche in London the same day in the afternoone*, London 1581 (*STC* 3099)

Bowler, H. (ed.), *Recusant Roll No. 2 (1593–4)* (Catholic Record Society lvii, 1965)

—— *Recusant Roll No. 3 (1594–5) and Recusant Roll No. 4 (1595–6)* (Catholic Record Society lxi, 1969)

Bradford, John, *The Hurte of Hering Masse. Set forth by the faithfull servant of god & constant Marter of Christ. Johnn Bradforth when he was Prisoner in the Tower of London*, London [1561?] (*STC* 3494)

—— *The Writings of John Bradford*, ed. Aubrey Townsend (Parker Society, 1848–53)

Breton, Nicholas, *A Merrie Dialogue betwixt the taker and Mistaker*, London 1603 (*STC* 3667)

A Briefe Censure upon the Puritane Pamphlet: Entituled, (Humble Motyves, for association to maintayne Religion established.), [English secret press] 1603 (*STC* 3519, *A&R* 141, *ERL* 47)

Brightman, Thomas, *A Revelation of the Revelation, that is, the Revelation of St. John opened clearly with a logicall Resolution and Exposition*, Amsterdam 1615 (*STC* 3755)

Bristow, Richard, *A Briefe Treatise of diverse plaine and sure wayes to finde out the truthe in this doubtful and dangerous time of Heresie: conteyning sundry worthy Motives unto the Catholike faith, or Considerations to move a man to beleve the Catholikes, and not the Heretikes*, Antwerp 1574 (*STC* 3799, *A&R* 146, *ERL* 209)

—— *Demaundes to be Proponed of Catholiques to the Heretikes Taken partely out of his late Englishe boke of Motives to the Catholike faithe, partely out of his intended Latin boke of the same matter*, Antwerp 1576 (*STC* 3801, *A&R* 148, *ERL* 53)

Broughton, Richard, *The First Part of Protestants Proofes, for Catholikes Religion and Recusancy (Taken only from the writings, of such Protestant Doctors and Divines, as have beene published in the raigne of his Majesty over this Kingdome)*, [English secret press] 1607 (*STC* 20448, *A&R* 160, *ERL* 100)

—— *Protestants Demonstrations, for Catholiks Recusance*, Douai 1615 (*STC* 20450, *A&R* 168, *ERL* 155)

Bruce, John (ed.), *The Diary of John Manningham, of the Middle Temple, and of*

Bradbourne, Kent, Barrister at Law 1602–1603 (Camden Society, o.s. xcix, 1868)

Buckland, Ralph, *An Embassage from Heaven. Wherein Our Lord and Saviour Christ Jesus giveth to understand, his just indignation against al such, as being Catholikely minded, dare yeelde their presence to the rites and publike praier, of the malignant Church*, [English secret press 1611]   (*STC* 4007, *A&R* 180, *ERL* 298)

Bullinger, Henry, *Two Epystles One of Henry Bullynger, wyth the consent of all the lernyd men of the Church of Tigury: another of Jhon Calvyn, cheffe Preacher of the Church of Geneve: whether it be lawfull for a Chrysten man to communycate or be pertaker of the Masse of the Papystes, wythout offendyng God and hys neyboure, or not*, [Antwerp 1544?]   (*STC* 4079.5)

Bunny, Edmund, *A Booke of Christian exercise, appertaining to Resolution, that is shewing how that we should resolv our selvs to becom Christians indeed: by R. P., Perused, and accompanied now with a Treatise tending to Pacification*, London 1584   (*STC* 19355)

Bunny, Francis, *Truth and Falsehood; Or, A Comparison betweene the Truth now taught in England, and the Doctrine of the Romish Church, with a briefe Confutation of that Popish doctrine. Hereunto is added an Answere to such reasons as the popish Recusants alledge, why they will not come to our Churches*, London 1595   (*STC* 4102)

Calendar of Letters and State Papers Relating to English Affairs, Preserved Principally in the Archives of Simancas, 4 vols, ed. Martin A. S. Hume, London 1892–9

Calendar of State Papers, Domestic Series, of the Reigns of Edward VI, Mary, Elizabeth I and James I, 12 vols, ed. R. Lemon and M. A. E. Green, London 1856–72

Calthorp, M. M. C. (ed.), *Recusant Roll No. I, 1592–3. Exchequer Lord Treasurer's Remembrancer Pipe Office Series* (Catholic Record Society xviii, 1916)

Calvin, Jean, *De vitandis superstitionibus, quae cum sincera fidei confessione pugnant, Libellus Johannis Calvini. Eiusdem excusatio, ad pseudonicodemus. Philippi Melancthonis, Martini Buceri, Petri Martyris Responsa de eadem re. Calvini ultimum responsum, cum appendicibus*, Geneva 1549

—— *The Mynde of the Godly and excellent lerned man M. Jhon Calvyne, what a Faithfull man, whiche is instructe in the Worde of God, ought to do, dwellinge amongest the Papistes*, [Ipswich] 1548   (*STC* 4435)

—— *A Sermon of the Famous and godly learned man, Master John Calvine, Chiefe minister and Pastour of Christes Church at Geneva, conteining an exhortation to suffer persecution for followinge Jesus Christe*, London 1581   (*STC* 4439.5)

Canisius, St Peter, *Certayne Necessarie Principles of Religion which may be entituled, A Catechisme conteyning all the partes of the Christian and Catholique Fayth*, trans. T. I., Douai [London] 1578–9   (*STC* 4568.5, *A&R* 840, *ERL* 2)

Cardwell, Edward (ed.), *Documentary Annals of the Reformed Church of England: being a collection of injunctions, declarations, orders, articles of enquiry, &c., from the year 1546 to the year 1716*, 2 vols, Oxford 1844

—— *Synodalia: a collection of articles of religion, canons, and proceedings of convocations in the province of Canterbury from the year 1547 to the year 1717*, 2 vols, Oxford 1842

Carlson, Leland H. (ed.), *The Writings of John Greenwood 1587–1590* (Elizabethan Nonconformist Texts iv, 1962)

Cecil, William, *The Execution of Justice in England*, ed. R. M. Kingdon, Ithaca, NY 1965 (first publ. 1583)

Certaine Sermons or Homilies Appointed to be Read in Churches in the Time of Queen Elizabeth I (1547–1571). A facsimile reproduction of the edition of 1623, 2 vols in 1, intro. Mary Ellen Rickey and Thomas B. Stroup, Gainesville, Florida 1968

Chaderton, Laurence, *An Excellent and godly sermon, most needefull for this time, wherein we live in all securitie and sinne, to the great dishonour of God, and contempt of his holy word. Preached at Paules Crosse the xxvi. day of October, An. 1578*, London 1580 (*STC* 4924)

Clay, W. K. (ed.), *Liturgical Services: liturgies and occasional forms of prayer set forth in the reign of Queen Elizabeth* (Parker Society, 1847)

Coke, Edward, *The Lord Coke His Speech and Charge. With a Discoverie of the Abuses and Corruptions of Officers*, ed. R. P., London 1607 (*STC* 5492)

Cooper, Thomas, *An Admonition to the People of England: wherein are answered, not onely the slaunderous untruethes reprochfully uttered by Martin the Libeller, but also many other Crimes by some of his broode, objected generally against all Bishops, and the chiefe of the Cleargie, purposely to deface and discredite the present state of the Church*, London 1589 (*STC* 5682)

—— *Certaine Sermons wherin is contained the Defense of the Gospell nowe preached, against such Cavils and false accusations, as are objected both against the Doctrine it selfe, and the Preachers and Professors thereof, by the friendes and favourers of the Church of Rome*, London 1580 (*STC* 5685)

Cooper, Thomas, *The Cry and Revenge of Blood. Expressing the Nature and haynousnesse of wilfull Murther. Exemplified In a most lamentable History thereof, committed at Halsworth in High Suffolk, and Lately Convicted at Bury Assize, 1620*, London 1620 (*STC* 5698)

Corderoy, Jeremy, *A Warning for Worldlings, Or a comfort to the godly, and a terror to the wicked. Set forth Dialogue wise, betweene a Scholler and a Travailer*, London 1608 (*STC* 5757)

Crowley, Robert, *A Deliberate Answere made to a rash offer, which a popish Antichristian Catholique, made to a learned protestant . . . Anno Do. 1575*, London 1588 (*STC* 6084)

The Declaration of the Fathers of the Councell of Trent, concerning the going unto Churches, at such time as hereticall service is saied, or heresy preached, [London secret press 1593] (*STC* 24264, *A&R* 357, *ERL* 47)

Dent, Arthur, *The plaine Mans Path-way to heaven*, London 1610 (first publ. 1601) (*STC* 6630)

Dillingham, Francis, *A Quartron of Reasons, composed by Doctor Hill, unquartered, and prooved a quartron of follies*, London 1603 (*STC* 6889)

The Discription, Causes and Discovery, or Symptomes of a Church Papist, or a Popish Protestant, which may stand in stead this Yeare, 1642. Which by Reason that this searching Parliament, and wonderfull Conjunction of happy Planets, hath proved so sickly and Crazy unto the Romish Constitutions, That is to be suspected that some of them will flye into Churches, for Remedy though not for Conversion, London 1642 (Thomason Tracts E143 [10])

Dod, John and Robert Cleaver, *A godly forme of householde government: for the ordering of private families*, London 1612 (first publ. 1598) (*STC* 5386)

—— *A Plaine and Familiar Exposition of the Ten Commandments With a Methodicall Short Catechisme containing brieflie all the principall grounds of Christian Religion*, London 1612 (first publ. 1604) (*STC* 6971.5)

Dove, John, *A Perswasion to the English Recusants, to Reconcile themselves to the Church of England. Written for the better satisfaction of those which be ignorant*, London 1602 (*STC* 7084)

Earle, John, *Earle's Microcosmography*, ed. Alfred S. West, Cambridge 1897 (first publ. 1628)

Edwards, A. C. (ed.), *English History from Essex Sources 1550–1750* (Essex Record Office xvii, 1952)

Elton, G. R. (ed.), *The Tudor Constitution: documents and commentary*, Cambridge 1982

Field, John, *A Caveat for Parsons Howlet, concerning his untimely flighte, and scriching in the cleare day lighte of the Gospell, necessarie for him and all the rest of that darke broode, and uncleane cage of papistes, who with their untimely bookes, seeke the discredite of the truth, and the disquiet of this Church of England*, London 1581 (*STC* 10844)

Fitzpatrick, Edward A. (ed.), *St Ignatius and the Ratio Studiorum*, New York 1933

Foley, Henry (ed.), *Records of the English Province of the Society of Jesus*, 7 vols, London 1877–84

Foxe, John, *The Acts and Monuments of John Foxe with a life of the martyrologist and vindication of the work*, 8 vols, ed. S. R. Cattley, London 1837–41

Frere, W. H. and C. E. Douglas (eds), *Puritan Manifestoes: a study of the origin of the Puritan revolt* (The Church Historical Society lxxii, 1907)

Fulke, William, *A briefe Confutation, of a Popish Discourse: Lately set forth, and presumptuously dedicated to the Queenes most excellent Majestie: by John Howlet, or some other Birde of the night, under that name. Contayning certaine Reasons, why Papistes refuse to come to Church, which Reasons are here inserted and set downe at large, with their severall answeres*, London 1581 (*STC* 11421)

—— *A Confutation of a Popishe and sclaunderous libelle, in forme of an apologie: geven out into the courte, and spread abrode in diverse other places of the Realme*, London 1571 (*STC* 11426)

—— *A Retentive to Stay Good Christians, in True Faith and religion, against the motives of Richard Bristow*, London 1580 (*STC* 11449)

[Garnet, Henry], *An Apology against the Defence of schisme. Lately written by an English Divine at Doway, for answere to a letter of a lapsed Catholicke in England to his frend: who having in the late Commission gone to the Church, defended his fall. wherin is plainely declared, and manifestly proved, the generall doctrine of the Divines, & of the Church of Christ, which hitherto hath bene taught and followed in England, concerning this pointe*, [London secret press 1593] (*STC* 711, *A&R* 353, *ERL* 167)

—— *A Treatise of Christian Renunciation . . . Whereunto is added a shorte discourse against going to Hereticall Churches with a Protestation*, [London secret press 1593] (*STC* 5189, *A&R* 357, *ERL* 47)

Garnier, Jean, *A briefe and cleare Confession of the Christian fayth. Containing an hundreth Articles, after the order of the Creede of the Apostles. Made and declared by John Gardiner*, London 1579 (*STC* 11620.7)

Gerard, John, *John Gerard: the autobiography of an Elizabethan*, trans. P. Caraman, London 1956

Gifford, George, *A Briefe discourse of certaine points of the religion, which is among the common sort of Christians, which may be termed the Countrie Divinitie. With a manifest confutation of the same, after the order of a Dialogue*, London 1598 (first publ. 1581) (*STC* 11847)

—— *A Dialogue between a Papist and a Protestant, applied to the capacitie of the unlearned*, London 1582 (*STC* 11849)

—— *Foure Sermons upon the seven chiefe vertues or principall effectes of faith, and the doctrine of election: wherein everie man may learne, whether he be Gods childe or no*, London 1582 (first publ. 1581) (*STC* 11857.5)

—— *A sermon on the parable of the sower taken out of the 13. of Matthew*, London 1582 (*STC* 11862.5)

Greenham, Richard, *The Workes of the Reverent and Faithful Servant of Jesus Christ M. Richard Greenham, Minister and Preacher of the Word of God*, London 1599 (first publ. 1598) (*STC* 12314)

H. B., *A Consolatory Letter to all the Afflicted Catholikes in England*, Rouen [London secret press] [1587–8] (*STC* 1032, *A&R* 59, *ERL* 10)

Harrison, William, *Deaths advantage little regarded, and the soules solace against sorrow. Preached in two funerall sermons at the buriall of K. Brettergh. The one by W. Harrison, the other by W. Leygh. Whereunto is annexed the life of the said gentlewoman*, London 1602 (*STC* 12866)

—— *The Difference of Hearers: An Exposition of the Parable of the sower Delivered in certaine Sermons at Hyton in Lancashire*, London 1614 (*STC* 12870)

Harrison, William, *Harrison's Description of England in Shakspere's Youth*, 2 vols, ed. F. J. Furnivall, London 1877 (first publ. 1577)

Hartley, T. E. (ed.), *Proceedings in the Parliaments of Elizabeth I, Volume I. 1558–1581*, Leicester 1981

Hicks, L. (ed.), *Letters and Memorials of Father Robert Persons, S.J.: vol. I (to 1588)* (Catholic Record Society xxxix, 1942)

Hide, Thomas, *A Consolatorie Epistle to the afflicted Catholikes*, Louvain [London] 1580 (first publ. Louvain 1579) (*STC* 13376, *A&R* 394, *ERL* 105)

Hill, [Edmund] Thomas, *A Quartron of Reasons of Catholike Religion, with as many briefe reasons of refusall*, Antwerp [English secret press] 1600 (*STC* 13470, *A&R* 400, *ERL* 98)

Historical Manuscripts Commission, *Reports*, London:
   First Report, 1874
   Twelfth Report, Appendix, Part IV (Rutland MSS), i, 1888
   Thirteenth Report, Appendix, Part I (Portland MSS), 1891
   —— *Appendix, Part IV* (Rye and Hereford Corporations MSS), 1892
   Fourteenth Report, Appendix, Part IV (Kenyon MSS), 1894
   Lord Montagu of Beaulieu, 1900
   Salisbury, Part XIX, 1965

The Holie Bible Faithfully Translated into English (Old Testament), 2 vols, Douai 1609–10 (*STC* 2207, *A&R* 107, *ERL* 265, 266)

Holmes, P. J. (ed.), *Elizabethan Casuistry* (Catholic Record Society lxvii, 1981)

Hooker, Richard, *The Works of that Learned and Judicious Divine Mr. Richard*

Hooker with an account of his life and death by Isaac Walton, 2 vols, ed. J. Keble, Oxford 1850

Hooper, John, *Later Writings of Bishop Hooper (together with his letters and other pieces)*, ed. Charles Nevinson (Parker Society, 1852)

—— *Whether Christian faith maye be kepte secret in the heart, without confession therof openly to the worlde as occasion shal serve. Also what hurt commeth by them that hath received the Gospell, to be present at Masse unto the simple and unlearned*, Rouen [London?] 1553 (*STC* 5160.3)

Hughes, P. L. and J. F. Larkin (eds), *Tudor Royal Proclamations*, 3 vols, New Haven–London 1969

Hussey, Arthur (ed.), 'Visitations of the Archdeacon of Canterbury', *Archaeologia Cantiana* xxvi (1904), 17–50

Kennedy, W. P. M. (ed.), *Elizabethan Episcopal Administration: an essay in sociology and politics*, vols ii and iii (*Visitation Articles and Injunctions 1575–1582, 1583–1603*) (Alcuin Club Collections xxvi–xxvii, 1924)

Kenny, Anthony (ed.), *The Responsa Scholarum of the English College, Rome: part One 1598–1621* (Catholic Record Society liv, 1962)

Knox, T. F. (ed.), *The First and Second Diaries of the English College Douay and an Appendix of Unpublished Documents* (Records of the English Catholics under the Penal Laws i), London 1878

—— *The Letters and Memorials of William Cardinal Allen 1532–1594* (Records of the English Catholics under the Penal Laws ii), London 1882

[Leslie, John], *A Treatise of Treasons against Q. Elizabeth, and the Croune of England, divided into two Partes: whereof, The first Parte answereth certaine Treasons pretended, that never were intended: And the second, discovereth greater Treasons committed, that are by few perceived*, [Louvain] 1572 (*STC* 7601, *A&R* 454, *ERL* 254)

Luttrell, Narcissus, *A Brief Historical Relation of State Affairs from September 1678 to April 1714*, 6 vols, Oxford 1857

McCann, J. and H. Connolly (eds), *Memorials of Father Augustine Baker and Other Documents Relating to the English Benedictines* (Catholic Record Society xxxiii, 1933)

Martin, Gregory, *A Treatise of Schisme. Shewing, that al Catholikes ought in any wise to abstaine altogether from heretical Conventicles, to witt, their prayers, sermons, &c*, Douai [English secret press] 1578 (*STC* 17508, *A&R* 535, *ERL* 117)

—— *The Love of the Soule Whereunto are annexed certaine Catholike Questions to the Protestants*, [Lancs. Birchley Hall press] 1619 (first publ. 1597) (*STC* 17506, *A&R* 530, *ERL* 363)

Matthews, J. H. (ed.). 'Records relating to Catholicism in the South Wales Marches', in *Catholic Record Society Miscellanea II* (Catholic Record Society ii, 1906), 289–304

More, St Thomas, *A dialogue of Cumfort against tribulacion . . . Now newly set foorth*, [Antwerp] 1573 (first publ. 1553) (*STC* 18082, *A&R* 549, *ERL* 25)

Morris, John (ed.), *The Troubles of Our Catholic Forefathers Related by Themselves*, 3 vols, London 1872–7

Morton, Thomas, *An Exact Discoverie of Romish Doctrine in the Case of Conspiracie and Rebellion, by pregnant observations: Collected (not without direction from our*

Superiours) out of the expresse dogmaticall principles of Popish Priests and Doctors, London 1605 (*STC* 18184)

Musculus, Wolfgang, *The Temporysour (that is to saye the observer of tyme, or he that chaungeth with the tyme.)*, [Zurich?] 1555 (*STC* 18312)

N. C., *The Pigeons Flight From Out of Noes Arke, over the floud, into the Arke againe. Resembling well, The fall of Heriticks, Scismaticks, &c. out of Holie Church, their continuance without, and returne againe*, [English secret press 1602–5] (*STC* 4291, *A&R* 188, *ERL* 352)

Nashe, Thomas, *The Workes of Thomas Nashe*, 4 vols, ed. Ronald B. McKerrow, Oxford 1966

Naunton, Robert, *Fragmenta Regalia*, [London] 1641

The New Testament of Jesus Christ Translated Faithfully into English, Rheims 1582 (*STC* 2884, *A&R* 567, *ERL* 267)

Nichols, Josias, *The Plea of the Innocent: Wherein is averred; That the Ministers & people falslie termed Puritanes, are injuriouslie slaundered for enemies or troublers of the State. Published for the common good of the Church and commonwealth of this Realme of England as a countermure Against all Sycophantising Pap[i]sts, Statising Priestes, Neutralising Atheistes, and Satanising scorners of all godlinesse, trueth and honestie*, London 1602 (*STC* 18541)

Notestein, Wallace *et al*, *Commons Debates 1621*, 7 vols, New Haven–London, 1935

A parte of a register, contayninge sundrie memorable matters, written by divers godly and learned in our time, which stande for, and desire the reformation of our Church, in Discipline and Ceremonies, accordinge to the pure worde of God, and the Lawe of our Lande, Middelburg [1593?] (*STC* 10400)

Peacham, Henry, *The Truth of our Times: Revealed out of one Mans Experience, by way of Essay*, London 1638 (*STC* 19517)

Peel, Albert (ed.), 'A Puritan survey of the Church in Staffordshire in 1604', *English Historical Review* xxvi (1911), 338–352

—— *The Seconde Parte of a Register being a calendar of manuscripts under that title intended for publication by the Puritans about 1593*, 2 vols, Cambridge 1915

—— and Leland H. Carlson (eds), *Cartwrightiana* (Elizabethan Nonconformist Texts i, 1951)

Perkins, William, *A Reformed Catholicke: Or A Declaration shewing how neere we may come to the present Church of Rome in sundrie points of Religion; and wherein we must for ever depart from them: with an Advertisement to all favourers of the Romane religion, shewing that the said religion is against the Catholike principles and grounds of the Catechisme*, London 1597 (*STC* 19735.8)

—— *William Perkins 1558–1602: English Puritanist*, ed. Thomas F. Merrill, Nieuwkoop 1966

—— *The whole treatise of the cases of conscience, distinguished into three bookes*, London 1608 (first publ. 1606) (*STC* 19670)

—— *The Work of William Perkins*, intro. and ed. I. Breward, Appleford, Berks 1970

[Persons, Robert], *A Brief Apologie, or Defence of the Catholike Ecclesiastical Hierarchie, & subordination in England, erected these later yeares by our holy Father Pope Clement the eyght: and impugned by certayne libels printed & published of late both in Latyn & English: by some unquiet persons under the name of Priests of the Seminaries*, [Antwerp 1601]   (*STC* 19391.5, *A&R* 613, *ERL* 273)

—— *A Brief Discours contayning certayne reasons why Catholiques refuse to goe to Church, Written by a learned and vertuous man, to a frend of his in England. And Dedicated by I.H[owlet] to the Queenes most excellent Majestie*, Douai [London secret press] 1580   (*STC* 19394, *A&R* 616, *ERL* 84)

—— *The Christian Directory Guiding men to eternall salvation, Devided into three Bookes*, (first publ. as *The First Booke of the Christian Exercise* 1582), Rouen 1607   (*STC* 19371, *A&R* 623, *ERL* 41)

—— *A Discoverie of I. Nichols Minister, misreported a Jesuite, latelye recanted in the Tower of London. Wherin besides the declaration of the man, is contayned a ful answere to his recantation, with a confutation of his slaunders, and proofe of the contraries, in the Pope, Cardinals, Clergie, Studentes, and private men of Rome*, [London secret press] 1581   (*STC* 19402, *A&R* 627, *ERL* 57)

—— *A Manifestation of the Great Folly and bad spirit of certayne in England calling themselves secular priests. Who set forth dayly most infamous and contumelious libels against worthy men of their own religion, and divers of them their lawful Superiors, of which libles sundry are heer examined and refuted. By priestes lyving in obedience*, [Antwerp] 1602   (*STC* 19411, *A&R* 633, *ERL* 169)

—— *Quaestiones Duae De Sacris alienis non adeundis*, [St Omer] 1607

Petti, Anthony G. (ed.), *The Letters and Despatches of Richard Verstegan c 1550–1640* (Catholic Record Society lii, 1959)

—— *Recusant Documents from the Ellesmere Manuscripts* (Catholic Record Society lx, 1968)

Pilkington, James, *The Works of James Pilkington B.D. Bishop of Durham*, ed. James Scholefield (Parker Society, 1842)

Pollen, J. H. (ed.), 'Father Persons' Memoirs', in *Catholic Record Society Miscellanea IV* (Catholic Record Society iv, 1907), 1–161

—— 'The memoirs of Father Robert Persons', in *Catholic Record Society Miscellanea II* (Catholic Record Society ii, 1906) 12–218

—— *Unpublished Documents Relating to the English Martyrs: vol. I 1584–1603* (Catholic Record Society v, 1908)

—— and W. MacMahon (eds), *The Ven. Philip Howard Earl of Arundel 1557–1595: English martyrs vol. II* (Catholic Record Society xxi, 1919)

Price, Sampson, *Londons Warning by Laodicea's Luke-Warmnesse. Or A Sermon Preached at Paules-Crosse, the 10. of October, 1613*, London 1613   (*STC* 20333)

Purvis, J. S. (ed.), *Tudor Parish Documents of the Diocese of York*, Cambridge 1948

Radford, John, *A Directorie Teaching the Way to the Truth in a Briefe and plaine discourse against the heresies of this time. Whereunto is added, A Short Treatise Against Adiaphorists, Neuters, and such as say they may be saved in any Sect or Religion, and would make of many divers sects one Church*, [English secret press] 1605   (*STC* 20602, *A&R* 701, *ERL* 19)

Raines, F. R. (ed.), 'A description of the state, civil and ecclesiastical of the county of Lancaster about the year 1590', *Chetham Miscellanies V* (Chetham Society, o.s. xcvi, 1875)

Renold, P. (ed.), *Letters of William Allen and Richard Barret 1572–1598* (Catholic Record Society lviii, 1967)

—— *The Wisbech Stirs 1595–1598* (Catholic Record Society li, 1958)

Rhodes, W. E. (ed.), 'The apostolical life of Ambrose Barlow, O.S.B.', in *Chetham Miscellanies. New Series. Vol. II* (Chetham Society, n.s. lxiii, 1909)

Robinson, Hastings (ed.), *The Zurich Letters 1558–1579 (Comprising the Correspondence of Several English Bishops and Others With Some of the Helvetian Reformers During the Early Part of the Reign of Queen Elizabeth)* (Parker Society, 1842–5)

Rogers, Timothy, *The Roman-Catharist: Or, The Papist is a Puritane. A Declaration shewing that they of the Religion and Church of Rome, are notorious Puritans*, London 1621   (*STC* 21250)

Ryan, Patrick (ed.), 'Diocesan returns of recusants for England and Wales 1577', in *Catholic Record Society Miscellanea XII* (Catholic Record Society xii, 1921), 1–114

Sander, Nicholas, *The Rise and Growth of the Anglican Schism*, ed. and trans. David Lewis, London 1877 (first publ. in Latin 1585)

—— *A Treatise of the Images of Christ, and of his Saints: and that it is unlaufull to breake them, and lauful to honour them*, Louvain 1567   (*STC* 21696, *A&R* 754, *ERL* 282)

Sanderson, Thomas, *Of Romanizing Recusants and Dissembling Catholicks. A Countermaund of a counterfeit Embassage (or An Answere to the posthume Pamphlet of Ralfe Buckland sometime, a Popish Priest, secretly pointed and published after his death about a yeere ago)*, London 1611   (*STC* 21711)

Selden, John, *Table-Talk: Being the Discourses of John Selden Esq; Or his Sence of Various Matters of Weight and High Consequence Relating especially to Religion and State*, London 1689

Sheldon, Richard, *A Sermon Preached at Paules Crosse: Laying open the Beast, and his Marks. Upon the 14. of the Revelations, vers. 9.10.11*, London 1625   (*STC* 22398)

Smith, Richard, *The Life of the Most Honourable and Vertuous Lady, The Lady Magdalen Viscountesse Montague, Written in Latin and published soon after her death by Richard Smith, D.D. and her Confessour. Now translated into English by C. F.*, [St Omer] 1627   (*STC* 22811, *A&R* 775, *ERL* 54)

Southwell, Robert, *An Epistle of Comfort, to the Reverend Priestes, and to the Honorable Worshipful, & other of the Laye sort restrayned in Durance for the Catholicke Fayth*, Paris [London 1587–8]   (*STC* 22946, *A&R* 781, *ERL* 211)

—— *An Humble Supplication to Her Majestie*, [English secret press] 1595 [1600]   (*STC* 7586, *A&R* 784, *ERL* 123)

The Statutes of the Realm, ed. T. E. Tomlins *et al*, London 1819

Strype, John, *Annals of the Reformation and Establishment of Religion and Other Various Occurrences in the Church of England During Queen Elizabeth's Happy Reign, (Together with an Appendix of Original Papers of State, Records and Letters)*, 4 vols in 7, Oxford 1824

Stubbes, Phillip, *Phillip Stubbes' Anatomy of Abuses in England in Shakspere's Youth A.D. 1583*, 2 vols, ed. F. J. Furnivall, London 1877–9 (first publ. 1583)

A Survey of the Booke of Common Prayer, By way of 197. Queres grounded upon 58 places, ministering just matter of question, with a view of London Ministers exceptions, [Middelburg] 1606   (*STC* 16450)

[Sutcliffe, Matthew], *A Briefe Replie to a certaine odious and slanderous libel, lately published by a seditious Jesuite, calling himselfe N. D. in defence both of publike enemies, and disloyall subjects . . . Hereunto is also added a certaine new Challenge made to N. D. in five encounters, concerning the fundamentall pointes of his former whole discourse*, London 1600 (*STC* 23453)

Sutton, Thomas, *Englands First and Second Summons. Two Sermons Preached at Paules Crosse*, London 1616 (*STC* 23502)

Talbot, Claire (ed.), *Recusant Records* (Catholic Record Society liii, 1961)

Tanner, J. R. (ed.), *Constitutional Documents of the Reign of James I AD 1603–1625*, Cambridge 1930

Tedder, William and Anthony Tyrrell, *The Recantations as they were severallie pronounced by Wylliam Tedder and Anthony Tyrrell: (sometime two Seminarie Priests of the English Colledge in Rome, and nowe by the great mercie of almightie God converted, unto the profession of the Gospell of Jesus Christ) at Paules Crosse, the day and yeere as is mentioned in their severall Tytles of theyr Recantations*, London 1588 (*STC* 23859)

A True and Perfect Relation of the Whole proceedings against the late most barbarous Traitors, Garnet a Jesuite, and his Confederats, London 1605 (*STC* 11619)

[Udall, John], *The state of the Church of Englande, laide open in a conference betweene Diotrephes a Bishop, Tertullus a Papist, Demetrius a usurer, Pandocheus an In-keeper, and Paule a Preacher of rhe [sic] word of God*, [London 1588] (*STC* 24505)

Vaux, Laurence, *A Catechisme or Christian Doctrine*, ed. T. G. Law (Chetham Society, n.s. iv, 1885) (first publ. Louvain 1568)

Vermigli, Peter Martyr, *The Common Places of the most renowned Divine Doctor Peter Martyr, divided into foure principall parts: with a large addition of manie theologicall and necessarie discourses, some never extant before*, London 1583 (*STC* 24669)

—— *A Treatise of the Cohabitacyon of the faithfull with the unfaithfull. Wherunto is added. A Sermon made [by Henry Bullinger] of the confessing of Christe and his gospell, and of the denyinge of the same*, [Strassburg] 1555 (*STC* 24673.5)

Viret, Pierre, *An Epistle to the Faithfull, necessary for all the children of God: especially in these dangerous days*, London 1582 (*STC* 24779)

—— *Of the principal points which are at this daye in controversie, concerning the holy supper of Jesus Christ, and of the masse of the Romish Church*, London 1569 (*STC* 24782)

W. C., *The Fatall Vesper, Or A True and Punctuall Relation of that lamentable and fearefull accident, hapning on Sunday in the afternoone being the 26. of October last, by the fall of a roome in the Black-Friers in which were assembled many people at a Sermon, which was to be preached by Father Drurie a Jesuite. Together with the names and number of such persons therein unhappily perished, or were miraculously preserved*, London 1623 (*STC* 6015)

Walsingham, Francis, *A Search made into Matters of Religion, by Francis Walsingham Deacon of the Protestants Church, before his change to the Catholicke*, [St Omer] 1609 (*STC* 25002, *A&R* 875, *ERL* 286)

Weston, William, *William Weston: the autobiography of an Elizabethan*, trans. Philip Caraman, London 1955

Whitgift, John, *The Works of John Whitgift*, 3 vols, ed. John Ayre (Parker Society, 1851–3)

Wiburn, Perceval, *A checke or reproofe of M. Howlets untimely shreeching [sic] in her*

Majesties eares, with an answeare to the reasons alleadged in a discourse therunto annexed, why Catholikes (as they are called) refuse to goe to church: Wherein (among other things) the Papists treaterous and treacherous doctrine and demeanour towardes our Soveraigne and the State, is somewhat at large upon occasion unfolded: their divelish pretended conscience also examined, and the foundations thereof undermined. And lastly shewed that it is the duety of all true Christians and subjectes to haunt publike Church assemblies, London 1581   (*STC* 25586)

Wigand, Johann, *De Neutralibus & Mediis. Grosly Englished, Jacke of both sides. A Godly and A Necessarie Catholike admonition, touching those that be Neuters, holding upon no certaine Religion, nor doctrine, and such as hold with both partes, or rather of no part, very necessary to stay and stablish Gods elect in the true catholike faith against this present wicked world*, London 1591   (*STC* 25613)

Worthington, Thomas, *A Relation of Sixtene Martyrs, glorified in England in twelve monethes. With a declaration. That English Catholiques suffer for the Catholique Religion. And That the seminarie priests agree with the Iesuites. In answer to our Adversaries calumniations, touching these two points*, Douai 1601   (*STC* 26000.9, *A&R* 917, *ERL* 350)

Wright, Thomas, *The Disposition or Garnishmente of the Soule To receive worthily the blessed Sacrament*, Antwerp [English secret press] 1596   (*STC* 26038.8, *A&R* 921, *ERL* 36)

Index